M000028788

Unassimilable Feminisms

Breaking Feminist Waves

Series Editors:
LINDA MARTÍN ALCOFF, Hunter College and CUNY Graduate Center
GILLIAN HOWIE, University of Liverpool

For the last twenty years, feminist theory has been presented as a series of ascending waves. This picture has had the effect of deemphasizing the diversity of past scholarship as well as constraining the way we understand and frame new work. The aim of this series is to attract original scholars who will offer unique interpretations of past scholarship and unearth neglected contributions to feminist theory. By breaking free from the constraints of the image of waves, this series will be able to provide a wider forum for dialogue and engage historical and interdisciplinary work to open up feminist theory to new audiences and markets.

LINDA MARTÍN ALCOFF is Professor of Philosophy at Hunter College and the City University of New York Graduate Center. Her books include *Visible Identities: Race, Gender and the Self* (2006); *The Blackwell Guide to Feminist Philosophy* (co-edited with Eva Kittay, 2006); *Identity Politics Reconsidered* (co-edited with Moya, Mohanty, and Hames-Garcia, Palgrave 2006); and *Singing in the Fire: Tales of Women in Philosophy* (2003).

GILLIAN HOWIE is Senior Lecturer in Philosophy at the University of Liverpool. She has edited *Gender, Teaching and Research in Higher Education* (2002); *Gender and Philosophy* (2003); *Third Wave Feminism* (Palgrave, 2004); *Menstruation* (Palgrave, 2005); *Women and the Divine* (Palgrave, 2008); and the forthcoming *Fugitive Ethics: Feminism and Dialectical Materialism*. She is the founder and director of the Institute for Feminist Theory and Research.

Titles to date:

> *Unassimilable Feminisms: Reappraising Feminist, Womanist, and* Mestiza *Identity Politics*
> by Laura Gillman

Forthcoming:

> *Further Adventures of* The Dialectic of Sex*: Critical Essays on Shulamith Firestone*
> edited by Mandy Merck and Stella Sandford

> *Hegel's Philosophy and Feminist Thought: Beyond Antigone?*
> edited by Kimberly Hutchings and Tuija Pulkkinen

> *Essential Re-Orientations*
> by Gillian Howie

> *Feminism and the Mexican Woman Intellectual from Sor Juana to Rivera Garza: Boob Lit*
> by Emily Hind

> *The Many Dimensions of Chinese Feminism*
> by Ya-Chen Chen

Unassimilable Feminisms

Reappraising Feminist, Womanist, and *Mestiza* Identity Politics

Laura Gillman

UNASSIMILABLE FEMINISMS
Copyright © Laura Gillman, 2010.

All rights reserved.

Portions of chapter 2 originally appeared as "Beyond the Shadow: Re-scripting Race in Women's Studies." *Meridians* 7.2 (2007): 117–41.

Portions of chapter 6 originally appeared as "*Con un pie a cada lado*/With a Foot in Each Place: *Mestizaje* as Transnational Feminisms in Ana Castillo's *So Far from God*," with Stacey M. Floyd-Thomas. *Meridians* 2.1 (2001): 158–75. An abbreviated version of chapter 6 appeared as "Revisiting Identity Politics in Contemporary *Mestiza* Thought: The Case of *Domesticana*." In *Identity, Migration and Women's Bodies as Sites of Knowledge and Transgression.* Ed. Silvia Borrego and María Isabel Romero Ruiz. Oviedo, Spain: KRK Ediciones. 2009.

First published in 2010 by
PALGRAVE MACMILLAN®
in the United States—a division of St. Martin's Press LLC,
175 Fifth Avenue, New York, NY 10010.

Where this book is distributed in the UK, Europe and the rest of the world, this is by Palgrave Macmillan, a division of Macmillan Publishers Limited, registered in England, company number 785998, of Houndmills, Basingstoke, Hampshire RG21 6XS.

Palgrave Macmillan is the global academic imprint of the above companies and has companies and representatives throughout the world.

Palgrave® and Macmillan® are registered trademarks in the United States, the United Kingdom, Europe and other countries.

ISBN: 978–0–230–62316–3

Library of Congress Cataloging-in-Publication Data is available from the Library of Congress.

A catalogue record of the book is available from the British Library.

Design by Newgen Imaging Systems (P) Ltd., Chennai, India.

First edition: July 2010

10 9 8 7 6 5 4 3 2 1

Printed in the United States of America.

I dedicate this book to my mother, Rosalie Gillman,
and to the memory of my 'other' mother,
Carmen (Cachita) Conchado Pita.

CONTENTS

SERIES FOREWORD

Breaking Feminist Waves is a series designed to rethink the conventional models of what feminism is today, its past and future trajectories. For more than a quarter of a century, feminist theory has been presented as a series of ascending waves, and this has come to represent generational divides and differences of political orientation as well as different formulations of goals. The imagery of waves, while connoting continuous movement, implies a singular trajectory with an inevitably progressive teleology. As such, it constrains the way we understand what feminism has been and where feminist thought has appeared, while simplifying the rich and nuanced political and philosophical diversity that has been characteristic of feminism throughout. Most disturbingly, the imagery restricts the way we understand and frame new work.

This series provides a forum to reassess established constructions of feminism and of feminist theory. It provides a starting point to redefine feminism as a configuration of intersecting movements and concerns; with political commitment but, perhaps, without a singular center or primary track. The generational divisions among women do not actually correlate to common interpretive frameworks shaped by shared historical circumstances, but rather to a diverse set of arguments, problems, and interests affected by differing historical contexts and locations. Often excluded from cultural access to dominant modes of communication and dissemination, feminisms have never been uniform nor yet in a comprehensive conversation. The generational division, then, cannot represent the dominant divide within feminism, nor a division between essentially coherent moments; there are always multiple conflicts and contradictions, as well as differences about the goals, strategies, founding concepts, and starting premises.

Nonetheless; the problems facing women, feminists, and feminisms are as acute and pressing today as ever. Featuring a variety of disciplinary and theoretical perspectives, *Breaking Feminist Waves* provides a forum for comparative, historical, and interdisciplinary work, with special attention to the problems of cultural differences, language and representation, embodiment, rights, violence, sexual economies, and political action. By rethinking feminisms' history as well as its present, and by unearthing neglected contributions to feminist theory, this series intends to unlock conversations between feminists and feminisms and to open up feminist theory and practice to new audiences.

—Linda Martín Alcoff and Gillian Howie

ACKNOWLEDGMENTS

It is a rewarding task to extend my gratitude to the many people who have provided me with help and support during the writing of this book and throughout my professional career. I was fortunate to receive an undergraduate education in Spanish at the University of California San Diego in the heyday of the *Chicana/o* movement. I want to thank two professors from that era, Ellen McCracken and Tomas Ybarra Frausto. It was in their classes that I initiated what was to become a lifelong passion for the Spanish language, literature, and culture, and learned what it meant to be a *gabacha*.

I have investigated the constructions of mistaken, imagined, and real identities in relation to values since the completion of my doctoral dissertation and first book, both of which focused on identity as a critique of humanism in Cervantes' *Don Quixote*. But it was my appointment in Women's Studies and an ensuing move in 1998 from the Department of Foreign Languages to the Department of Interdisciplinary Studies at my university that caused me to shift my research interests and teaching areas from Eurocentric to Americentric and global realities. Working within an interdisciplinary, ethnic studies context brought me into contact with a number of colleagues who have sustained me intellectually.

I would like to thank womanist ethicist Stacey Floyd-Thomas for sharing with me the richness of her insights on the womanist identity. The collaboration that we shared in some form or another for close to a decade, culminating in the publication of her book, *Mining the Motherlode: Methods in Womanist Ethics* (2006), allowed me to deepen my appreciation of the womanist vision. The Women and Gender Studies research group on Space, Place, Race, and Identity has encouraged me to develop a more interdisciplinary understanding of some of the ideas I developed in chapter 5 around migration, transnationalism, and identity. I thank the members of that group for revitalizing my thinking on these issues: Gena Chandler, Maria Elisa Christie, Minjeong Kim, Katy Powell, Emily Satterwhite, and Barbara Ellen Smith. Many other departmental colleagues and affiliates including

Ingrid Banks, Toni Calasanti, Gary Downey, Nikol Alexander-Floyd, Michael Herndon, Sharon Johnson, Elizabeth Struthers-Malbon, Terry Kershaw, Neal King, Karl Precoda, and Janell Watson have listened thoughtfully and provided feedback on my presentations of various portions of this book throughout the different stages of its development. There have also been numerous students over the years, whose critical questions and dissonances have helped me to hone my conceptual frameworks: Laura Agnich, Anisa Ali, Elizabeth Arnold, Megan Baumgardner, Shawn Braxton, Clarence Brown, Blair Fornville, Ashley Mannes, Alex Perez, Marie-Belle Perez Rivera, Liz Roots, Elie Smith, Lisa Tabor, Ashley Tomisek, John Walsh, and Kristin White.

I would like to thank those colleagues who have read all or some portions of the manuscript. My writing partner, Nikol Alexander-Floyd, has been instrumental in providing me with feedback on all aspects of the manuscript. I also want to thank Jennifer Browdy de Hernandez for her careful reading and feedback on several chapters. I am thankful to the Future of Minority Studies group, including Linda Martin Alcoff, Michael Hames-Garcia, Satya Mohanty, and Paula M. L. Moya, among others, who have read portions of the manuscript, and whose own work has inspired me to flesh out the mediated nature of experience. My graduate research assistants, Ellie Smith and Jongmin Lee, have provided important editorial assistance in the various stages of completing the manuscript. I have also benefited greatly from the support of the Palgrave Macmillan team, including the series editor, Linda Martin Alcoff and the anonymous reviewer, who have shown interest in this project, as well as Palgrave Macmillan editors Lee Norton and Brigitte Shull.

I also want to acknowledge the benefit I have gained from audience comments and questions at panels where selections of this work were presented, including the Collegium of African American Research Conferences in Cagliari, Italy in 2001 and in Tours, France, in 2005; the Ethnicity and Public Memory Conference at Lewis and Clark College, Portland, Oregon in 2007; the Identity, Migration and Women's Bodies as Sites of Knowledge and Transgression Conference at the University of Malaga, Spain, in 2008; and *El Mundo Zurdo*: An International Conference on the Life and Work of Gloria Anzaldúa at the University of Texas at San Antonio, in 2009.

I have learned the most about theories of racialized gender and the interconnections between race and poverty when I have been able to test them out within community settings and community workshops. I want to thank the following friends and colleagues who have taken and/or continue to take the risk to believe that we can face the challenges of sorting out the complexities of our shared social reality by confronting our conflicting perspectives on who we are as a community, the causes of inequality, and how we got here, starting from our own spaces of identity: Laura Agnich, Sandy Bernabei, Shawn Braxton, Clarence Brown, Mary Connerly, Elaine Carter, Ellington Graves, Kwame Harrison, Bob Leonard, Shewanda Marie Muhammad, Wayne Muhammad, John Ryan, Marcy Schnitzer, Tonya Smith-Jackson, and Ray Williams. I also want to thank fellow community organizers David Billings, Pat Callair, Deena Hayes, Monica Walker, and the White Caucus of the Undoing Racism Group of Greensboro, North Carolina.

I am most grateful to my partner, Don, for his willingness to listen to my aspirations and frustrations while writing this book, and for helping me understand that I could participate in non-academic activities in the process, just for pure recreation. Finally, I am forever indebted to my parents, Aaron and Rosalie, both for their unconditional love, and for the cultural legacy they have bequeathed to me, which, by necessity, has obliged me to question the issue of identity and the notion of the self as something worthy of exploration and defense. It is a legacy that not only will I continue to struggle to understand over the course of my life, but one that I have in turn passed on, for better or for worse, to my sons, Eduardo and Sean.

CHAPTER 1

Introduction: Reconceptualizing Identity Politics in a Post Identity Politics Age

As the first decade of the twenty-first century is rapidly coming to a close, another book on identity politics might be considered anachronistic. Popular, political, and scholarly opinions have it that we live in a post identity politics age. The '80s' and '90s' debates over essentialism have long ago subsided, but not before raising important questions about the self in relation to identity that have yet to be successfully resolved. The antiessentialist view that prevailed causing those debates to come to a close at the end of the '9 0s provided an important insight that also came to be, ironically, the most important obstacle to the effectiveness of an ongoing feminist project. That insight consisted in the claim that universal understandings about women's physical or metaphysical nature are false; there is no fixed, universalizing biological essence, nor are there sociocultural patterns of conduct, activities, or structures of feeling that bind all women together as a group. Whether celebrating women's biological traits or social attributes in order to compensate for racist and patriarchal representations, or simply deconstructing the mind/nature dichotomy in order to dismantle Western binary thought that marginalized women in the first place, feminists, so the argument goes, had mistakenly reproduced stereotypical femininity. They had indulged either in an over-attentiveness to naturalized conceptualizations of the body or in the celebration of ahistoricized and abstract stereotypical attributes, such as nurturing and caring.

Such a fortuitous conclusion has now allowed for the possibility of raising new questions about the relationship of raced and gendered embodiment to social practices and meanings, as well as for interrogating the possibility of creating an epistemological and ontological ground, however shifting, for talking about and acting on behalf of "women." This book attempts to seriously conceptualize and illuminate such possibilities. I highlight some of the legitimate arguments posed against identity attachments, in particular, the arguments against essentialism, and deconstruct the illegitimate ones, most especially, those that claim that identities are intrinsically oppressive. I also offer a defense of identity as a necessary mechanism for developing reliable knowledge; I posit that identities serve as the justification for our decision and meaning making procedures as well as political action.

This study takes as its starting point the bifurcation of feminist thought that developed on the heels of those debates as feminists sought to address a clear need to understand the implications of antiessentialism on feminist thought and activism. An early essay by Nicholson and Fraser, "Social Criticism without Philosophy: An Encounter between Feminism and Postmodernism," noted the infelicitous coincidence of two strands of American feminist thought in the '80s: one heavily influenced by Derridean deconstruction and Foucaldian discourse analysis, and another that articulated frameworks for a micropolitics of identity and difference, effected by working-class women and women of color (Nicholson and Fraser 1990, 33). The intense theoretical reconsideration of the concept of the self as a singular, unitary, and coherent subject in both camps led to very different conclusions about antiessentialist identities, even as both borrowed conceptual insights and arguments from each other to some extent.

The most extreme version of postmodernist feminism has been fueled by certain assumptions about the deterministic nature of sexual difference, namely, that all attempts to define a gendered identity trigger normative roles or behaviors to which women must conform. and thus function as an exercise of power. I elaborate on this topic in greater detail in chapter 2. For now, suffice it to say that postmodern feminists view the category "women" as phantasmatic, having no objective basis in reality. As recently noted by Alison Stone, postmodern feminists, such as Judith Butler, Moira Gatens, and Elizabeth Grosz, among others, hold a view of bodies as so thoroughly articulated within culture, that they cannot conceive of sexed embodiments outside of social practices and discourses (Stone 2004, 7). Thus, for example, according to Judith Butler, our gendered identities do not exist except through our doing or performing of them (Butler 1990, 9). The implication of such a view is that in the absence of any natural attributes or properties that are attributable to all women, there is no longer any means to posit a feminist epistemology, that is, a better knowledge about social life that women have because of their experiences as women.

In fact, the crisis of truth that feminists evoked in raising the specter of legitimacy with regards to the patriarchal foundations of Eurocentric thought and cultural traditions led postmodern feminists to the conclusion that no truth claims—not even those discovered and sustained by feminists—can be considered to provide the conditions for absolute certainty.[1] Such a conclusion effectively delegitimated the notion of a 'feminist' knowledge that could be derived from women's experiences and validated and acted upon by women as a means to achieve empowerment. Human agency thus became decoupled from human subjectivity, and is now seen as only being exercised as a strategic essentialism. Postmodern feminists' underlying plea to fellow feminists has been that we must simply "get beyond" identity politics. Hence, feminist epistemology—based on the belief that our gender, at its intersections with other categories of identity, does and ought to influence our conception of knowledge—is seen by the postmodern feminists as an "impossible project."[2]

For others, most notably, women of color, the emphasis on difference politics led to a very different view. They argued that because the category of "women" needed to be conceptualized more broadly in order to include a diversity of female subjectivities, it had a diverse, proliferating content. By maintaining the social construction of different gender identities and practices while still highlighting the ontological and social dimensions of racialized gendered identity, it remained possible to theorize both the different *and* shared ways in which women experience real social problems because they are women (rape and other forms of violence, reproductive restrictions, difficult access to education and work, workforce discrimination and segmentation, and, in the case of subaltern women, racism, xenophobia and homophobia).

An emphasis on difference politics, moreover, highlighted the fact that the category "women" could be retained, without subjecting those included in this category to normative understandings of sexual difference. Insofar as identities are unstable and fluid social categories, the meanings of one's identity are discovered, adopted and/or revised as differently located embodied subjects actively engage in the process of interpreting and evaluating both the meanings of their identities and social categories to which their identities have been indexed within the social world. Within this camp, thus, it is argued that to erase identities is to forego the very possibilities for radicalizing consciousness, so that it becomes possible to become a "feminist," a "new *mestiza*," "*mujerista*," or "womanist."

This book engages these divergent forms of thought for the purpose of indicating not only the excesses of postmodernist feminism but also the deleterious impact of these excesses on minority women's thought and activism. It offers a reappraisal of the viability and value of identity politics at a juncture in which admittedly a shift in feminist thought is underway from an identity-based or feminist epistemology to a postmodernist or postfeminist, postracial epistemology. In opening up the discussion of identity, it is not my aim to resurrect the old controversies over essentialism, but to put them behind us by dispelling the essentializing depictions of identities that are brought up by neoconservative pundits as well as by those on the Left whenever one attempts to present a defense of identity politics or just simply theorize identity as a feminist practice.

Thus, a primary goal of this book is to make the claim that even while there is an attempt to submerge, render obsolete, or reessentialize them, identities are anything but anachronistic. Importantly, identities continue to drive contemporary feminist thought, as well as popular cultural and political discourses. Identities matter—particularly for those whose visible identities (of race and gender) place them disadvantageously with respect to social power, and who therefore have a stake in claiming and explaining their identity. But they also matter to those who are closest to the center of power and wish to stay that way. This only becomes evident, however, when the identity practices of subaltern groups make visible their opaque and apparently neutral identities.

The Senate confirmation hearings of *Nuyorican* Judge Sonia Sotomayor that are in progress as I sit down to write this introduction illuminate the tremendous sway identities hold and will continue to hold over people as well as how identities will be vehemently reasserted whenever there is an attempt to submerge or purposefully obfuscate them. *Nuyorican*s and Latinas/os turned out *en masse* at rallies held in cities and towns throughout this nation, in support of Sotomayor's candidacy. Democrats remained quietly pondering the stark contrast between the post-racial rhetoric that Obama had used during the 2008 presidential campaign and the overt racial-ethnic and feminist identity politics of his Supreme Court pick. In the meantime, Conservatives sought to politically use the judge's forthright expression of her identity to derail her appointment to the Supreme Court.

When asked what she meant by the 2001 remark, that "a wise Latina woman with the richness of her experiences would more often than not reach a better conclusion than a white male who has not lived this life," this first *Nuyorican*/Latina to be nominated to the Supreme Court shrewdly pointed to the overwhelming social facticity of identities by stating that in her entire career "no words that [she] has ever said or written have received so much attention." Additionally, her subsequent response—that her consideration of the lived experiences of Latinas/os as resources for better understanding human needs would only enrich the rational basis of legal decision-making, not just for Latinos, but for everyone—effectively dispelled two concerns. First, her enlarged vision of objectivity offered a cogent response to the Grand Old Party's (the Republican Party) concern with regard to the narrowness or bias of her judgment capacities. Second, in dismantling their portrayal of her as someone who encourages irrational behavior of "groupthink," Sotomayor also succeeded in exposing their offense as a deflective strategy that aimed to keep their own subjective interests covert and intact. Ultimately, Sotomayor refused to acquiesce to the GOP condition that she "get beyond identity" politics; this refusal was overtly mandated by neoconservative Abigail Thernstrom in her commentary on the nomination, as rights of passage into the "white, male club" (2009).

The Senate Confirmation hearings are revealing of the striking similarities between neoconservatives and postmodern feminists, insofar as they both aim to drive identities underground. While their reasons might be quite different, the negative effects of their attempts to bury identities are the same. Rather than working to construct theories that aid in eliminating human suffering produced by social inequality, postmodern feminists only serve to deepen confusion around identity politics sown by neoconservative pundits as well as by the eroding politics of the Left, best epitomized in President Obama's postracial campaign and presidential rhetoric. In so doing, this strand of feminist thought delimits our progress toward understanding the ongoing practices and effects of racism and sexism ever present in our social structures and institutions, including the academic ones of which feminism forms a part.

This book works to move beyond the entanglements posed by the dominant strands of postmodernist feminist thought through an analysis of the identity politics practiced by womanists and *mestiza* feminists. Womanism draws upon political modalities and resistance practices that are complementary to Black feminist thought. Womanist thought, however, remains distinct from Black feminism insofar as womanists labor to identify and maintain their ties to Black nationalist ideologies and discourses. There are different womanist camps, some of which are secular, but the dominant one that I focus on here derives its theoretical frameworks from the disciplines in which its members are primarily located—the fields of ethics and religion.

In my analysis of identity politics, I first examine the ways in which womanist and *mestiza* feminist thought have respectively engaged and advanced postmodernist thought by fostering more nuanced frameworks for understanding intra-group differences while continuing to affirm the stability of group identity, grounded in spatial-temporal relations. Second, I locate womanist and *mestiza* modes of intellectual inquiry and mobilizations at the crossroads of a range of disciplines, theories, and social movements that offer new spaces for projecting radical, nonessentializing subjectivities. Finally, I apply a postpositivist realist framework to womanism and *mestiza* feminism, a mode of inquiry primarily but not exclusively indebted to American pragmatism, a school of thought that rejects both foundationalism and antifoundationalism in favor of an experimental and practical understanding of experiential knowledge (Rosenthal 2003, 43). Postpositivist realism is aligned with and further advances a pragmatic approach to identities insofar as it foregrounds a view of human consciousness as an awareness that results from the interactivity of human subjects with the natural and social world of which they form a part.[3]

Postpositivist realism seeks to address some of the intrinsic limitations of postmodernist discourses, most notably, its denial of the possibility of an objective truth other than that which is discursively constructed, and its uneasiness with respect to claims about the relationship of experience to knowledge about the self, as well as about the real or natural world. Applying postpositivist realist theoretical claims to womanist and *mestiza* thought and activism, I argue more specifically that womanists and *mestiza* feminists have worked to develop theoretically mediated interpretations of their experiences. In the process, they have not only gained a truer, more objective knowledge of the nonarbitrary elements of our world, but have also constructed interpretive schemas that have allowed them to refute with greater epistemic reliability the dominant ideologies and institutions that have distorted their identities and constrained their agency.

A theory-mediated postpositivist realist notion of identity formation and identity politics that I employ here resonates with womanist and *mestiza* feminist frameworks of identity in three ways. Like womanism and *mestiza* feminism, postpositivist realism offers an alternative to the skeptical stance of postmodernism that denies identity altogether as an epistemological resource as well as to the positivist position that recognizes knowledge as only that which is self-evident.

Like womanist and *mestiza* feminist thought, postpositivist realism also highlights identities as both constructed and ontologically real. By "real," I do not mean that identities are fixed and essentialized, but rather, are linked to organic beings that exist extra-discursively and, as is the case with all organic beings that exist in the natural world, are subject to change. Postpositivist realists, like womanists and *mestiza* feminists, also view identities as sources of erroneous interpretations as well as sources of theory-mediated knowledge that can better serve the interests of subaltern individuals and social groups.

In effect, by affirming reinforcing, and further fleshing out existing womanist and *mestiza* feminist intellectual resources, postpositivist realism contributes to womanist and *mestiza* feminist thought. I highlight here two key interrelated concepts informing postpositivist realism that I examine throughout this book: objective location and moral universalism. Objective knowledge might appear at first glance to be antithetical to experiential-based theories of knowledge. Embodied experiences constituting identities are often portrayed in womanist and *mestiza* feminist thought as resources of subjective and intersubjective knowledge about Black or *mestiza* women. Knowledge constructions developed by womanists and *mestiza* feminists are often produced and sustained, moreover, within enclosed self-contained spaces—womanist or *chicana/mestiza* activist organizations, including women's discussion groups and parish groups in the Church, and academic sites, including journals, conferences, consultations, and caucuses. These spheres have helped Black women and Latina women achieve their goals without concern, as womanist Katie Cannon notes, about having their "realities be verified in institutions of higher learning where the dailiness of [their] authentic experiences cannot be proven by scientific methodology" and where they can thus be free to construct knowledge about themselves and their communities outside of "the fixed rules or absolute principles of the white-oriented, male structured society" (Cannon 2006, 19; 1988, 4).

From a postpositivist realist perspective, however, identities are both the subjective *and* objective locations from which one must make sense of the world (Moya 2000b, 17). A basic claim of postpositivist realism is that social knowledge is not simply out there in the world waiting to be apprehended, but is always derived from embodied experience. Further, experiences only come to be experiences as we interpret them. Because postpositivist realists posit a cognitive conception of experience, one that depends upon our narratives and paradigms for their illumination, it becomes possible to understand experience as having a conscious element. Thus, although error is always possible, experiences can, when subjected to empirical and theoretical verification processes, yield objective knowledge about the social realm and about women's lives, that is, the meanings of what it is to be female within specific contexts (Mohanty 2000, 39).

By "women's objective location," then, I mean the ways in which women are positioned within and refer to the external context of spatial-temporal relations in which they find themselves inserted in the real world. Women's identity as location or what Linda Alcoff refers to as positionality, always conceived as fluid and relational, indicates that women's embodied identities are constituted within specific social-spatial/temporal practices and structures. Insofar as the meanings of those experiences are ambiguous and nondeterminate, and therefore open to interpretation, women can, as active agents, use their position to learn the meanings of their identity, and in the process, negotiate and reconstruct them, constituting themselves as social and political subjects (Alcoff 2006, 148–49). Furthermore, when individuals develop reliable theoretical accounts of the social world, their claims about the social world and their justifications for their actions based on their knowledge claims are not applicable only to the identities of the group in question, but rather to the world we all share. I can thus affirm that such epistemic claims have universal value. Going by this view, identities contribute a "more nuanced universalist view of human needs and vulnerabilities, as well as—by implication—human flourishing" (Mohanty 2000, 62).

The concepts of objective location and universalism, as I demonstrate from a variety of angles throughout this book, help to address a number of arguments leveraged against experiential knowledge that have limited its widespread application within feminist and other academic forms of inquiry. First, the notion of experience as objectively as well as subjectively constituted dispels the postmodernist view of experiential knowledge as arbitrary, radically subjective, or at best intersubjective. At the same time, the notion of all knowledge as subjective as well as objective dispels positivist conceptions of knowledge as a detached, neutral enterprise, or what Mohanty terms "a view from nowhere" (2000, 36).

Second, insofar as objective and subjective knowledge are no longer seen as incompatible, there is no longer any justification for keeping subaltern knowledge within separate, private spheres, marginalized from objective academic inquiry. Instead, feminists within academic corridors need to become acquainted with approaches that highlight theory-mediated experience as the basis of objective inquiry. In this manner, subaltern women's theories that provide important reservoirs of oppositional knowledge can take a central place in mainstream academic theory as well as in all social institutions that seek to reflect true and objective understandings of society.

Third, the interconnectedness of objectivity with universalism has important implications in terms of how theory-mediated knowledge is to be extrapolated and used outside of the location from which it originated. Insofar as specific experiences point to the universality of human experience, experiential knowledge can never be cast as pertinent or true only with respect to the location from which it originated. In terms of different feminisms, this means that it would not be considered acceptable to talk about "feminisms" as separate sets of frameworks for political action, as such an absolute separation denies the rule of "general applicability" of women's experience to the varied practices and understandings of what it means to be constituted as female and how to operate within that category with moral and political agency.

Using the above-referenced arguments, as well as the general framework of postpositivist realism and of other social theories that seek to explain the cognitive status of experience, I work to demonstrate in a variety of ways throughout this book that white feminist, Black feminist, womanist, and *mestiza* feminist thoughts must remain unassimilable to one another. The respective positional perspectives that Black feminists, womanists, and *mestiza* feminists develop and employ derived from group-related experiences that occur at different social and cultural locations, and are shaped by different interpretive traditions and values that have historically remained in conflict with Western interpretive paradigms and values—the legacy of white feminist thought.

Assimilative attempts, often expressed in feminist circles as a "politics of inclusion," jeopardize an antiessentialist project by both reinforcing the elements that groups share, and by minimizing the difference in power that social hierarchies produce. Yet at the same time, the concepts of general applicability, cultural translatability, and commensurability of knowledge require that differently situated feminisms/womanisms remain open to one another in order to fill in the gaps of our understanding that result because our experiences are necessarily curtailed to particular locations. I thus posit a view of universalism as one that can only be articulated through particular experience, and as one that will aid in the adjudication of competing and conflicting knowledge claims. I will show how this is modeled within womanist and *mestiza* feminist texts.

I further suggest that unassimilablity should not be viewed as negative, that is, as having a balkanizing effect on women's organizational structures and movements; instead, it is to be seen as being productive–epistemically, and, ultimately, politically. A situated universalism is productive insofar as it can facilitate the use of positional perspectives as the means to identify and evaluate the background assumptions and epistemic consequences of differently positioned individuals and groups. In the process, we can learn the different ways in which our location with respect to social power "produces forms of blindness just as it enables degrees of lucidity" (Mohanty 2000, 60). Because such reciprocal interactivity requires egalitarian relations, the exercise of such interactivity must be consciously engaged if it is to happen without appropriation. In an era where social stratification is increasing at home and globally, we must not, as Seyla Benhabib affirms, "shy away from knocking down the 'parish walls'" (Benhabib 1992, 228). The goal here is not, at least initially, to seek solidarity, but rather to initiate a much-needed preliminary step that would allow solidarity to become a realizable future goal: the consideration of the possibility of learning from identities. For how can we make sense of the Other's goals or agenda if we do not even conceive of identities, that is, conscious experience, as the principle mechanism people have for developing justifications that motivate meaning making procedures, reasoning, and action?

I said above that I use postpositivist realist insights to *affirm, reinforce,* and further *flesh out* Black feminist, womanist, and *mestiza* thought because clearly, the notions of objectivity and universalism are, implicitly or explicitly, already a foundational part of their frameworks. The elucidation of the indexical relationship of the raced and gendered self to social categories, structures, and institutions in the real world lies at the heart of the paradigms of intersectionality and the constitutive models of identity, originally developed by the Combahee River Collective and further honed by feminists of color. These frameworks aim to demonstrate that subaltern women's knowledge can provide objective knowledge about social reality. Latina/ *mujerista* ethicist Ada María Isasi-Díaz, whose theories on the interpretive traditions of Latinas I apply to Ana Castillo's novel *So Far from God* in chapter 5, also labors to explain how the subjective experiences of Latinas can provide objective knowledge about the social world. She states up front that the interpretive traditions from which Latinas operate, by virtue of being incorporated into everyday practice, have attained objective status (Isasi-Díaz 2004a, 183–84).

The urgency of moral universalism is also placed center stage in Alice Walker's definition of womanism that is detailed in chapter 2, and applied as a hermeneutical concept to her novel *The Color Purple* in chapter 3. The second and fourth parts of her definition speak to the need for Black women to maintain universalism as a goal, the former with respect to the universality of Black womanhood, and the latter, with respect to feminism. And this must be accomplished as the very means to specify the particularity of their identities. For her part, womanist Katie Cannon defends the universality of womanhood. She argues that it is necessary to theorize differentiated gender. Comparative analyses of racialized gender help us to avoid parochial dispositions. This can best be accomplished by foregrounding the universality of women's lives. Precisely because of the social fact that identities are fluid and relational, womanists must insist on refraining from building their scholarship only from Black sources, as womanist Cheryl Sanders has advocated. Cannon writes:

> As one of the senior womanist ethicists, I am issuing advance warning to new womanist scholars, both actual and potential, that Sander's devaluation of credibility consequent on such a conservative framework of Black-sources-only encourages guesswork, blank spots and time-consuming busy work, the reinvention of the proverbial wheel over and over again. Having struggled so long and hard at the intersection of race, sex, and class, African-American women scholars cannot allow the suspicion of fraudulence to spread and contaminate the creative horizons in womanist research and writing. Staying open-minded as heterogeneous theoreticians may prove to be the most difficult ethical challenge in securing and extending the legacy of our intellectual life. (Cannon 1996, 131)[4]

Cannon, arguably the most noted womanist theologian, affirms, then, the need for linking womanist and feminist scholarship, and implicitly, politics as well.

Within the context of *mestiza* feminism, as I show in chapter 4, Gloria Anzaldúa, Sandra María Estéves, and Miriam Jiménez Román's theory-mediated portrayals of their multiply raced selves point to *mestizaje* and *mulatez* as the context for keeping universalism foregrounded. Their mixed race identities keep open the possibility of translatability of cultural knowledge. In my discussion of everyday popular practices of *Chicanas/mestizas* in chapter 5, I work to exemplify how interpretive traditions of *domesticana*, shared by *Chicanas*, have applicability within the broader social and institutional practices of Anglo society in which *mestiza* culture is embedded.

My views on the unassimilability of identities as well as my interest in learning how experience can serve as sources of mystification as well as of self and social knowledge are shaped by my own experiences. I grew up in Seattle in the aftermath of World War II, along with three other siblings, in a white, middle-class household. My parents were first generation Americans of Russian-Jewish descent. As noted in the literature of how Jews became white, postwar Jewish culture celebrated its resonance within mainstream Anglo culture through its shared cultural intellectual traditions, a resonance that, together with other circumstances such as phenotype, made it quite easy for American Jews not only to accept the construction of Jewishness as a "model minority," but also, eventually, to remove the racial-ethnic status of "off white" and become assimilated into whiteness (Brodkin 1998, 150–55; 182–84).

My own family trajectory demonstrated what anthropologist Karen Brodkin calls the "dialectic of racialized ambivalence," a dialectic that characterized Jewish identity in the era beginning with post World War II and ending with the Vietnam war. Assimilation was something to be desired, because it brought the comforts and rewards of a middle-class lifestyle as well as the freedoms that this country promised (183). But it also meant learning and adopting the practices of whiteness, which meant recreating oneself as American by distancing oneself from Blackness. In my own experience, the ambivalence produced by the conflicts between whiteness and Jewishness manifested itself as an overriding sense of shame and stigmatization. This intergenerational family legacy, passed down through the paternal line, became a permanent mark of my otherwise erased ethnoracial identity, a mark that, much to my confusion, others did not seem to see. What remained unmarked and backgrounded for me, on the other hand, are the ways in which the conflict/discrepancy between white Jewishness and Blackness inform the experiential structure of whiteness, which is also my ethnoracial legacy. But then, the very fact of its unmarkedness indicates the relative effectiveness of my own assimilation into whiteness.

These experiences have shaped my focal points of intellectual interest, modes of inquiry, interdisciplinary collaborations, and feminist and racial politics. The questions I raise here around identity have been informed by a desire to understand my identity through relational learning, that is, from the vantage point of other languages, cultures, and races. A cluster of experiences has allowed me to question issues of identity more deeply: my formal training in Spanish Cultural and Literary Studies, the years that I lived within a *chicana/o* setting in my early college years at the University of California in San Diego, and the many years I lived in Spain. Additionally, my experiences as an activist and community organizer around feminism and race, as well as my professional collaborations, have informed my vision of identity. From intense dialogues about the effects of inequality within community workshop settings as well as from the professional relationships I have forged with feminists, womanists and Black feminists within the context of working within a Women's Studies program embedded in an Ethnic Studies enclave of my university, I learned that coalition building is limited when the epistemic status of identity is not acknowledged.[5]

Thus, both my formative and professional experiences have justified my own perspectives on identity. They are not justified because they are my experiences, but because they provide an account of the social world that meshes with what I know about it, by making visible the background assumptions that are constitutive of my conscious social experience. It is because of these experiences that I have come to believe that by focusing on identity-based politics, which are claims about the social and epistemic significance of identities, it is possible to avoid the emotional and social-psychological injuries that accompany assimilative demands, false consciousness, and the fruitless expenditure of resources on failed coalition building.

Additionally, such claims provide important empirical and theoretical explanations of the social structure, including the notions of patriarchy, white supremacy, and ethnocentrism, helping us to better understand how our social/cultural system obscures, discounts, or renders arbitrary certain experiences as sources of knowledge while rendering others meaningful, "true," and objective. At a more personal level, as I hope to have indicated, such claims help me to make visible my own investment in whiteness that remains partially obscure to me but that is constitutive of my identity, and that I continuously labor to bring into focus. I outline this process of hermeneutical self-recognition throughout this book, but with particular salience in the conclusion of chapter 5.

I begin chapter 1 by revisiting the debates around differences and the strategies for inclusion and solidarity within feminist discourse that surfaced as white feminists responded to the identity-based movements of the '80s and '90s as well the development of postmodern feminist thought that has developed subsequent to those early debates. I read the dominant expressions of this body of theory as a denial of identity-based politics. To demonstrate this intent, I deconstruct Susan Friedman's *Mappings: Feminist and*

Cultural Geographies of Encounter and Robyn Wiegman's *American Anatomies*, teasing out the embedded tactics of discursive racial power. I then turn to a postpositivist realist account of identity, elaborating on the overview in this introduction.

In chapter 2 I examine womanism as an evolving identity formation that surfaces at the interstices of academic discourses, historical and aesthetic periods, cultural productions, and nationalist mobilizations. I analyze the dominant strain of womanist thought, drawing upon Alice Walker's definition. I highlight the specificity of race-gender formation as a site of social conflict, cultural/ideological meaning, and political organization. I further indicate the resonance of Walker's womanist reinterpretive anthropology with the epistemological concerns of postpositivist realism, namely, the exploration of experience as a source of real knowledge as well as of social mystification.

In the four remaining chapters I develop the concept of location as another way of articulating the raced, gendered body. Insofar as human subjectivity is so intimately bound to and defined by the social world in which it is situated, I interrogate constructs of time and space as forms of cognition that aid human subjects in the task of understanding themselves and the social world. In this regard, we can understand the constitutive nature of embodied female subjectivity as "bits of social and political theory" (Mohanty 2000, 57). In contradistinction to postmodern concepts of space and time as both counterposed to one another and at the same time equally unmappable and incoherent, and in contrast to positivist understandings of space as static and time/history as closed and contained to the "past," I draw upon an understanding of spatiality and temporality as interactively and multiply conceived, insofar as they are intimately linked to the human subject. I thus posit an understanding of the body as the location where human experience and self-recognition assume spatial and temporal dimensions. I argue that while articulated within temporal and spatial contexts not necessarily of their own making, embodied subjects can also develop oppositional temporal and spatial practices, located in the body, as they begin to undertake the conscious effort of linking their experiences to their historical and spatial environments.

For instance, when a social actor perceives past time in relation to the remembrance of an historical event in which he or she was a participant, by deploying memory mechanisms located in the body such as those invoked by the senses and emotions, the meaning of an event becomes spatialized. In this regard, a subject's embodied mnemonics of the past, as opposed to the historian's version of the subaltern subject's past, can provide a context in which the human subject may discover the broader historical context in which the meanings of his or her identity have been produced, and the consequences of that history within the present. Similarly, the notion of spatiality I develop here considers space as intrinsically linked to the located experiences of embodied subjects and to the history(ies) and interpretive traditions/mnemonics they bring to the space(s) they inhabit. We can understand space as spatialities when we consider the different cultural and social locations of social actors within a given space, locations that develop internally, within individuals, as well as externally, between individuals and groups. Insofar as human subjects are a constitutive part of space, that is, embodied space, they are capable, through conscious reflection on their experiences, of providing knowledge about social relations within the specific time/space in which they are located.

In chapter 3 I focus on the notion of embodied memory in Alice Walker's prototypical womanist novel, *The Color Purple*. I conceptualize embodied memory as lived, self-actualizing memory. The body is the "site" of history, a site that challenges the static representation of "truth" as represented in the authoritative discourse of history. I further indicate how the collective embodied contexts of the African American community allow the protagonists to engage a cognitivist critical praxis that facilitates their development of a historiographical consciousness.

In chapter 4 I review the challenges facing Latinas in defining racialized gender, given their racial heterogeneity. I argue that an identity politics of *mestizaje/mulatez* is fundamentally an interrogation of the various racial economies in which Latinas/*mestizas* are located, as a result of various colonialist and imperialist projects. I draw upon the philosophical foundations of Human Geography, notably, of hermeneutics and phenomenology, to conceptualize the notion of the body as an ontological metaphor of place. The body, conceived thus, is an interpretive schema that is not only caught up as another object within the social world's organization, but also one that actively participates, as subject, in the structuring of social experience and in the construction of reality. Through an analysis of the autobiographical works of Gloria Anzaldúa, Sandra MaríaEstéves, and Miriam Jiménez Román, I retrace the crisscrossing of domains of meanings, located in the body, whereby the domain of hegemonic understandings of raced, classed, and gendered meanings open themselves up to the particular lived, spatialized experiences of the narrative subjects. I argue that these writers conceptualize their embodied identities as ontological metaphors, a conceptualization that allows them both to understand their identities within existing economies of meanings, as well as to reorganize their identities.

In chapter 5, I use the lens of popular geography, a subfield of human geography that attends to the reproduction of social identity through everyday practice to explore a particular set of everyday social-spatial practices in Ana Castillo's novel, *So Far from God*, that of *domesticana*, a concept referring to the domestic spaces that *Chicanas/mestizas* inhabit, as well as the habits, patterns of interactions, and practices that take place within them. I argue that as the female characters within Castillo's narrative draw upon *domesticana* as a set of interpretive traditions, they begin to operate within multiple temporalities and spatialities. This, in turn, allows them the opportunity to compare the meanings and values of disembodied rationality as grounded in Western modernity that have proven to be deleterious to their survival with their own conceptualizations of embodied rationality, derived from *domesticana* traditions. I end with an exploration of how social practices implemented by subaltern women, pertaining to diverse temporalities and spatialities, can help adjudicate between competing conceptualizations of reason and truth, as well as deepen our understanding of the processes for recognizing and negotiating them across the divides of our different locations.

CHAPTER 2

Reimagining Identity Politics in the New Millennium: A Postpositivist Realist Approach

Introduction: Revisiting the Difference Question in the '70s, '80s, '90s, and Beyond

Dating back at least to Barbara Christian's seminal article, "The Race for Theory," women of color feminists have implemented a sustained critique of postmodern feminism, viewing it as a threat to feminist goals (Christian 1987). Christian then echoed the sentiments of many women of color feminists when she noted that it was not theory that was the problem, but its hegemony within academic circles, in particular, its silencing of the discourses and theories of feminists of color that were just beginning to take hold as postmodernist theory surfaced (1987, 53). New generations of feminists of color have continued the work of developing important critiques of postmodernist discourses even as they have sought to understand and acknowledge the positive implications of postmodernist thought for subaltern women's agendas. They have also developed compelling theoretical alternatives for making salient the experiential realities of subaltern communities as resources of knowledge, some of which I will examine in detail here and throughout this book.

At the same time, however, cultivating what has been broadly defined as identity politics, Black feminists, womanists, Latina, and Asian American feminists have also continued to carve out shared group interests and perspectives, based on their own group's collective experiences. I define identity politics here as a set of political practices fostering a collective empowering subjectivity by offering members of marginalized groups a different perspective on themselves and the world. Monika Gagnon has correctly described identity politics as "the self-naming and self-identification of individuals and communities around a common identity category in order to make a political intervention" (Gagnon 2000, 22). Although subaltern communities have historically practiced such processes, I focus in this work on the particular deployments of identity politics in the post–World War II civil rights period by Latina feminists, Black feminists, and womanists, within the broader context of U.S. society and on the debates that theories of identity emerging from such deployments sparked off within feminist circles as well within the social movements against which they have pushed. These include *chicano* and Puerto Rican nationalist movements, and Black Nationalism respectively.

The debates around identity within the ranks of feminism developed at a specific historical point, in the '80s and '90s, in response to important economic and social shifts developing in American society as well as globally, associated with neoliberalism. As noted by Lisa Duggan, neoliberalism emerged with full force during this period, drawing on classical liberalism's utopianism of benevolent free markets and minimal government to advance the specific interests of U.S. economic elites. Supported by new democrats, traditional conservatives, and neoconservatives alike, this pro-business activism had as a central aim the honing of corporate profits by dismantling the limited U.S. welfare state and other social formations aimed at the downward redistribution of wealth. By drawing upon a rhetoric of privatization and personal responsibility, proponents of this activism were able to achieve and at the same time mask their own identity politics, one which functioned to bring about an "upwardly redistributive impetus" (Duggan 2003, 14).

Women of color feminists negotiated their identity politics partly at least in response to the aforementioned developing social conditions. Black feminism, for example, as noted in the Combahee River Collective Statement, developed an anticapitalist orientation that took into account economic oppression and its imbrications with patriarchal and white supremacist ideologies. Black feminist scholarship examines upward distribution through reforms that effectively dismantled the welfare state, and the effects of such redistributions on Black women and their communities, especially the pathologization of the Black family and the demonization of Black women (Alexander-Floyd 2007, 5–6; 81–83). Women of color feminists also developed a sustained critique of racism within feminism on the one hand, and sexism within Black, *chicano*, and Puerto Rican nationalisms on the other.

Although such critiques on the part of feminists of color have obliged Women's Studies as a discipline to engage self-reflexively with these nationally based identity politics, and even to adopt their theoretical insights, notably those of intersectionality and constitutive models of identity, Women's Studies has been generally reluctant to develop more fully the interconnections of such theories to the community experiences to which they correspond in order to better understand unassimilable differences (Collins 1990, Combahee 1982; Crenshaw 1991). Quite to the contrary, the increased attention that feminist theory has given in the last decades to identity divisions has only led to feminisms' general abandonment of identity politics and a reorientation toward postmodernist theories that decenter or dismantle human subjectivity as well as human agency.

In order to evaluate these shifts, it is important to consider the kinds of knowledge production, practices, and politics of feminism that the abandonment of identity politics does or does not make possible. A good part of my aim in this investigation is to clarify the often understated and opaque investments scholars have in producing certain types of knowledge and excluding others in their practice of feminism. A primary goal of this work, then, is to marshal different types of feminist, minoritarian and other academic discourses with the aim to illuminate the knowledge producer's interests as part of what is examined. These discourses include, primarily, postpositivist realism, which I will define below, critical race theory, revisionist social theory including social postmodernism, Cultural Studies, and critical pedagogy.

Another equally important and interconnected goal of this chapter is to clarify and defend a revised understanding of the notion of objective knowledge, highlighting not only the context-dependent nature of all knowledge, but also the ways in which social contexts and social localities that individuals and groups occupy both constrain and enable what can possibly be felt, known, and valued. My belief that accurate knowledge about social identities and realities is both possible and desirable is informed by my commitment to use feminist thought to respond more adequately to the real problems of our era, including, most notably, growing social stratification and poverty, revitalized forms of patriarchy and racism. With these goals in mind then, I offer in the subsequent text some justifications for a reappraisal of identity politics and its utility for feminist thought.

A central claim that I make in this and successive chapters is that while admittedly identity politics has not evolved unproblematically from its first expressions of contestation against social hierarchies, it has nonetheless facilitated the emergence of subaltern groups from the margins of power to reclaim their suppressed identities as resources for their collective empowerment. Significantly, identity politics has helped those who are socially marginalized to obtain the radical insight that domination is systematically structured into relations between social groups. This key insight has allowed socially marginalized women to refigure difference more complexly in relation to community membership and social responsibility, as well as to construct oppositional identity formations of racialized gender that can serve as acts of resistance against neoliberal and neoconservative agendas.

Importantly, critical perspectives on identity politics, spearheaded by women of color in the decades of the '70s and '80s, have been fundamental to the formation of discourses and social mobilizations that seek a radical renewal of democratic society. Indeed, the theoretical interventions of women of color, including Black feminism, womanism, Latina feminisms, and Asian American feminisms, are premised on the assumption that there is a fundamental link between subjects and structures and between subjects and their histories. As Patricia Hill Collins points out, this link is made evident by the fact that in spite of the varying positions members of minority groups may occupy within the categories of gender, social class, ethnicity, age, and sexuality, their participation in a collectivity means that they continue to have shared experiences due to their common location in relations of power. An analysis of the fluidity of boundaries between interlocking categories of identities, such as race, class, gender, and sexuality, help us, moreover, to better understand how structural power can impact members of an oppressed group differently, depending on the referent or situation. Yet even with extreme modulations, members of a group continue to experience the ongoing effects of inequality, a fact that results in and underscores group stability (Collins 2004, 249).

Beyond revealing the compelling arguments that theorists and activists provide on behalf of the ongoing necessity of the projects of identity politics, I also argue that the general trend within U.S. feminism to dismiss identity politics—whether out of a defensiveness toward its reactionary character, a profound skepticism toward modernist understandings of identity, or, alternately, out of a weariness to deal with the complexities that arise when addressing the differences in power that diversified gender identities invoke—is done so at a historical conjuncture when conservatives are appropriating racial discourses that minoritarian women's groups have honed for their own empowerment. By failing to attend to the theoretical possibilities for the reformulation of a politics of identity, the feminist agenda not only runs the risk of being co-opted from without but also from within its own ranks.

In this book I draw upon the theory of postpositivist realism as my primary, but not exclusive, frame of reference.[1] Over the last decade, scholars have adopted postpositivist realism in order to contest postmodernist claims that identity politics is philosophically and socially unjustifiable, a claim that is reflective of postmodernists' general skepticism of epistemological foundationalism within contemporary thought (Mohanty 2000, 31–33). Developed initially by Satya M. Mohanty in his essay, "The Epistemic Status of Cultural Identity: On *Beloved* and the Postcolonial Condition," postpositivist realism engages the intellectual traditions of American pragmatism and analytic philosophy (including epistemology, social theory, and the philosophy of science), drawing upon the works of such scholars as Richard Boyd, Donald Davidson, Charles Peirce, W.V.O. Quine, and Hilary Putnam (Mohanty 2000). Taking seriously as its goal a politics of social struggle and public culture, postpositivist realist understandings of identity theorize subjectivities not only as constructed but also as 'real' social categories of race, class, and gender—categories that are linked in varying and complex ways with social arrangements in the world as well as with one's material and epistemological interests. Because identities refer outward, it is not only politically expedient but also epistemologically possible to use lived experiences as a venue for gaining objective knowledge of the self and the social world through a comparative analysis of conflicting and incompatible explanations (Mohanty 2000, 55–57).

As I will demonstrate throughout this study, postpositivist realism provides new frameworks for redefining social identity, based on a naturalist-realist account of the self that considers sensorial and affective realms of the lifeworld as sources of experiential knowledge lodged in the body, as well as recognizes the cognitive status of experience (Mohanty 2000, 32–33). By this I mean that knowledge is never posited as free from theoretical bias, as postmodernists and positivists would have it. Nor is it naively assumed to correlate to self-evident understandings of experience. Instead, identities are viewed as theoretically mediated, and therefore dependent upon our ability and our willingness to understand and explain the various possible types and degrees of accuracy or error regarding our social and political situations. As an ideal of inquiry rather than an achieved condition, postpostivist realism aspires to be epistemically and politically productive. As such, it begins with the basic premise that being able to understand and explain one's identity and social situation in relation to one's historical circumstances and the cultural meanings of one's embodiment is a fundamental precondition of being able to effectively act on behalf of one's own interests for the purpose of emancipatory action (Mohanty 2000, 53–54).

Postpositivist realism has captured the attention of minority scholars working within the arenas of Multicultural Education, Philosophy, Literary Studies/Cultural Studies, and other disciplines, precisely because it provides additional intellectual resources that they can use to further fortify and legitimize their cultivation of social formations and theoretical practices against such critiques. Since the early '90s, a number of feminist scholars, including Linda Martín Alcoff, Johnella Butler, Sandra Harding, and Paula M.S. Moya, have engaged postpositivist realism to correct previous theoretical misconceptions as well as to articulate a new progressive feminist politics of identity by redrawing the lines of connection between experience, personal understandings, and public meanings.

Among these scholars, Alcoff and Moya have contributed a significant body of scholarship in this arena. Moya has been instrumental in introducing the basic tenets of a postpositivist realist method of inquiry as well as applying them to literary and multicultural discourses in order to better distinguish the epistemic and political consequences of various forms of *chicana/o* identity politics. Alcoff has drawn from analytic epistemology and metaphysics as well as from phenomenology and hermeneutics to nuance the various configurations and meanings of realism, highlighting the co-participation of human beings in its constitution, while affirming the limitations of discursive or linguistic manipulation of human subjectivity and the world. As I will indicate in detail in chapter 5, Alcoff brings together the theoretical insights of phenomenology and hermeneutics to further develop the notion of identities as "interpretive horizons," the perspectival mediations that subjects undertake to make sense of the world and the specific material embodied situatedness from which such interpretations are derived (2006, 94–113).

In this chapter I develop an analysis of the relevance of postpositivist realism to feminism. In particular, I indicate its utility for culling out the limitations of current theoretical orientations, that of postmodern feminism, with regard to the feminist goal of empowerment and liberation. I begin with a brief overview of theories pertaining to postmodernism and provide a critical overview of the terminology and evolving debates around social identity and identity politics that developed in the '80s and '90s in response to the development of feminist and subaltern women's mobilizations of the '70s and '80s. This is by no means an exhaustive overview, but rather one that signals the various positions that feminists assumed, the problems that such positions posed, and the various solutions that feminists sought as the debates took their course. I use the overview to critique the strategy of strengthening feminist movement through postmodern theoretical directions.

Following a review and clarification of terminology deployed within a number of discourses and debates developing in the last decades of the twentieth century, I develop an analysis of the ideological implications of specific feminist applications of theories that dismiss identity. I use as examples two works, *Mappings*, by Susan Stanford Friedman, and *American Anatomies*, by Robyn Wiegman, both published in the '90s, that directly engaged the debates around essentialism and identity, and sought to provide orientations for studying inequality and/or for implementing solidarity and coalition building that sidestepped identity as a basis for feminist politics and coalition building. In doing so, I hope to provide compelling arguments that point to the justification of a widespread development and deployment of social theories, including critical pedagogy and social postmodernism, that, like postpositivist realism, can effectively aid women of color theorists as well as white feminists, such as myself, in achieving the liberatory goals we claim as our own.

The works of Friedman and Wiegman provide a useful starting point for my analysis of identity politics. In their respective works, each scholar aims not only to critique and dismantle identity politics, but also to offer an ameliorated frame of reference for feminist thought. Moreover, their approaches are not merely random examples of feminist approaches to gender analysis, but set the stage for and are reflective of current antihumanist theoretical trends within feminism, based on the rejection of the belief in the autonomy of the human subject, and of the concept of human agency. Wiegman, for example, suggests that because subaltern identities of women are unassimilable, it becomes necessary to disarticulate gender from identity, seeking counter- knowledges not in social identity but rather in a reinterpretation of feminism's own problematic epistemic imbrications with modernist thought (Wiegman 1995, 181–93).

For her part, Friedman proposes an incorporation of various differentiated feminisms into a unified locational feminism, or what she calls a "relational positionality," based on and achieved by playfully moving beyond difference through performances and dialogics (Friedman 1998, 74–82). I argue, alternatively, that the respective theoretical approaches by Friedman and Wiegman only serve to rearticulate the very racial projects within feminist thought that they aim to dismantle.[2]

I end the chapter with a formulation of an anti-foundationalist, oppositional identity politics and its potential to fortify the social practices of differentiated women's spheres or publics.

THEORY AS CO-OPTATION: THE BAIT AND SWITCH TACTIC

There is a tendency in more sophisticated and elaborate gender standpoint epistemologists to affirm "an identity made up of heterogeneous and heteronomous representations of gender, race, and class, and often indeed across languages and cultures" with one breath, and with the next to refuse to explore how that identity may be theorized or analyzed, by reconfirming a unified subjectivity or "shared consciousness" through gender. The difference is handed over with one hand and taken away with the other.

Norma Alarcón (1997, 295)

Postmodernist feminisms take on the question of identity and difference within the context of postmodernity and the economic philosophy of neoliberalism that justified it. Postmodernity refers to a set of social and geopolitical formations shaped by postmodernist cultural forms, more flexible modes of capital accumulation, and global reconfigurations that have "led to further consolidation and exacerbation of capitalist relations of domination and exploitation" (Alexander and Mohanty 1997, xvii). Globalization and postmodernity are inextricably linked (Harvey 1989). According to conventional Marxist formulations, both discourses represent identity as a commodity to be reintegrated into newly organized markets. Fredric Jameson affirms, for example, that postmodernity and globalization exert a standardizing force on identities in order to create consumers for American global markets (Jameson 1984).

Additionally, postmodernist discourses reject modern theory's notion of social coherence and patterned social processes, such as integration, domination, and exploitation (Baudrillard 1983; Jameson 1984). Rather than examine the disjunctures between differing processes of gender and racial formations produced within the framework of relations of global capitalistic relations, postmodernists have instead opted to reject the analytic utility of the categories of race, class, gender, and sexuality. Thus, in conjunction with theorizing the phenomenon of social fragmentation on a global scale, postmodernists argue that the philosophical subject that shaped the conceptions of representation and social coherence in modern philosophy and social theory has been superseded. The cultural/philosophical formation that accompanied the historical situation of late capitalism is now viewed as a fictive construct that is utilized as a tool of power and discipline as is reality (Foucault 1977), which evaporates into a contingent play of simulacra (Baudrillard 1983, 31–32).

In contrast to Enlightenment thinkers who believed people capable of grasping the foundations of knowledge and achieving a relatively unambiguous understanding of the external world with the aim of transforming social conditions, postmodernists view modern theory's notion of epistemic foundationalism as a myth, one that only functions to repress human spontaneity and difference. In sum, postmodernists reject the basic meta assumptions of modern social theory: the authority of positivistic science as a means to ascertain knowledge about the self and the world, and the totalizing features of Enlightenment rationalism, in particular, the notion of meta narratives that has given rise to understandings of the unified goals of history, such as universal emancipation, social coherence, and the autonomous, stable subject (Antonio and Kellner 1994).

Feminist scholars were quick to engage these discourses in order to better understand the effects that the new global structures, cultures, and subjects would have on women's struggles for agency, identity formation, and empowerment, and to more adequately assess the social conditions affecting women. Throughout the '80s, poststructuralist and post-Marxist feminists thus developed a significant body of postmodern theory that continues to have a palpable impact on feminist thought today. Proponents of these theories, including Judith Butler, Donna Haraway, and Joan Scott, among others, have had a pervasive influence on feminist thought in the last decades. These scholars argue that the construction of meta narratives that bring into being the civilizing subject, based on the legacy of an Enlightenment faith in science and reason, had been developed to legitimate violence against women and subaltern communities in the form of political repression and cultural homogenization. The construction of meta narratives has resulted, they argue, in the strengthening of centralized systems of power, such as mass culture, that eradicate particularity and block the creative forces of language and desire (Butler 1990; Haraway 1990; Scott 1991).

Within the camp of philosophical subject formation, more particularly, postmodernist feminists have made salient the ideological underpinnings of representational practices of modernity, exposing the interconnections of language, power, and subjectivity. In doing so, they have worked to demonstrate the failure of Enlightenment rationality to determine absolute meaning as well as to expose in contemporary empirical practices an inability to transcend the ideological and economic conditions that create and reproduce systems of inequality. Postmodern feminists contend, moreover, that social coherence, as well as conceptions and representations of the real, are the result of mythic constructs and textual signifiers that have been eclipsed in postmodern society. Accordingly, enactments of the identity "woman" are never real, because they are never separate and apart from the discursive practices of modernity that differentiate and regulate subjects in the first place, and are necessarily subjected to hermeneutical problems that accompany social signification.

Postmodernist feminists have not directed their skepticism with regard to Enlightenment notions of rationality, objectivity, and the universality of knowledge exclusively toward its legacies in the empirical methodologies of modern science and social sciences, but also toward the epistemologies and politics of minoritarian groups, including some forms of feminism, which have in effect remained loyal to modernist accounts of identity, purportedly against their own interests. Thus, postmodernist feminists point out that minoritarian women's essentialized definitions of race and gender, definitions that view identities as concrete and fixed, led to their social exclusion in the first place.

Postmodern feminists further argue that by accepting their identity as naturalized or biologically determined, members of subaltern groups mistakenly believe they inherently hold authenticated knowledge of their self and of others in their group by virtue of their shared location. By creating a politics based on the assumption that they are best situated to interpret their individual and collective experiences, as well as the workings of domination and oppression more broadly, subaltern communities in effect reproduce the dominant behavior of coercing sameness against which they pushed. Postmodern feminist critics propose, alternatively, that there is liberation to be found both in recognizing that there is no empirical basis that structures our experiences of self and our social realities, and in exposing the ways in which binaries work interdependently within discourses to create systems of power and subjugation.[3]

The protracted debates over identity that developed in the '70s, '80s, and '90s within feminist camps began with polarized positions. The position held by women of color theorists, as well as by standpoint theorists in general, held that knowledge claims about women's lives must be grounded in women's everyday life and experiences. Reality about women's lives can be objectively known, these critics argued, if one uses women's experiences—experiences that are not fully discursively appropriated—to study it. In a 1972 conference paper that Sandra Harding subsequently included in an anthology on standpoint theory, Dorothy Smith expresses this view when she states: "To begin from direct experience and to return to it as a constraint or 'test' of the adequacy of a systematic knowledge is to begin from where we are located bodily" (2004, 29). Similarly, in a 1993 essay collected in the same volume, Sandra Harding affirmed: "[T]he fact that subjects of knowledge are embodied and socially located has the consequence that they are not fundamentally different from objects of knowledge" (2004, 133). In her 1986 essay, "Learning from the Outsider Within: The Sociological Significance of Black Feminist Thought," Patricia Hill Collins advocated a Black women's standpoint, arguing that Black women's marginal status within academia provides them with a particular perspective or standpoint which they can use to produce accurate analyses of race, class, and gender, and, more particularly, analyses about the lives of Black women (1986).

The method here consists not only in exposing knowledge production as imbricated in systems of power, based on race, class, and gender hierarchies, and as a mechanism for the reproduction of such systems, but also in liberating women from such systems. It was largely in response to such methodologies that the 'strong' postmodernists and poststructuralists proposed to eliminate the authority of experience. They argued that insofar as the meanings of experiences and identities are not transparent, they cannot be explained outside of cultural and discursive productions of intelligibility—social narratives, codes, paradigms, and ideologies. Identities and identity politics, so the argument goes, are simply not adequately accountable to the epistemological and political significance of identities (Scott 1991).

But as the debates around identity, knowledge, and power developed, feminist scholars working in the overlapping arenas of women of color feminism, feminist epistemology, the philosophy of science, and cultural criticism advanced a nonessentialized subjectivity. For example, Black feminists, womanists, and Latina feminists sought to clarify the distinctions between their nonessentialist portrayals of identity and the essentialist identity politics that came into being under the auspices of Black Power, Black Liberation and *La Raza* movements respectively. My analysis in successive chapters elaborates on the nature of such distinctions and the extent to which individually and collectively such distinctions were achieved. Proponents of feminist standpoint theory, such as Patricia Hill Collins and Sandra Harding among others, further elaborated and/or explained their standpoint methodologies in order to more fully acknowledge the fluidity of identity and the difficulties and challenges of interpreting social experience (Collins 1998; Harding 2004).[4] Cultural feminists, such as Diana Fuss, and Elizabeth Meese, also attempted early reformulations of the essence versus constructivism controversy, primarily through a revision of deconstructive practices, highlighting the strengths and limitations of each polarized component, and examining the politics driving these two positions (Fuss 1989; Meese 1986).

In the late '80s and '90s, feminists continued to develop theories that could transcend the problems posed by essentialism. Some post-modern feminists developed a new rubric more in consonance with feminists' normative commitments. In doing so, they labored to remain accountable to the subjective understandings and mobilizations of members of subaltern social movements as central components of a democratic society while recognizing the need to provide more nuanced frameworks for explaining the complexity of identity. A salient example of this orientation is Linda Nicholson and Steven Seidman's edited volume *Social Postmodernism: Beyond Identity Politics* (1995).

In her essay in this volume, "Politics, Culture, and the Public Sphere: Towards a Postmodern Conception," Nancy Fraser elaborates on the concept of subaltern counterpublics, defining them as "discursive arenas where members of subjugated groups invent and circulate counterdiscourses" (Fraser 1995, 290). She argues that the elaboration of oppositional interpretations of self and community that subaltern groups undertake within these discursive sites, moreover, ultimately expand possibilities for social contestation and enacting democratic processes (291–92). Accordingly, Fraser conceptualizes the public sphere as made up of a constellation of dialectally related public spheres. Fraser's concern, however, is not with retaining or affirming group-based identity, that is, with affirming group recognition that exists extradiscursively as a mechanism for achieving social justice. She proposes instead the notion of counterpublic, articulated as a discursive tool or weapon, to de-institutionalize hierarchical patterns that prevent access, participation, and parity. She gives the example of how the parallel subaltern counterpublic of the U.S. women's movement gave rise to new discursive arenas, including terms such as sexism, sexual harassment, date rape—terms that made salient oppositional interests and needs, and functioned over time to ameliorate women's condition within the public sphere (291).[5]

Iris Marion Young's essay in the same volume postulates a theory of seriality, one that also aims to facilitate a dialectical dynamic of identity, thereby avoiding essentialist portrayals of the subject (1995).

Seriality is a concept that allows for the recognition of the category 'women,' but extricates women from having to define themselves according to any common natural or metaphysical characteristics. Without requiring women to have any common physical or metaphysical traits or social situation seriality posits that women form part of a series because they experience the effects of social forces, including sexism, racism, and classism (1995, 197; 205).

In the same volume, Chantal Mouffe provides another example of a more moderate version of postmodern identity. She acknowledges that the deconstruction of women's identity is a necessary precondition for a radical democratic politics but 'women' as a category can exist as a "precarious status," providing the basis for feminist struggle. For Mouffe, however, the goal is not that feminists should seek a separate identity for women, but should discard the idea of such an identity instead. The work of feminist politics should be simply to examine how the female subject is constructed in multiple discourses, in a manner that reproduces women's subjugated status (328–29).

Insofar as the above-referenced critics work to retain in some manner the notions of group identity, they provide "constructive as well as deconstructive analyses of the social" (Nicholson 1995, 9). Nonetheless, because identity articulated as embodied experiences shared by a collectivity remains distinctly muted in these theories, with the category 'woman' being viewed, alternately, as discursive, randomly organized, or as a provisional and inferior status that must be overcome, these moderate postmodernist conceptions of identity fall short, at least in my estimation, of offering compelling solutions to social inequality. It is significant to note, moreover, that there are a number of social movement theorists focusing on women's movements that emphasize the importance of understanding women's identity as based not on some temporal condition, but rather on the ongoing realities of women's lives, based at least partly on some of the natural properties pertaining to women.

Jane Jenson's work on feminism in France exemplifies this approach. Focusing on the abortion issue during the second wave of feminism as the lynchpin of transformational change, she argues that women's ability to reproduce and to make decisions about their fertility are components of existence that are specific to women's lives, that is, their identities. Moreover, by making the interpretations of their identity as well as of their needs and demands based on their interpretations recognized, Jenson argues, French feminists were able to bring about change in the status of women, as evidenced in effective policy change around abortion legalization (Jenson 1985, 12–13).

The abortion issue, moreover, is key because it signals, as social movement theorist Jean Cohen points out, a transformation in women's identity as political subject, insofar as the discourses on abortion reform caused a shift in women's understanding of their bodies as well as a shift in the relationship of their embodied selves to the state (Cohen 1996, 198–99). Jenson also notes that public recognition of a new identity of women within political discourse due to changed state policy in the area of reproduction was important not just because it expanded the arena of political discourse, but also because the abortion campaign that resulted in new policies created new sites for women to further develop their identities as different from men's, and to have their identities be recognized (Jenson 1985, 15). Such a view of identity and difference, however, is arguably quite different from Fraser's emphasis on full participation as the ultimate goal for which feminists should struggle. Precisely because they are women, their different concerns justify the ongoing need to affirm identity, rather than to dispel it simply because some measure of parity has been achieved.

In her study of Uruguayan women's social movements, political scientist Erica Townsend-Bell also underscores the importance of a deepened understanding and recognition of the ongoing relevance of racialized gender identity. Indeed, this social movement theorist makes the claim that women activists are effective coalition builders only when they are capable of acknowledging the salience of identities. In exploring the lack of success that Uruguyan women's organizations experienced in attempting to build multiracial coalitions, she found that among the groups she studied, conflicts that prevented further negotiations tended to occur precisely because members of the diverse organizations held different conceptualizations of race as well as different considerations of the relevance of racial identity with regard to the process and outcome of gender mobilization (Bell 2007).

It is interesting to note, nonetheless, that the more moderate theoretical directions that the above-referenced critics have set forth, directions that at the very least leave open the possibility for negotiating a politics around identities, have been largely overshadowed by the looming presence of the earlier, more extreme renditions of postmodernist feminism, as espoused, for example, by Butler, Haraway, and Scott. Indeed, the camp of corporeal feminism that also surfaced in the '90s, and included such figures as Claire Colebrook (2002), Elizabeth Grosz (1994), and Judith Olkowski (1999), among others, worked to elaborate and extend their orientation. Concerned with the domestication of feminism, these theorists reflected an eagerness to indicate feminism's increased resonance with the evolved orientation of European philosophy, in particular, the Deleuzian conceptualization of the subject as a constitutive fiction.

For example, rather than viewing the material body and the experiences that constitute embodied identity as the external expression of a deeper psychical self that can provide meaning, Elizabeth Grosz, in her work *Volatile Bodies*, posits the body not as an organic, unified subjectivity, but rather as "a series of surfaces, energies, and forces, a mode of linkage, a discontinuous series of processes, organs, flows, and matter." (Grosz 1994, 120). According to this perspective, embodied identity is never related to identification or the self-identical concepts that inform the raced or gendered subject, but rather to the mobilization of bodily processes that, in their temporal inscriptions, function to destabilize, deform, and disorder unified meaning.

These more excessive or extreme strains of postmodern feminist thought have unwittingly generated a type of social theory that has had the overall effect of disengaging feminist thought from the goals of social justice, and from the local identity-based movements that spawned such goals. In the arena of philosophical postmodernism, as noted by Peter McLaren, postmodernists have demonstrated modernist theory's inability to construct "a vocabulary or epistemology that is able to render the world empirically discoverable or accurately mappable" (McLaren 1994, 196). Yet, at the same time, postmodernists have failed to replace modernist theories of the social with better theories that can more adequately address social change. In effect, such radically skeptical perspectives on the theoretical foundations of modernist theory have stymied progressive action by rejecting not only modernism's problematic contributions but also its valuable ones, namely, the resources it has provided for the projects of social theory that take into account the need for broader and more complex perspectives on contemporary differentiated social formations as well as social interdependencies.

As the adoption of postmodern theoretical critiques of the philosophical subject has become palpable in feminist scholarship throughout the '80s and '90s, so has it become more difficult for feminist scholarship to reflect more centrally on how the scholarly and cultural practice of decentering identities and meaning is itself a product of particular historical realities. By failing to ask such questions, we as feminist scholars run the risk not only of contributing to the concealment of those very material conditions that have produced fragmented and socially marginalized identities, but also of undertheorizing the current proliferating processes of racialized gender, ultimately depicting as unnecessary the various mobilizations of feminists of color who have, since the '70s, worked within the academy to theorize.

At the same time, because of the subject of their theorizing and their deployment of analytic tools that are privileged within the academy, postmodern feminists have located themselves in elevated positions within academic Feminist Studies, garnering both academic prestige and economic profitability in the form of endowed chairships, status, and spiraling salaries (Alexander and Talpade Mohanty 1997, xvi; Ebert 1996, 179–80). For women of color within the ranks of Women's Studies, however, the types of analytic tools they may prefer to adopt—and identity politics is certainly one of them—pose a number of risks to their integration into academic culture, both in terms of access to intellectual and material resources as well as in terms of professional promotion. Thus, while Women's Studies as the academic arm of the women's movement has been instrumental in acting as a site of contestation with regard to racist, sexist, and homophobic representations of minoritized social subjects, and in also ameliorating the professional enfranchisement of women of color within the ranks of Women's Studies, there continues to be a growing disjuncture between the divergent and contested theories we produce in the name of social justice, and the resulting exacerbation of social marginalization experienced by women of color both within the institution of higher education and within the U.S. macrostructure.

Regrettably, the more extreme strand of postmodern feminism has become aligned with the very tendencies of late capitalism and global processes it critiques. Proponents of these lines of critique have failed to investigate the internal contradictions of globalization, thereby opening up a broader terrain of potential consumerism of women's cultures and political realities. Additionally, insofar as postmodern feminists share with neoconservatives and neoliberalists a common view of identity and identity politics, while admittedly motivated by quite different rationales, they also frequently implement analogous processes of cultural representations of women of color and their communities. Such processes rely on the marketization strategy of appropriation, a strategy that exposes the underlying interconnection between capital and culture. Womanist theologian Katie Cannon defines appropriation in the following manner:

> [T]he concept of appropriation has to do with the act of preempting, usurping, confiscating—possessing the power to seize and control a people's resources without authority or with questionable authority. Within the terms of this critique, the social process of appropriation

means the taking over of someone else's culture, and, I would add, someone's educational capital or discourse, more or less with desire beforehand to convert the thing taken over to one's own use. (1996, 131–32)

In the following section, I identify the theoretical resources that women of color feminists as well as critics working within the fields of Sociology and Cultural Studies have developed in order to clarify identity-formation processes as well as the co-optation of oppositional frameworks of racialized gender identity. I then examine the means by which such appropriations have been reabsorbed within feminist thought, using two works published in the '90s as examples: *American Anatomies*, by Robyn Wiegman, and *Mappings*, by Susan Stanford Friedman.

IDENTITY POLITICS AS SOCIAL STRUGGLE IN FEMINIST THOUGHT AND PRAXIS

Oppression is not a game, nor is it solely about language—for many of us, it still remains profoundly real.

(Collins 2004, 253)

The notions of identity formation and identity projects lay the groundwork for theorizing identity politics. Theories of intersectionality and constitutive models of identity that women of color have contributed to feminist thought have advanced our understandings of racialized gender identity formation as a constellation of social structures, processes, and representations. Identity is not shaped by one identity category alone, but rather by the varying and intersecting categories of class, gender, and sexuality. The Combahee River Collective's Statement continues to be one of the most powerful statements on the ways in which Black women experience multiple oppressions, and its impact on the politics of Black women is crystallized in the following excerpt:

> We believe that sexual politics under patriarchy is as pervasive in Black women's lives as are the politics of class and race. We also often find it difficult to separate race from class from sex oppression because in our lives they are most often experienced simultaneously. (16)

Omi and Winant's notion of racial formation further contributes to contemporary understandings of identity formation. These scholars decouple race from biological essence, depicting it instead as a fundamental organizing principle that structures social relationships, practices, and meanings of racial categories (Omi and Winant, 1986, 61–62). Racial meanings, moreover, are constantly shifting, as individuals and groups negotiate them through their social interactions (1986, 66–69). Additionally, according to Omi and Winant, racial formations are constituted by "projects" that are both symbolic (representational) and structural. Racial formation, in this regard, both organizes social life according to racial meanings and provides interpretations that are ideologically informed, justifying a group's power or control of resources (intellectual, social, and economic) along racial lines (Omi and Winant 1994, 56–61). The challenge at hand for social justice scholars who wish to diminish human suffering caused by dominant racial ideologies is to identify the ways in which individuals and groups, through contestation over racial meanings, form and reformulate their identities as they experience them within particular lived conditions (1986, 66–69).

Within recent decades, transnational corporate control of the global economy and global politics has accompanied and/or taken the place of various state formations in the construction of racial, gendered hegemonic projects. Political systems, within both state and global terrains, continue to be organized racially, carrying within them the "stigmatizing signifier" (Winant 2004, xv). Within this context, it becomes important to consider how racial projects within U.S. state and global formations are masked by a rhetoric and racial project of postracialism, one that eminently prefers an incorporative or integrative resolution of racial difference, while rejecting the conflict models of social change adopted by post–civil rights social movements. As an ideological construct, the interpellation of hegemonic incorporation or assimilation is always rearticulated with new linkages and in new contexts. (Winant 2004, xix). Beyond state formations, it becomes necessary to attend to the diverse "re-racializing" processes that comprise globalization—a "system of transnational social stratification under which corporations and states based in the global North dominate the global South" (Winant 2004, 131).

The field of Cultural Studies also takes up racial identity projects in order to understand and intervene in the relations of culture and power as they relate to difference. Like Sociology, this discipline in the '80s attempted to field the complex ideological interconnections between structures and cultures. In the dominant forms of representation that grew out of the historical legacy of neocolonialism and slavery, now called the "old racism" or the "old cultural politics of difference," people and objects were deemed to have unproblematic universal meanings. In the "new racism," categories of identity and culture are viewed as caught between social formations, daily life, and representational practices. For cultural theorists as for social theorists, the cultural project conceives of cultural representation not merely as a description or explanation of an image representing an object, or of something observed within the social world, but as a mechanism through which complex and conflicted cultural and political meanings are circulated, exchanged, contested, and transformed (Hall 2003).

Within the "new cultural politics of difference," that developed in response to the increased hybridization of the U.S. society, there is no unifying discourse on race or gender. As people who have the power to enable signification of things ascribe meaning and value to identities in order to secure the preeminence of whiteness, racial meanings and practices within discourses and representation become sites of conflict and struggle (Hall 2003, 19). The dominant cultural practices of representation, whether exercised in the political media by conservative groups in the name of cultural or national unity or by progressive cultural workers within popular culture, are unavoidably ones in which cultural theorists unwittingly become co-participants, as members of the culturally dominant group. Indeed, cultural theorists create the sites of struggle. But they also create the weapons for that struggle in the form of new articulations of racial and gendered meanings. These often include postracial, integrative rhetoric used to ward off the threat that the oppositional racial and gendered projects fomented by social movements pose to their centrality.

It is precisely against this assimilationist and market rationality impetus that Robyn Wiegman pushes in her work *American Anatomies*, yet in a manner that dismantles rather than affirms the recognition of subaltern subjectivities. Wiegman critiques subaltern communities of women for relying upon incorporative and integrative political strategies insofar as such strategies naturalize embodied identities, foster the homogenization of identities into singular configurations 'Blacks' and 'woman,' and make them ripe and available for commodification. She also critiques the neoliberalists, because they espouse and implement a postracial integrative logic and politics that reinforce hegemonic social structures. Her antidote to such gestures is to focus her critical attention on more historically contingent discursive articulations of racialized gender rather than on an analysis of a natural conception of raced and gendered bodies (1995, 10–11).

She implements such an analysis by examining sexual difference as it appeared in scientific discourses on race in the eighteenth and nineteenth centuries, generating a series of analogies and differentiations between Africans and women.

In what follows, I provide a critical summary of the arguments Wiegman uses to defend "a politics of disloyalty" to assimilative tendencies in and outside of feminist discourse. I then provide a "critical commentary" section, in which I examine her rearticulation of racist projects, with an aim to expose the types of liberation tactics that she claims to be conceptualizing in the name of feminism. I focus my critical review on two arguments that Wiegman uses to justify the disarticulation of gender from both identity and experience. A first claim is that the principle strategy of identity politics used by Black feminists, the creation of oppositional identity formations, has already been appropriated and dismantled by reactionary neoliberalist strategies, thereby justifying the demand for new theoretical approaches. She proposes the denaturalization of identity. A second claim is the unassimilability of the Black woman into the public sphere, thereby rendering moot any attempt on the part of subaltern women to reclaim identity.

Claim #1: The Market economy has effectively dismantled counter-identity formations

American Anatomies focuses on retracing the processes by which identities, throughout history as well as in contemporary society, have been constructed within a cultural economy informed by technologies of visibility or corporeal signifiers, including skin color and skull shape, that inform a "real" or naturalized epistemology of the body, and that function to maintain and reproduce white supremacy and patriarchy. Refusing to follow the more commonly held intersectionality-based approaches to thinking about social identity, Wiegman does not attempt to construct new linkages between 'Black' and 'woman,' categories of identity that have been respectively elided within hegemonic feminist and Black nationalist discourses. Such efforts, she argues, would only reinstantiate the inclusivist tendencies of post-1960s politics, and reinscribe the logic of visibility that has historically contributed to Black women's historical erasure (Wiegman 1995, 7). Although she affirms that identity politics was not a mistaken effort, she concludes that because hegemonic racial practices have evolved in response to its successes, the articulation of identity as a political force and framework for disarticulating inequality is no longer viable (5).

Armed with this rationale, Wiegman initiates the process of dismantling identity by first negating an epistemology of the flesh pursued within the framework of Black feminist identity politics. She then proposes a critique of the oppositional identity formations pursued through such an epistemology, for they not only unwittingly contribute to the naturalization of difference that informs modernity, but also, in their invocation of race, class, and gender as knowable or known categories, such oppositional identity formations assume that these categories are fully adequate to the task of critiquing relations of domination. Referencing bell hooks' *Feminist Theory: From Margins to Center* as a prototypical example of Black feminist political demands to make visible the subjectivities and histories of the cultural margins, Wiegman affirms that methodological centrality does not extract Black women from their historical invisibility. Herein she is referring to the fact that as feminism and Black Power have respectively proven, woman has been elided with whiteness and Blackness with maleness, resulting in newer and more complex social exclusions for Black women (77).

Due to the fact that the desire for incorporation that is aimed for in the re-centering project does not create evidence of an advancement of democratic principles of equality, Wiegman opts to "intervene in the decontextualized and specular incorporation and absorption of identities that now characterize the popular visual realm" (5). Still foregrounding race, class, and gender, Wiegman proposes that these are not transhistorical, natural, or metaphysical categories, but rather historically contingent constructs. She then explores the various historical contexts in which sexual difference becomes imbricated with racial difference, attending not to Black women, but to cultural relations among Black and white men, as a means to grasp both the contingent production of Black masculinity, and also concomitantly, the historical erasure of Black women.

Critical Commentary

While Wiegman asserts that there is no certainty that the re-centering projects of Black feminism will foster an advancement of democratic principles of equality (189), and therefore there is no reason to privilege and pursue such projects, I would posit that there are in fact empirical indicators of democratic advancement within academic Women's Studies programs and departments in recent decades. The numerical representation of women of color at various ranks as professional faculty within Women's and Gender Studies has significantly exceeded the incorporation of women of color in other fields. The Executive Summary of the National Women's Studies Association

Report, "Mapping Women's Studies," posted on the NWSA Web site, states that women of color represent roughly 30 percent of Women's Studies faculty in post-secondary degree-granting institutions as opposed to 19 percent in other disciplines nationally (2007). It is therefore possible, given such indicators, to assume that theories of intersectionality spawned by Black feminists as well as other feminists of color—explanatory models that illuminate how women of color's self-understanding and political interests are shaped by power relations that frame their lives—have been largely responsible for a changed consciousness and praxis within feminist thought. Even as feminism remains coded as white, academic Women's Studies has created new spaces of theoretical negotiation within the cultural and political hegemony of feminism that have forced an effort to hire more diverse faculty as well as to diversify the curriculum and programming.

It is interesting to note the ease with which this critic folds under the difficulties posed by assimilative tendencies, an ease that raises suspicions with regard to Wiegman's ideological investments. Herein, it is useful to reference the conflict model of racial difference, based on Stuart Hall's study of popular culture, that she invokes at the beginning of her study to justify the abandonment of identity politics. Citing Hall extensively, Wiegman claims that the cultural dominant's appropriation and commodification of subaltern identities within the realm of popular representations developed as a tactic to ward off the success of identity politics and the social movements that coalesced in the second half of the twentieth century, creating a requirement that cultural workers abandon identity as the central framework for understanding inequality today (1995, 5).

What she fails to note, however, in Hall's discussion of the appropriation of 'Black' in popular culture, is that central to his line of inquiry about what constitutes cultural politics and the crisis of cultural identity within the global postmodern is the Gramscian notion of *struggle* over cultural hegemony and of *negotiation* of dominant and subordinate positions across and within the hybrid forms of the dominant culture and Black popular culture (1992, 21–25). Like Gramsci, moreover, Hall does not see identity, in this case "the Black," as disappearing as a grounded phenomena. Quite to the contrary, he argues that as popular culture has become the dominant form of global culture, cultural bureaucracies have seized control of interpretations of race, using them as a technology to accrue power and capital. As a result, Black identity shifts, creating a mixed or hybrid character of 'Black' within cultural representations.

Moreover, as cultural critics become more adept at detecting the complexities of such cultural mixing, Black cultural criticism has also shifted. In this phase of its aesthetic, Black cultural criticism now also investigates the hybrid forms of Black cultural aesthetic resulting from the interconnections between inherited African traditions and the cultural repertoire resulting from the Black diasporic experience, which in turn has appropriated and incorporated various European ideologies, cultures, and institutions (28). More importantly, Hall makes salient that it is particularly within this new phase of a Black cultural hybrid aesthetic and dialectic that cultural hegemony opens itself up to the play of power, refashioning and revaluing but not throwing out its epistemology of the body. Herein, the 'popular' form of the 'Black'—that is, the various differentiated representations of the distinctiveness of the historical experiences of subjugated life from which popular communities draw their various cultural traditions, memories, self-understandings, modes of expressiveness, and resilience—is strategically fought over so as to avoid representing them as "low and outside" (1992, 26).

While Hall himself highlights the pivotal role of the body and the materiality of experience as resources of knowledge, Wiegman appropriates Hall's notion of commodification to argue against an epistemology of the flesh. Yet by arguing thus, she maintains "Blacks" and "women" in a decoupled and invisible state while omitting Hall's analysis of the Black body as cultural capital, a central component of his essay. Thus, Hall argues that within the various contexts of the subordinated lives of the diasporic 'Black,' the body often serves as cultural capital that can be used as "canvases of representation" on which to test out alternative repertoires of lived experience. Regardless of the variability of Black traditions and figures in popular cultural representations, Hall affirms that it is possible to detect "the experiences that stand behind them" and that point to "a discourse that is different—other forms of life, other traditions of representation" (27). Indeed, good popular cultural representation, that is, one that engages experience, helps to make salient "which Black popular culture is right on, which is ours, and which is not" (29).

Critical race perspectives deployed across a variety of disciplines coincide with Hall's theoretical insistence on contestation and struggle within representation as the primary strategy available to subaltern communities for advancing democratic ideals, in particular, those that can shift dispositions of power. Working within the interdisciplinary arena of American Studies and Anthropology, Arlene Dávila, for example, focuses on those aspects of neoliberal culture that foreground the various cultural strategies and discourses promoted by corporations, residents, and government policies for the purposes of entrepreneurial success.

Dávila does not challenge or wish to eradicate marketing and consumption because she recognizes these activities as sites that provide openings for marginalized groups and others who care to expose the neoliberal project (2004, 11). She argues that "a disavowal of race and ethnicity, or of the 'messiness' of identity politics, is not yet warranted" (2004, 21). This is because the destabilization of hegemony does not require the dismantling of identity based on race, but rather a transformation in the managing and deployments of cultural and racial-ethnic identities, implemented within government programs and policies as well as within cultural representation (2002, 21). Moreover, identity politics represents an important recourse of contestation against trends prioritizing marketable racial and gendered identities for economic gain and/or development that wish to extricate cultural representations from ethnic or racial memories and politics of identity (11).

For her part, cultural critic Susan Willis argues that the body is a valuable source of cultural capital. Indeed, commodity culture offers a new venue that Black cultural workers may use as a privileged context for creating and affirming Black embodied identity. She shows how Kobena Mercer uses the example of the "Fro," a hairstyle that was not a naturalized expression of difference, but rather a representational strategy, to indicate how market culture can serve as a venue for Black cultural expression, functioning within the public domain as a form of social subversion precisely because white Americans (hippies) believed it was a natural hairstyle related to African Blacks, and desired to appropriate it for their own back-to-nature movement (Willis 1991, 181).[6] In her examination of the musical videos of Michael Jackson, Willis further affirms that Black artists working within cultural terrains largely determined by the white male-dominated system of capitalist production and reified by the fetishizing nature of commodity, can find "a zone of contention," within cultural representation. Importantly, representation serves as a context for developing contestation that can deny and defy the commodified image (Willis 1991, 194).

It is important to note, moreover, that the rejection of an epistemology of the flesh, one that articulates gender and race with particular identities in the world through re-centering projects, is now practiced more broadly within Women's Studies, to the detriment of the empowerment of subaltern communities. Thus, we are now witnessing an important shift in the naming of administrative units of academic feminism and in the types of analysis that are now possible within them, as Gender Studies becomes grafted onto and in some cases supplants Women's Studies. Such a shift was initially conceptualized in the '90s as a means to foment within Women's Studies a more fully integrated framework that allowed for a relational analysis of gender, since social-sexual identities are considered to be constructed relationally, and to make this framework available to other academic disciplines. However, the theoretical content of Gender Studies—gender identity, gender relations, and gender difference—is subsumed under this new lens with its various components—as already complete social facts, available for comparison or correlation (Seremetakis 1994).

Such a shift fails to take into account the fact that women's social realities and experiences are unfinished historical projects as are the concepts we use to define them. And just as the social identities of women are forged through representations and narratives that register historical experiences, so Women's Studies is the register of institutional narratives of the women's movement and of women's culture more generally. As such, Women's Studies continues to revise and rearticulate the concepts we use to piece together historical reconstructions of racialized gender as well as contest discourses of power that created those concepts, including those of the institutions in which it finds itself imbricated, disallowing itself to be absorbed or completely identified with them. A salient example of the difficulties posed by the attempt to contain or reduce the social experiences of women within the frame of relationality and gender relations, disarticulated from identity, can be gleaned from the second claim that Wiegman makes.

Claim #2: The unassimilability of the Black woman into the public sphere

Wiegman draws upon Foucault's notion of 'the end of man' to draw attention to the notion of the recent (modernist) invention of subjectivity, triggered by a rupture in the episteme of Western culture. She thus argues that subjectivity cannot serve as a transcendental foundation of knowledge. Instead, subjectivity manifests itself as an 'effect' of particular discontinuities in the history of thought. It is these ruptures that Wiegman highlights and examines. Retracing the instantiation of racialized gendered hierarchies since their inception in the cultural and scientific debates about race in the eighteenth and nineteenth centuries, Wiegman argues that race surfaced as the effect of the organization of Western knowledge during this era, triggered by scientific and aesthetic approaches to vision, along with philosophical understandings of embodiment and disembodiment dating back to enslavement.

In her analysis of Frederick Douglass's 1853 tale "The Heroic Slave," Wiegman posits that following Abolition, the African American male was able to enter the discursive site of human signification by adopting a rhetoric of sexual difference, evidenced in the textual production of the slave narrative. The African American male's potential success in achieving citizenry depended upon his ability to achieve corporeal abstraction and capacity for rational thought, as his white male counterpart. Nonetheless, lynching remained as a threat to such aspirations (74–75). The social practice of lynching, a technology of visibility, constituted individuals as subjected objects of power-knowledge relations. Lynching produced certain types of individuals, in this case, the feminized masculine body, and then produced a normalizing effect onto this newly constructed individual.

At the same time that the African American male was able to achieve citizenry, Wiegman argues, the Black woman's efforts to gain entry into the sphere of political rights was prohibited:

> In the struggle for citizenship in the post-Civil War years, for instance, the Black female could only be insinuated into enfranchisement, so thorough was her gendered disqualification from the public sphere. No longer chattel, she nonetheless was without recourse to the patronymic of citizenship—that right of self-possession—that governed the legal and political discourses of the public realm. (68)

Because Black women were unable to exchange the deviant corporality associated with Blackness for discorporation, as their male counterparts had done, they were excluded from signification within political discourses, remaining as the sign of deviant corporality (76).

Critical Commentary
Gender Studies, as other disciplines, constructs its own content according to what it wishes to study, for example, the questions it wants to ask, and what knowledge it wishes to foreground. Herein, Gender Studies chooses to examine women in terms of their points of social intersections with men, now including racial and sexual difference as well. But this type of correlation hardly grasps the scope of women's socio-historical and cultural realities. Nowhere is this more evident than in Wiegman's thesis of the production of sexual difference with regard to African American men and women, resulting from the Black male's entry into the public sphere, apparently through the acquisition of literacy, and, consequently, his apparent achievement of corporeal abstraction. In essence, Wiegman has taken the public/private distinction as a readymade social fact that undergirds

sexual difference, and legitimizes women's subordination and containment. In doing so, she has unproblematically bought into white supremacist patriarchal presuppositions, which in turn has led her to correlate 'public' with such attributes as 'masculinity' and 'rational, abstract thought. By contrast, she identifies 'private' with 'deviant corporeality' and 'subordination.'

In contradistinction to the above-referenced line of inquiry, one that keeps Black women in a fossilized state of disenfranchisement, Black cultural critics as well as some feminists have critiqued the public/private distinction in recent decades, in the hope of dismantling this binary. Houston Baker, for example, suggests that Black Americans have always located their unique forms of expressive publicity in a complex set of relationships to other forms of American publicity. The public sphere, conceived as Black, decenters and pluralizes a single authoritative public, fostering a "black counter-authority of interpretation" (Baker 1995, 14). The Black public sphere thus transforms the notion of public sphere into an expressive and empowering self-fashioning (Baker 1995, 13–15).

Black feminist scholarship in both the first and second waves has focused its attention on the ways in which post-slavery oppression, including lynching, has unwittingly created the social conditions under which Black women's identities evolved differently from those of white women. As noted in this scholarship, Black women were able to participate in a variety of decentered public spheres, in contrast to white women, who remained trapped within the cult of domesticity. If lynching reflected a white supremacist practice that ensured and legitimated white male political and economic power, it did so through a re-entrenched control of white women, ultimately bringing about white women's participation in such strategies. In effect, in exchange for assuming the responsibility of keeping the white race pure, white women were able to protect their status as women by gaining some measure of power over Black and all working-class women. But they did so at the cost of both being contained within the domestic sphere and supporting a system based on race and class domination (Carby 1985; White 2001).

Finding themselves located outside of the protection of the ideology of womanhood, Black women entered the public realm, along with their male counterparts, to protest their worsening social conditions throughout the nineteenth century. Black women's participation in the Black church, specifically through the Women's Convention, an auxiliary of the National Baptist Convention, as well as the Black women's club movements, allowed them the opportunities to organize against racial discrimination as well as sexism within the church.

Ironically, as Evelyn Higginbotham has noted, the failure of the first wave of Black feminists to critique the good (white)/bad (Black) woman dichotomy, and that of their counterparts in the second wave, was what led Black middle-class church and club women into the public realm. Thus, within the church as well as the Black club movement, Black women engaged a politics of respectability, one that, far from keeping them subjugated to patriarchal understandings of womanhood, allowed them to counter racist practices (Higginbotham 1993; White 2001, 34–37).[7]

Black feminist historian Elsa Barkley Brown further demystifies the commonly held assumption on the part of scholars of "an unbroken line of exclusion of African American women from formal political associations in the late-nineteenth century" (1995, 112). Barkley Brown problematizes the public/private dichotomy when applying it to the Black community. She notes that it is possible to identify both internal and external political arenas within the public realm. In the years following Emancipation, Black women were completely enfranchised in the internal one, participating in all public forums, including parades, rallies, mass meetings, and conventions (124). When Black men obtained legal franchise, Black women continued to intervene in the internal arena of politics, and most importantly, entered the external one. Barkley Brown cites the value of collective autonomy that permeated the political organization of the Black community as well as helped shape the contours of its worldview. African American women and men understood the legal franchise as a "collective possession" that gave Black women and men alike the ability to participate in decisions with regard to the reconstruction of African American families, and the development of communal institutions (128).

Indeed, Barkley Brown argues that the focus on the concept of formal or official disenfranchisement obscures Black women's ongoing participation in the internal political sphere. Black women's early participation in the Republican and Constitution conventions preceding the Black male's legal enfranchisement, their participation following their franchise through their participation in political meetings in large numbers, and their organization of political parties, such as the Rising Daughters of Liberty, not only challenged the public/ private distinction that would, as Wiegman asserts, permanently disqualify women from social inclusion and identity, but also deftly challenged the privileging of public political participation itself as the lynchpin of patriarchal and white supremacist power (126). Barkley Brown posits that Black women played an instrumental role both within the internal and external spheres of politics that resulted in

Black enfranchisement.[8] While Black women's contributions reflect an early public presence and visibility that counters Wiegman's assertion of the impossible linkage of "Blacks" and "woman," the very splintering of the public sphere into external and internal, the former formally integrated into the dominant white public sphere and identified with enfranchisement and the latter relegated by necessity to the Black public sphere, was produced out of necessity, precisely because of Black women's exclusion from the public realm of formal politics.

If Wiegman's work offers us an instance of a particularly salient camp of feminist thought, one that rejects identity on the basis of its insidious effects on women, Susan Stanford Friedman's work, *Mappings: Feminism and the Cultural Geographies of Encounter*, offers a diametrically opposed alternative in the name of the democratic advancement of women of color: that of assimilation and inclusivity, an orientation also pervasively championed within feminist thought.

Claim #1: Positing a new theory of locational feminism

Drawing on postcolonial and postmodern theories of difference, Friedman advocates for a shift away from the splintering of feminisms into distinct identity-based movements toward a singular "locational feminism." Such splinterings, she argues, have only created obstacles to the advancement of feminism's goal of solidarity. In this regard, she proposes that we move our focus away from what she calls a "feminist commitment to difference" because it has led us into ideological and strategic impasses and a crisis in coalition feminism (Friedman 1998, 71–72).[9] In her quest for feminist solidarity, she first affirms that the reunification of feminism into one site requires geopolitical or transnational literacy, one that is "built out of a recognition of how different times and places produce different and changing gender systems as these intersect with other and different and changing societal stratifications and movements for social justice" (5). Further, she argues that locational feminism, while encouraging an ongoing examination of difference, "undertakes a difficult negotiation between insistence on multidirectional flows of power in global context and continued vigilance about specifically western forms of domination" (6).

Finally, she urges feminists to desist from racially based conflictive exchanges, ones that, she claims, are manifest across three detrimental cultural narratives or scripts that feminists, depending on their social location, opt to reproduce: scripts of denial (white feminists denying their racism), accusation (feminists of color accusing white feminists of not being honest about their racism), and confession (white feminists wallowing in guilt about their racism) (41–47). Friedman suggests that feminists should deploy mimetic processes that restore the suppressed principle of sameness to feminist discussions of identity by imitating the linguistic play, dialogics, and performativity cultivated by women of color theorists and artists. She references and analyzes Maria Lugones' notion of "curdling," Gloria Anzaldúa's *mestiza* or borderlands consciousness, and Ann Deavere Smith's notion of performance and travel. She posits that the mixing or hybridity of forms between different subjectivities reflected in these concepts call into question, like Homi Bhabba's notion of colonial mimicry, the natural authority of difference, and highlight the constructedness of all identities. Friedman argues that by using such hybridity as a source of radical or transgressive play, feminists can make real their utopic longing for relationality across difference (78).

Critical commentary
Like Wiegman's proposal of the rejection of centered identity(ies), Friedman's locational feminism reproduces and veils the asymmetrical power relations that have separated white feminists and feminists of color. Following her overview of locational feminism, Friedman offers a representation of scripts that delegitimize the conflict and dissent emerging from women of color's discursive interventions, emphasizing the arbitrariness of such scripts. She changes the modes of struggle by using two strategies: the racial alibi and the paradigm reversal. As womanist ethicist Stacey Floyd-Thomas and I argue in a paper entitled "Bounded Cultures" presented at the 2001 National Women's Studies Association conference, the racial alibi is produced for the purpose of putting oneself in a place beyond contestation and condemnation while remaining situated at the center of feminist discourse. To do so, the (white) person, identified within racial discourses as victimizer, shifts attention off the power she is currently exercising by putting herself in the role of the victim, normally occupied by the person of color, while putting the victim in the place of the accuser or victimizer (Gillman and Floyd-Thomas 2001).

As I argue below, the alibi is used to ward off the threat of power that feminists of color are perceived to be exercising through their interventions. It is used to keep out of the dialogue a critical engagement with the theories that women of color produce out of their experiences. However, the logic of the alibi is made manifest under more careful scrutiny of its objective. Indeed, the alibi is used at that point in the conversation at which the analysis of privilege might cause a more exacerbated discomfort, lack of theoretical authority, or has begun to create a shift in our understandings and praxis of feminism. The alibi is interjected opportunely, so that the power and agency of women of color feminists remain attitudinal but not legitimized institutionally.

Friedman employs various versions of the script of the racial alibi as she begins her discussion of discursive complementarity and relational positionality. She first draws upon Black feminist Ann duCille's understandings of racialized gender to counter duCille's script of accusation, and then to adopt duCille's theory of theoretical complementarity. Friedman begins with an analysis of some claims made by duCille in her essay "The Occult of True Black Womanhood." She disaffiliates from the victimizer's role when she states that as an American woman of European descent she could be aligned with those other white academics, described by duCille, whose "desire... to write about Black women, (for example) all too often includes a failure to include real Black women in the discussion or to understand Black women as cultural producers rather than simply as objects of the racial gaze" (1998, 38).

Friedman seeks to dodge potential critique against her by using this citation so that she will not be aligned with white power. But she also wants to thwart the potential that duCille's insights have for disrupting whiteness. She thus rejects duCille's suggestion that white feminists reflect on what motivates their incursions into the arena of Black Studies and/or race. She claims that it is unfair that she should be prohibited from saying anything about race simply because she is white: "Nonetheless I cannot accept the notion that the racial privilege of my whiteness should enforce my silence about race and ethnicity, issues of vital ethical and political importance not only in the United States but also in a global context... . Yet I ask that you hear me out" (38). With this discursive gesture, Friedman places herself in the role of victim while placing duCille in the role of the victimizer who delimits, controls, and accuses. At the same time, she claims that the conflict, apparently initiated by duCille, is unnecessary and unfair.

Friedman goes on to appropriate duCille's concept of "complementary theorizing," a method of achieving intercultural dexterity through dialogue. She does not engage with duCille's ambivalent desire to both erect boundaries around the site of Black feminist thought in order to avoid the potential of being objectified, and have Black feminist thought impact the academy. Instead, she uses duCille's term to redirect feminist discourse to Homi Bhabba's concept of fluid identities. Bhabba's concept serves as the gateway to Friedman's introduction of scripts of relational positionality, which she claims feminists should adopt in order to undertake "a search for common ground" (46). At this point in the criticism, the covert aim of the alibi, which is to re-center whiteness, becomes manifest through omission. Friedman writes out of her analysis the crux of duCille's dilemma—her struggle to situate herself within the bounded site of Black Studies in order to mark and protect her own subjectivity as a person with relative powerlessness within the academy while simultaneously contesting the notion of marginalization. Friedman bypasses the difference that power makes in order to re-project a unified coalitional feminism based on the idea that all identities are fluid. In effect, she argues, power can flow from different racial locations: "Scripts of relational positionality...acknowledge that the flow of power in multiple systems of domination is not always unidirectional. Victims can also be victimizers" (48).

Friedman reproduces this ironic maneuver of placing white feminists and feminists of color in analogous positions of disempowerment as she proceeds to analyze the victim paradigm of race relations within feminism. Here, Friedman cites Anzaldúa's published description of racial conflict that developed in a course she taught on U.S. women of color. In the referenced article, Anzaldúa wrestles with articulating racial difference, made salient in the tension resulting from the decentering of white privilege as it was experienced among 'mujeres-de-color,' 'Jewishwomen,' and 'white-women.' Friedman disrupts Anzaldúa's rescriptings by literally bracketing the observations that she and her students of color make with respect to their experiences of marginalization, converting them into scripts of accusation:

> But gradually *the mujeres-of-color* became more assertive in confronting and holding whites accountable for their unaware, "blocked" and chronically oppressive ways [accusation]. ...When white-women or Jewishwomen attempted to subvert the focus from women-of-color's feelings to their own feelings of confusion, helplessness, anger, guilt, fear of change and other insecurities [confession], the women-of-color again and again redirected the focus back to *mujeres-de-*color [accusation] (44).

By converting feminists of color into the aggressor through her own rescriptings, or at the very least making aggressive interaction appear to be reciprocal, Friedman masks the hierarchical racial relations in which white feminists and feminists are located. Moreover, rather than engaging Anzaldúa from that position of marginalization, she inserts the rescriptings in Anzaldúa's narrative to justify placing white students, and, by extension, herself in the place of the accused victim. While Friedman states that her purpose in critiquing racial scripts is to decenter whiteness and end arbitrary conflict, she in fact reappropriates discursive power by re-orienting her readers empathically toward the feelings of discomfort, guilt, and disempowerment of the white feminist.

The glossing over of difference that has as a major goal the assimilation of feminisms into a singular locational feminism takes a very particular form in Friedman's text. I call this form "paradigm reversal." Rather than proposing that women of color feminists adopt mainstream feminist agendas or methodological approaches as a means to obtain unity, Friedman proposes that white mainstream feminists adopt the paradigms of people of color, for instance, Bhabba's notion of hybridity and Anzaldúa's *mestiza* or borderland theories. Accordingly, the white feminist subject should now understand herself as analogous to the woman of color subject. Sharing a hybrid and fluid identity, white feminists and feminists of color may traverse boundaries of difference into a common ground of solidarity, where the forging of connections can occur between women who are different yet struggling against similarly complex oppressions.

The paradigm reversal and ensuing equivalence theory fail to take into account, however, that the liberatory processes that women of color have developed in order to shape their identities are not arbitrary, but rather pertain to particular lived realities of oppression that are simply not shared. While it may indeed appear to be politically expedient to seek narrativities of subjectivity based in relational positions in which power circulates in more than one direction, allowing for the possibility of "connection across racial and national division" (63), it is illusory. The search for this new theoretical direction seems to imply not only that the notion of hybridity of identity serves the function of acting as a buffer against the dangerous excesses of difference-talk, but also that such efforts at this theoretical redirection are a benign effort on her part, as savior, to mitigate the dangerous excesses enacted by women of color feminists that threaten to cause the demise of feminism (103). The reversal paradigm, whereby the victim of oppression is transformed into the potential perpetrator, is lynchpin to a re-racializing project that demands not only an incorporative notion of racial difference, but also a particular type of incorporation—one that rejects conflict models of difference in favor of a playful dialogics and performativity of difference generated by women of color—purportedly with the aim to enact democratic relationality that can refashion identity and power.

Friedman thus engages a new cultural politics of difference. For example, she is motivated by a desire to achieve unity and inclusivity through the resolution of difference, to use dialogue as the privileged means to achieve mutual understanding across difference, and to use playfulness as a preferred form of exchange, over and above direct confrontation. Yet her implementation of assimilation models is based on the assumption that all women, regardless of their different racial or ethnic communities, share such ideals and values. More significantly, Friedman's locational epistemology assumes that the performativity of race and gender is intended to avoid conflict caused by asymmetrical power relations rather than trigger it; that women of color feminists intended such techniques to be deployed by white women as a means to bridge differences; and, that a playful dialogics could actually convey the same meanings of resistance, regardless of the social location of the performer. Quite to the contrary, as Ien Ang points out, the difficulty of difference cannot be resolved through dialogue. Indeed, the very desire for resolution only results in prematurely overlooking the inescapability of difference that affect women's lives, and would require coerced inclusivity of women of color into the overarching feminist structure, one that has itself remained unexamined (Ang 1995).

Friedman's unexamined assumptions cause her to enact a white feminist identity politics with an aim to appropriate the emancipatory strategies of women of color feminists, thereby ascribing meaning and value to Smith's notion of performativity and travel to all identities—including her own—in order to mitigate the threat to whiteness that identity-based social movements forming around identity engender. Her work stands in contrast to a more innovative approach to relationality, posited by Ella Shohat. In her definition of multicultural feminism, Shohat uses women of color theories and methodologies to posit a radical relationality that definitively decenters and pluralizes feminism. She thus argues that because racial-ethnic as well as gender and sexual hierarchies and identities are always located within particular histories and spaces as well as move across and through other histories and spaces, no unified narrative of gender is possible. In a transnational world structure where identities are more complexly reconfigured, Shohat proposes drawing upon the strengths of women of color's methodologies while at the same time staging diverse political focal points of resistance or what she calls a "multifronted constellation of struggles that can synergistically meet and mutually reinforce one another" (Shohat 1998, 15).

CONCLUSION: FORMULATING AN ANTI-HEGEMONIC, ANTI-FOUNDATIONALIST IDENTITY POLITICS

In order to take the questions of identity, difference, and power seriously, we must recognize that the rapid shifts in feminist knowledge that have occurred over the last decades, caused both by social changes as well as by inadequately examined processes of institutionalization that have themselves developed in response to such changes, have hardly allowed academic Women's Studies a chance to evaluate the constructs it has embraced within the context of its own normative commitments. Thus, for example, obtaining multicultural literacy with regard to the theoretical concepts cultivated by feminists of color, the basis for Friedman's transnational locational feminism, is insufficient theoretically in terms of a feminist project of social justice. Because we bring our own ideological investments into our discursive arenas, a greater literacy of marginalized women's cultural theoretical concepts does not necessarily lead to a newfound understanding, nor does it explain how to use that perspective to begin to transform the feminist project. Similarly, Wiegman's and other feminist postmodernists' disarticulation of gender from identity is insufficient. Representational processes do not go away just because we suddenly understand the deleterious effects of a visible economy. Moreover, feminist and other progressive scholars are still in the process of reformulating ideological concepts as these relate to categories of social identity.

In view of the above-referenced impasses that keep feminist thought in oscillation between the absolutist positions of experiential foundationalism identified with modernity, and an unyielding skepticism identified with the stronger versions of postmodernism, I suggest that feminism cannot be politically effective if it cannot lay claims to particularized moral truths about the structural causality of identity. I propose, therefore, along with other postpositivist realists, that we begin by viewing identity as 'real,' that is, as at least in part existing independently of our mental or discursive representations of it, and as constituted by experiences that causally condition but do not determine what we can know about ourselves. From a postpositivist realist perspective, the judgments and interpretations that one makes of the experiences that comprise one's identity, while always changing and in a process of continual verification through contestation, are, therefore, valuable sources of theory-mediated knowledge of the self and the world.

Objective knowledge about one's social context can be obtained when one tests out how accurately one's understandings (emotions, feelings, beliefs, and values) correlate or refer to real features in the world. Realist understandings of identity acknowledge, moreover, that objectivity relies on an epistemology of the flesh, an epistemology that affirms that social beings, in the process of being an integral part of the natural and social world, both defined by and challenging its laws, develop particular kinds of knowledge and social practices in order to enhance their own moral situation (Moya 2002, 16). This process, however, often involves nuanced and challenging negotiations that include, as Mohanty affirms, "making buried explanations explicit, by examining the social and political views that are involved in what seem like purely personal choices and predilections" (Mohanty 2000, 57).

In sum, the revised identity politics that I am proposing as a paradigm for contemporary feminist thought expands upon earlier feminist and cultural critiques of the more pernicious essentializing elements of identity politics, including, those undertaken by women of color as they have evolved their theories. My analyses of the identity politics of womanists and *mestiza* feminists in the following chapters will bring feminist thought beyond its present articulations. First, I provide evidence of how womanist and *mestiza* feminist thought have respectively engaged postmodernist arguments, fostering more nuanced, nonessentialized frameworks for understanding intra-group differences while continuing to affirm the stability of group identity and group politics. Second, I draw upon the intellectual resources of postpositivist realism, namely, its processes of inquiry and systematic conceptualizations of the cognitive status of identities. Third, I examine such systematic procedures in light of the interpretative schemas womanists and *mestiza* feminists have already developed when engaged in processes of social contestation in order to refute with greater epistemic reliability the dominant ideologies and institutions that have distorted their identities and constrained their agency. Finally, I show how the schemas womanists and *mestiza* feminists develop represent deeply contextualized social practices informed by temporality, spatiality, and memory that explain more accurately the social and natural world. Their schemas thus indicate that their beliefs, values, and actions in the world are anything but arbitrary.

By integrating these approaches, I strive to cultivate a politics of recognition rather than of inclusion. I further labor to facilitate a politics of influence by indicating how womanists and *mestiza* feminists have used and can use their theory-mediated schemas to foster constructive paradigms that will disseminate their values, modes of consciousness, and politics into public arenas. And, by providing the means by which it is possible to evaluate the accuracy of knowledge claims, I hope to justify the liberation struggles in which we as feminists are engaged.

CHAPTER 3

Womanisms at the Interstices of Disciplines, Movements, Periodizations, and Nations

It never surprises me when Black folks respond to the critique of essentialism, especially when it denies the validity of identity politics, by saying "Yeah, it's easy to give up identity, when you got one." Should we not be suspicious of postmodern critiques of the "subject" when they surface at a historical moment when many subjugated people feel themselves coming to voice for the first time.

(hooks 1990a, 28)

The above quotation calls attention to the liberation of subjugated identities as a site of struggle. hooks highlights Black people's yearning to wrest their subjectivities from the stronghold of postmodernist colonizing discursive practices. Such yearnings are transformative, hooks argues, only when those who are oppressed challenge such practices, thereby creating the impetus for the construction of alternative liberatory discourses.[1] In this chapter I engage this site of struggle by challenging certain types of academic theories that correlate identity politics with movements and periodizations in order to deny their epistemological underpinnings as well as their politics. I argue that by drawing upon the interdisciplinary insights of the fields, among others, of Literary Studies/Cultural Studies, Religious Studies, Sociology, and Anthropology, as they intersect with Feminist Studies, Critical Race Studies, and diaspora/transnational theories, womanist scholarship reveals Black women's writings as liberation narratives. These narratives are informed by a politics that derives from cultural spaces inhabited by Black women.

Womanist scholars enact individual and collective processes of resistance against various forms of oppression, whether departing from ethical or theological frameworks, anthropological or sociological analyses, deconstructive methods related to Literary Studies/Cultural Studies, or interdisciplinary orientations constituted by the integration of more than one of the aforementioned approaches. Such a project requires a centering of Black women's experiences, and includes more generally a social analysis of the conditions in which the Black community operates, an interrogation of the formation of African American spiritual life as a source of empowerment, and a deconstruction of all of the oppressions that limit self- and collective determination. Since asking questions about the ways in which the lives of Black women are limited by hegemonic practices has immediate personal implications for the womanist scholar who forms part of the community she is researching, the self-reflection of the scholar becomes an integral part of the methodological process. As such, the autobiographical data or subjective perspectives supplied by the womanist scholar, is, as I will demonstrate, as important for testing out methodological assertions as are the social texts and contexts that are the objects of their critical analyses.

I begin this chapter with an examination of those arguments that delegitimate identity politics as they affect womanism not just in the sense of it being a movement, but also as a set of discursive practices emerging from Black women's critical reflection on shared histories of oppression. My purpose is to contribute to the womanist effort to break the force of a normative gaze promoted by academic theories on both liberal and conservative fronts that casts all identity politics as essentialist. This ahistorical gaze undermines the epistemological potential of womanist discourse by placing it within a false dialectic with respect to the more academically accepted theories of postmodernism. Essentialist claims not only deny the dynamic and evolving processes of race, class, and gender formations of Black women, but also reify Black women's location within the discursive spaces of political movements, aesthetic categories, academic disciplinary discourses, and nations. In order to challenge such false dichotomizations, I contextualize womanist theories within Black postmodernist theoretical frameworks that make salient group differences within specific relations of rule while affirming the stability and continuity of group identity. In distinguishing between hegemonic and Black postmodernism, I hope to illuminate the influences that womanist identity politics and discourses exert on such theoretical positions and the effects of such an influence for developing a more nuanced understanding of Black female subjectivities.

After positioning womanist thought within a number of U.S. academic discourses and debates, I define womanist thought within the context of a dominant academic branch of womanism, that of womanist theology and ethics. I explore womanism within and against African cultural traditions, traditions that U.S. womanists refashion and translate into present realities for the purpose of interpreting and responding to specific experiences of racism visited upon Black people in the United States. In order to provide the historical context of womanism, I then trace the hybridization of cultural traditions that results as Black women writers and scholars engage with other U.S. minority discourses and thought. I focus particularly here on Alice Walker's definition of womanism. Finally, I examine womanist interventions in cultural debates that are currently developing on difference and transdifference and/or diaspora studies. I address the points of contention between womanist critiques of racial difference and hybridity and diasporan theories of difference.

What follows, then, is a re-mapping of some of the ongoing and evolving polarized modes of thought within which womanism finds itself imbricated, ones that put in diametrical opposition the entrenchment of hegemonic theories of identity and minority identity politics; essentialism and postmodernism; multiculturalism as separatism versus multiculturalism as inclusiveness; and movements of coalition based on cultural and/or intellectual reciprocity versus cultural and intellectual appropriations. These polarizations are of crucial importance because they raise questions of authorization, agency, and power with regard to the epistemic significance of Black women's identity formation, and the meaning of Black women's cultural production within the academy.

Throughout this chapter I push beyond such polarizations by suggesting how womanist concerns about identity and knowledge resonate with postpositivist realist epistemologies in their foregrounding not of the deferral or impossibility of knowing through experiences informing identity, but rather of the epistemic status and political salience of identity. I indicate the various ways in which womanist scholars and cultural workers, according to their individual disposition, intellectual training, geopolitical location, and generation, acknowledge and to what extent they acknowledge in their writings that identities can be both real and constructed, epistemically grounded, and at the same time nonessentializing. Herein, I examine womanist writings along the essentialist/antiessentialist modernist/postmodernist continuum. The following analysis, while not exhaustive in its disentangling of these tensions, attempts to present the intrinsic logic of Black women's positionings within these debates.

PERIODIZATIONS: WOMANISM AT THE INTERSTICES OF MODERNISM AND POSTMODERNISM

In the decades following the civil rights movement, the fields and respective orientations of Feminist Studies and Black Studies articulated understandings of femaleness and Blackness through the fostering of radical constructions of centered her/histories of the female and/or Black subject. These newly centered subjectivities effected important shifts in U.S. culture and in the academic field of Cultural Studies wherein the sociocultural concept of unity, used to characterize Western culture and the universal Western subject, was now being replaced with notions of the fragmented postmodern subject. The demise of the modernist project was thus initiated within a U.S. context as a micropolitics of difference surfaced and organized itself within movements such as Black nationalism and feminism. Redefining for themselves the modernist project of liberal democracy while laying the idea of the universal Western subject to rest, Black nationalist intellectuals of the 1960s, influenced by a much longer trajectory of Afrocentric thought informing the study of African and African American people, propagated an ideal of culture rooted in racially specific experiences (Dubey 2003, 33), while in the 1970s, radical white feminists propagated an ideal of culture rooted in gender-specific ones. Each of these movements in turn proliferated and splintered, creating multiple and competing theories of identity and political struggle.

Within the Black nationalist tradition of the '60s, an ideal or essential identity of Blackness was constructed in order to resolve the ambivalences of double-consciousness. Within this tradition, members of the African American community were defined by themselves and others in terms of the extent to which they aligned with core cultural Black values (Gwaltney 1980, xxiii). Grounded in a syncretic mix of African and non-African religious beliefs, secular myths and rituals that were in turn founded on a cyclical Judeo-Christian understanding of history, such values propagated a vision of African Americans as a disinherited people. Produced by the brutalities such as enslavement, cultural degradation, and alienation from public identity, rights and self-worth that were inflicted on Black humanity in the New World, this disinheritance has been rightfully described, as "natal alienation" (West 1992). But these same values also foreground the individual and collective resilience of Black America in the face of such disinheritance, experienced as invisibility, and the will to achieve justice as a root foundation of their culture. Intrinsic values linked to this cultural foundation include a tragicomic vision of life and an enduring faith in the redemptive power of suffering, patience, perseverance and compassion, dignity, and courage. The embodiment of this cultural orientation facilitated the hope and possibility for African Americans to become agents of their own destiny, both as individuals and as a community (Bell 2004, 49; West 1992).

African American values, however, were never pure nor static. From the antebellum period to the present, African Americans have had to address the ethical ambiguity of racism, sexism, and classism—carving out ethical practices to follow within specific historical and sociocultural contexts while mastering or combating the ubiquitous negative orientations that the value patterns of white society encouraged. This demanded critical examination of conventional morality as well as inversions of and departures from normative moral and ethical assumptions (Cannon 1988, 76–77). In this century, as revealed in the Black Arts Movement of the late '60s and satirized in the neo-Black Aesthetic Movement of the '80s and '90s, for example, there was a plethora of responses to these core standards (Bell 2004, 50–51; Gibson 1995).

Indeed, when viewing Black Nationalism within the context of Afrocentric traditions more broadly, it is evident that there always were multiple and competing theories about the ways in which peoples, communities, and cultures of African descent were to be placed at the center of intellectual inquiry and political struggle, ranging from a European Marxist tradition to an 'authentist' perspective that resists Eurocentrism (Ransby 2000, 217–19). Afrocentric paradigms espoused by Molefi Asante and other Afrocentric scholars, since the publication of his book *Afrocentricity: The Theory of Social Change* in 1980, endorsed more ahistorical cultural understandings of race and, by extension, gender; understandings rooted in African cultural systems of the past. Other scholars, however, particularly Black feminists and womanists, contested the emplacement of the culture of African people in a historical and cultural vacuum. They represented African culture as the product of a dialectic of political struggle, between people of African descent and those of other cultures, as well as between African Americans and others of the African diaspora (Bell 2004, 75–93; Ransby 2000).[2]

Similar struggles over the meaning of feminist culture arose within the context of cultural feminism of the 1970s. During this time, feminists reappropriated patriarchal ideologies defining the female 'nature,' in order to valorize female attributes that had been dehumanized. Claiming culture as an ordered system of meaning by which groups of people explain their world and make their assessments, cultural feminists proactively worked to define women's cultures as different from those produced by men. Thus, according to 'relative deprivation' arguments developed during the second wave of feminism, women's cultures were considered unique from dominant male cultures, as a result of women's experiences within a sexual division of labor, marked by economic subjugation and attending social ills, including sexual exploitation and violence (Roth 2004). Women's cultures were further deemed unique because they pointed to a desire to foment a female counterculture that evolves out of women's anatomy, and is free of masculinist values. Cultural feminists thus offered essentializing responses to misogyny and sexism, by valorizing female traits or invoking homogeneous representations of motherhood or womanhood (Echols 1989).

For women of color, however, the impetus of feminist mobilization in the second wave of feminism was not to be found in relative deprivation with respect to their male counterparts. Rather, it came out of their heightened awareness of a more complex network of structural inequalities between women in different racial/ethnic communities and of the different ways in which they experienced race and class inequalities within social structures relative to white feminists. Because of such perceived differences, moreover, women of color's social identities and correlated political movements had different and separate developments, and were organizationally distinct during the second wave of feminism (Roth 2004, 31–46). The multi-layered cultural fracturings of both raced and gendered subjectivities, as summarized above, put into question the correlation that has traditionally been made in academic circles between minority identity politics and a modernist essentialism. The splinterings of movements and identities suggest instead that there is a more complex imbrication of the postmodern within the modern.

Indeed, the postmodern, defined as a universal crisis of subjectivity and critique of the universal Western subject, is its increasing implication in mainstream or white, Western, and male culture (Harper 1994, 12–13). Such belated categorizations have been widely noted by minority critics. Wahneema Lubiano thus affirms in reference to the postmodern crisis of identity that the decentering of the authority of Western cultural productions and subjectivities can hardly be considered as a crisis for African American Literary and Cultural Studies, where suspicion about modern Western meta-narratives have had a much more extensive history (Lubiano 1991: 154, 160; 1995, 94–95). Or, as postcolonial critic and geographer Doreen Massey argues: "For those who have been cast as the 'Other,' that is, all other inhabitants of the world, those subjected to slavery and various forms of colonial rule, such a crisis of home or 'place' and culture (cultural identity) as experienced over time has been fractured since the emergence of the repressive political formations of colonial rule as evidenced in its literature" (1993, 122–23).[3]

It is certainly understandable that some scholars have categorized Black cultural nationalism and some forms of feminisms as postmodernist, insofar as they employed racial and/or gender-specific experiences to critique the alleged universalism of modern Western humanism. Nonetheless, attributions of essentialism to these minority identity politics is to an extent justifiable when examining the persistence of a hegemonic binary logic that pervasively extends into their discourses. Thus, even while projecting a particular radical subjectivity in their contextualized notions of home, culture, and identity, such oppositional consciousnesses become defined respectively within their own oppressive binary structure according to such a logic, for example, Black cultural identity or Blackness as male within the theoretical constructs and day-to-day operations of the Black Power movement; and women's cultural identity or femaleness as white within the dominant strain of cultural feminism of the '70s. Under these conditions, arguing that minority identity politics decenter the universalizing logic of the subject becomes problematic. Soja and Hooper thus underscore the strategic nature of modernist identity projects that resulted in the reinstantiation of binary understandings of difference:

> Modernist identity politics characteristically projects its particular radical subjectivity, defined within its own oppressive binary structure, as overarchingly (and often universally) significant. Whether or not this totalization and essentialism is actually believed, its powerful mobilizing effect is used strategically in attempts to consolidate and intensify counter-hegemonic consciousness 'for itself' and on its identified 'home ground.' (1993, 186)

This is, ultimately, what leads hooks to cast the Black liberation movement as a modernist rather than postmodernist project:

> During the sixties, Black Power movement was influenced by perspectives that could easily be labeled modernist. Certainly many of the

ways Black folks addressed issues of identity conformed to a modernist universalizing agenda. There was little critique of patriarchy as a master narrative among Black militants. (hooks 1990a, 25)

Linda Alcoff analogously critiques white cultural feminism, affirming that it is ill-suited to analyze the complexities of multiple oppressions faced by women of color:

> The simultaneity of oppressions experienced by women such as Moraga resists essentialist conclusions. Universalist conceptions of female or male experiences and attributes are not plausible in the context of a complex network of relations, and without an ability to universalize, the essentialist argument is difficult if not impossible to make. (1997, 335)

Driven in part by such limitations, and in larger part by intrinsic motivations to claim those female subjectivities left out of preexisting minority discourses, new articulations of postmodern theories of identity rooted in Black Studies, Ethnic Studies, and Postcolonial Feminisms, such as those of bell hooks, Cornel West, Iris Marion Young, and Diana Fuss, were spawned in the decades of the '80s and '90s. These critics theorized new spaces for projecting radical, nonessentializing subjectivities, positing a multivoiced postmodernism that pursued a commitment to radical social change while still honing the politically suggestive critical foundations of radical modernist identity politics (hooks 1990a, 5; Soja and Hooper 1993, 187; West 1992, 19–36).

The aforementioned scholars explored the continuing implications and effects of modernity in the postmodern Black experience, generated by the perpetuation of racialized politics and projects. Radical postmodern critical practices include a problematizing of Eurocentrism as a form of power. Such theoretical practices expose the ways in which larger discourses produce and reproduce difference as a means to maintain social and spatial divisions from which hegemonic groups stand to benefit. They also expose the struggles of members of subjugated groups against differentiation and divisions. The purpose here is to take up the modernist project of mobilizing a radical subaltern subjectivity around an epistemological critique of such orderings of difference in order to denaturalize and/or dismantle these binaries.

Toward this end, African American postmodernism or radical postmodern Blackness builds on African American modernism's epistemological insights in order to engage in a process that demands the privileging of ongoing reconstructions of difference over and above the quest for hegemonic modernism's narrative coherence. It demands, therefore, a foregrounding of what is not known—what has been or is being erased or written out of the grand narratives or larger discourses, that is, all that is socially marginal to the modern. It also, however, foregrounds all that is left out of the partial, subaltern ones. It focuses on the exploration of intergroup differences, based on gender, class, sexuality, and citizenship. This epistemological project is attentive to the processes of erasure as well as the processes of discursive reconstruction and recuperation (Gibson 1995; Hesse 1993, 166; Lubiano 1995, 95).[4]

Womanism, a discourse and set of methodological practices encoding the collective experience and struggles of African American women, fits centrally into the above-referenced political camp, alongside and in contestation to these various movements. As a social movement and academic field of inquiry that for two generations has cleared a space for Black women's voices to enter political and intellectual dialogue, womanism has developed various strands of political thought and praxis that can be distinguished from one another by their differing foundational definitions, priorities, and political practices.[5] I focus, here, however, on the dominant articulations of womanism within the academy, that of womanist theology and ethics. Womanist scholars working within these disciplinary terrains work to transcend essentializing epistemologies by engaging different Black subjectivities, while at the same time affirming identity as grounded in specific social spaces that delimit and condition those subjectivities.

While Black feminism has had a longer history in forging an activist and scholarly agenda, dating back to Black cultural nationalist projects of the '70s and '80s, womanist movement and thought, emerging in the early '80s, have absorbed Black feminist oppositional discourses and also carved out their own social theories.[6] The exact differences, points of tension, and overlappings of these two movements have been debated among Black feminists and womanists within the academy, particularly in terms of each movement's varying degrees of identification and solidarity with white feminist and Black Power politics, as well as in their relationships with other women of color movements nationally and transnationally (Collins 1998, 60–70; Phillips 2006, xxxii–xxxvi).[7] Rather than clarifying the objectives and agendas of each, the debates tend to reinforce the very binaries that both Black feminists and womanists attempt to eradicate through their interrogation of tripartite oppression, namely, their valorization of gendered identity over that of racial identity or vice versa.

A more productive strategy for distinguishing womanism from Black feminism would begin with a consideration of the ways they are differentially located within academic disciplines and the distinct methodological tools that their respective disciplines offer for studying the effects of marginalization in the lives of Black women as well as their modes of resistance. Thus, while Black feminists have worked primarily in the fields of Sociology, Literary Studies/Cultural Studies, and History as a means to illuminate core themes impacting the agency of Black women, including work, family, motherhood, controlling images, and sexual politics, womanist scholars work primarily in the areas of Ethics and Theology, and draw on the disciplinary frameworks and methodological tools of Literary Studies, Sociology, History, and Anthropology in order to better demonstrate Black women's methods for creating ethical theological frameworks that they apply to such themes. The institutional frame of Black women's scholarship impacts the choice of naming oneself Black feminist or womanist. Moreover, the Black woman scholar's orientations are going to be informed by the different intellectual traditions that are constitutive of her discipline(s) as well as by the academic and collegial connections that she makes within them (Mitchem 2002, 89).

Joy James suggests, moreover, that Black women scholars working in the terrain of social inequality are located on a continuum of thought (1999, 11–12).[8] According to the logic of the continuum, it might be most appropriate to consider these two strands of Black women's liberation theories as complementary political modalities that function as resistance-oriented practices and expressions that are also distinguished by differences conditioned by the scholar's academic emplacement, as evidenced in the language they use to articulate resistances (Townes 1995; Bobo 2001, xv). The ideological identification and overlap of the two movements are made salient, moreover, in the pervasive practice, adopted by both Black feminists and womanists, of citing each other's work. In the following section, I engage the content of womanist scholarship in order to define its specific theoretical and methodological contours, ones that emerge from historical excavations of cultural identity.

WOMANISTS IN SEARCH OF
THE HISTORICAL BLACK EXPERIENCE

Perhaps the deepest and most dramatic issue in the Afrocentric discussion is the struggle over images of God and God's people. It is a struggle over the anthropology and origins of what we now call world religions, especially those now considered to be the Abrahamic religions, Judaism, Christianity, and Islam. The womanist response actually is not a response but a position, one that roots God in the Spirit who is loved. The womanist position is that we cannot know, but we can love and strive boldly. Ultimately we will adopt Afrocentrist ideas and strategies insofar as they heal us, take us back to the old landmarks, empower us to lead and guide others to liberation, and help us to build a compassionate world. Only those kinds of Afrocentric ideas are also womanist.

(Townsend-Gilkes 1995, 42)

A pervasive area of distinction if not discontinuity between Black feminism and womanism can be noted in the extent to which womanist scholars emphasize religiosity as the underpinning of their frameworks. While it is also possible to make the claim that Black feminist literary analysis uncovers African religious traditions and cosmology in Black women's writings, there is a clearly stated objective within the work of womanist ethicists and theologians to deploy frameworks of religiosity systematically in order to render intelligible both the realities of and resistances to tripartite oppression in the lives of Black women. Accordingly, womanist scholars of religion provide critical reflection on the ways in which Black women have been constructed historically within the church, in relation to the African American community, and in society. They additionally seek to reconstruct knowledge about Black women and their contributions to American history by excavating ethnographic accounts of Black women's experiences that have been rendered invisible by formal institutions. As womanist theologian Linda Thomas affirms:

> Womanist theologians bring to the center the experience and knowledge of those marginalized by a complex layering and overlapping by race, gender, and class experiences of all groups, inclusive of those with privilege and power. Thus, as we explore this multiple effect dynamic, we pose the question: If historically suppressed voices were central to our thought processes, would our conception of the world and analytical sensibilities be any different? If we pursue such epistemological dynamics as the personal/experiential or theoretical/scholarly, what influence would this endeavor have on the reconstruction of knowledge? (1998, 496)

While recognizing that cultural identities are subject to a continuous play of history, culture, and power, womanists excavate the past in order to articulate the multiple contexts in which Black women's oppression has been experienced and resisted, how Black women have individually and collectively been positioned within histories of power, and how they have negotiated the circumstances of their identities within specific times and spaces while responding to public versions of Black womanhood. Womanist theologian Katie Cannon espouses "human archaeology" as a method of womanist investigation. This method can be likened to Toni Morrison's investigation of the interior lives of her characters' lives. She thus states that this entails "a kind of literary archeology: on the basis of some information and a little bit of guesswork, you journey to a site to see what remains were left behind and to reconstruct the world that these remains imply" (1987, 112). According to Cannon, human archaeology is a process of remembering that entails using the body as a site of recovery of knowledge that has been rendered invisible by patriarchal white supremacy. As Cannon states:

> This theme of embodiment as rememory, and rememory as reincarnation, is a basic motif in human archaeology. Flesh houses memories—the color of flesh, the reproductive character of flesh, and the manifold ways that the flesh of African women is the text on which androcentric patriarchy is written. (1998, 9)

Womanist scholars of religion provide an epistemological emphasis that is recuperative. The relationship between identity, politics, and culture is made salient as womanists reconstruct culture, allowing the symbolic resources available to them to serve as a flexible frame of communication for the purpose of clarifying the ethical contradictions posed by social forces beyond their control, and the ensuing social responses that result from the real-lived experience of such contradictions. Sociologist Michael Brake views such resources as the very context of cultural expression that members of minority subcultures draw from in order to negotiate their identities as defined by the sociosymbolic systems pertaining to the dominant culture (1985, 1–29). A womanist interpretative anthropology would thus consist in collecting data from the repositories of Black women's lives. This data would be gleaned from cultural texts that crystallize such expressions, including fiction, biography, and autobiography, and also from the lives of living Black women through the collection of their unedited speeches, by engaging them as "human documents" (Thomas 1998, 496–97). Womanist scholars thus deploy what womanist theologian Linda Thomas refers to as a "self-reflective sensitivity about the historical factors giving rise to oppressed voices" (1998, 497).

Because of their understandings of Black women's ideological and material emplacement within history, womanists gravitate to Afrocentricism, seeking in its modes of thought a resource that helps African Americans "negotiate life in a white racist society" (Douglas and Sanders 1995, 9). Womanists share some basic ideological principles with Afrocentrists, in particular, with the principles espoused by Molefi Asante. Such principles are informed by a philosophical perspective, determined by history that aims to effect a liberatory and curative conversion from a Eurocentric conditioned white consciousness to an African American and African-centered one. An Afrocentric approach empowers Black women to create and/or recontextualize ritual in order to reinforce this new consciousness (Williams 1995, 46).[9]

Womanist affinity to Afrocentrism has caused some Black feminists to see womanist scholarship as just a gendered appendage of Black, male-controlled modes of thought. However, while conforming to some Afrocentric principles, womanism has an agenda that is distinct from Afrocentrism as well as from Black Power politics. As the reference quoted at the beginning of this section indicates, the tensions that womanists experience stem from the fundamental need to make visible Black women's social positionings as divergent not only from that of white women, but also from that of Black men. Thus, even though womanist scholars criticize the Eurocentric worldview for having served the interests of racial hegemony, calling instead for the use of African American role models and cultural symbols for interpreting the realities of African American peoples, they also critique Afrocentrism for idealizing traditional gender roles developed out of African kinship traditions that were in fact oppressive to women. The perpetuation of ideas within Asante's Afrocentricism, as womanist Delores Williams points out, "make it a convenient instrument (along with white feminism) for helping to hold white male supremacy in place in the United States" (1995, 53). Womanist identity politics thus enacts a critical Afrocentrism, one that takes all forms of power into critical account while remaining focused on historical reconstructions of Black people and providing comprehensive analyses of the evolving nature of race-gender formations.

As a first step to empowering Black people in general and Black women in particular, womanist analysis thus begins with the premise that African social institutions, such as the extended family system, as well as a symbolic universe that extends, informs, and defines such institutions, including cognitive systems, linguistic patterns, and rituals governing social exchanges and behaviors, were not lost during enslavement. Rather, this inherited cosmology has been retained as a continuing force in Black American life, becoming encoded in cultural expressions as well as in sociocultural practices. Indeed, Black Americans in general and Black women in particular have adapted such cultural repositories to the evolving social and cultural circumstances within white American society.

As a context of shared cultural signification, the revision and adaptation of cultural encodings and representations on the part of Black women scholars, writers, and activists to the circumstances of Black women's lives, has additionally served to 1) articulate cognitive and emotional alternatives that give value and meaning to their identities as Black women and American citizens that would otherwise be viewed as substandard by normative white culture; 2) foster a spiritual wholeness in the psyches of Black women and their communities that have otherwise been ruptured by economic exploitation, sex discrimination and structural racism; and 3) keep alive a political praxis relevant to the particular sociohistorical realities of Black women and their communities through various historical and contemporary phases: The Middle Passage, enslavement, Reconstruction, Northern Migration, urbanization, industrialization, and the era of advanced capitalism. Notions of cultural continuity and acculturation are germane to a politics of identity. They allow for an understanding of both Black attitudes toward assimilation into American life and Black cultural patterns as the very conditions for preserving Black cultural identity in its full humanity. The identity narratives of Black women are encapsulated in Alice Walker's coinage and definition of womanism, as charted in the next section.

WOMANISM: DEFINITIONS, EPISTEMOLOGIES AND CRITICAL INTERDISCIPLINARY APPLICATIONS

Black women's literary tradition is a particularly rich venue of cultural expression. As feminist theologian Katie Cannon and other womanists have demonstrated, Black women's writings offer particular versions of Black history that make salient the variegated responses of Black women to the restrictions imposed by tripartite oppression. Black women's literary tradition distances itself from the notion of art-for-art's sake, and urgently foments the tradition of a literature of necessity (Cannon 1988, 78). Such objectives are not surprising, given that by the late 1960s, African American women writers had self-consciously undertaken a reclaiming of Black women's history and selfhood, testifying in their narratives to lived histories, or imagining and filling in the gaps between incomplete or distorted versions of

Black women's histories to retell the various paths of resistance that Black women have taken.[10]

Award-winning novelist Alice Walker first introduced the term womanism in a piece of short fiction in 1979 (Phillips 2006).[11] As an artist entering the continuum of a Black women's literary tradition that had started long before yet had never been made accessible to her as it had not formed part of the literary canon, Walker sought to further advance that tradition separately, not only in her own writing but also in naming her identity as womanist. She thus sought to convey the particularities of Black women's sociohistorical realities and cultural-symbolic frame of reference. Walker introduced the term in order to reflect a perspective on the role of Black women's fiction, one that could capture in its multifarious forms the values of her community in her own time as part of the cultural legacy inherited from earlier historical periods. She also wanted to articulate the objectives of her art, namely, to make central the ways of knowing and being of Black women.

Walker indeed theorizes the pathways of Black women's identity development along the continuum of radical subjectivity, traditional communalism, self-love, and critical engagement, each of which are identified with the consecutive but interrelated four parts of Walker's definition (Floyd-Thomas 2006a, 8–11). More than being just a literary aesthetic or poetics, the four womanist tenets became the foundational tenets of a political movement and a set of interpretive practices that facilitate the implementation of moral agency outside of social parameters that have been imposed both inter- and intra-communally upon Black women. These four tenets facilitate a revisioning of history in order to make visible the historical struggle of Black women against oppression, and an interrogation of Black women's cultural expression as a revision of women's culture and women's politics.

In the first part of the definition of womanism, Walker satirizes the standard dictionary meanings. She mimics its format at the same time that she poeticizes and politicizes the name womanist, by providing meanings that would be inaccessible to those who collect definitions for these official documents. Walker thus explains that womanist is the opposite of being girlish and is the appropriate name for a Black feminist or feminist of color. It derives "[from] the Black folk expression of mothers to female children, 'You acting womanish'" (1983, xi). While the word indicates the willfulness of the adolescent "[w]anting to know more and in greater depth than is considered 'good' for one," it is viewed as positive in that it reflects an induction into and an education on womanhood whereby the young

Black woman grounds herself in the knowledge she inherits intergenerationally from her mother or other women, and grows that knowledge, in order to be "[r]esponsible. In charge. Serious" (xi).

In this first part of the definition, knowledge is connected to the particular goal of being responsible to one's own sociohistorical realities and to one's community. Thus, a dynamic encounter between Black women facilitates a maturation or developmental process that causes the younger woman to learn about the realities they share, including models for behavior—"outrageous, audacious, courageous"—that will allow her to transcend the lessons taught to her, even by other women, in order to further elaborate her own developed subjectivities (xi). This self-actualizing process will allow her not only to survive, but also to reshape those models of behavior in such a way as to enable her to subvert the triple jeopardy of racism, sexism, and classism in the particular manifestations in which she encounters them.

A second tenet of the politics of womanism that forms part of Walker's definition and that builds on the first is that of communalism. Walker negates all forms of hierarchical orderings of identity that have devalued women. She begins by rejecting homophobic attitudes, affirming and giving value to Black women's sexual fluidity. She claims that a womanist "loves other women, sexually and/or nonsexually" (xi). She affirms Black women's culture and the continuum and range of women's emotional responses, from her emotional vulnerability to her emotional resilience: "Appreciates and prefers women's culture, women's emotional flexibility (values tears as natural counterbalance of laughter), and women's strength" (xi). Though at times claiming the right to separatism, in order to protect women's emotional health, insofar as the effects of sexism as well as racism can be emotionally draining, Walker still insists on embracing the Black community in its entirety, "male and female" (xi). Walker makes a strong claim in this passage for communal wholeness among Black people. This can be strived for, she argues, by embracing a universalist framework for valuing Black people, based on the unique contributions that comprise Black culture. She thus affirms the importance of rejecting those inherited and internalized white supremacist frameworks such as pigmentocracy, colorism, and physiognomy.[12]

Walker celebrates the different hues of the peoples of the African diaspora in a teaching that a mother passes down to her daughter: "'Mama, why are we brown, pink, and yellow, and our cousins are white, beige, and black?' Ans.: 'Well, you know the colored race is just like a flower garden, with every color flower represented'" (xi). By bringing to bear this folk lesson, Walker argues that only when there is critical questioning of difference, along with the rejection of dominant modes of thought and expressions that dehumanize self and community, can Black people recognize the various contributions of its individual members, even within the most oppressive of circumstances, and learn to become resources to the community. Walker further exemplifies communalism through the notion of traditional capability, derived from an inherited legacy of collective resistance to oppression. Walker invokes the figure of Harriet Tubman to embody and define this value: "Traditionally capable, as in 'Mama, I'm walking to Canada and I'm taking you and a bunch of other slaves with me.' Reply: 'It wouldn't be the first time'" (xi).

The third part of the definition focuses on the theme of redemptive self-love. Walker dismantles the false stereotypes of the Black female body that have rendered Black women an easy target of economic and sexual exploitation as well as of violence, causing them to look with self-hatred upon their own bodies and bodily pleasure. Walker seeks to reconnect mind and spirit with the body and its pleasures: "Loves music. Loves dance. Loves the moon, *Loves* the Spirit Loves love and food and roundness. Loves struggle. *Loves* the Folk. Loves herself. *Regardless*" (xii). Womanist Michele Jacques notes that Walker's "call to love herself 'regardless' is one of the most foundationally holistic and revolutionary political actions African-American women can take" (1995, 145).

Walker's design to draw interconnections between the various dimensions of womanist identities culminates in the fourth part of her definition. Walker addresses a basic conundrum. On the one hand she wishes to be connected to white women because she appreciates women's culture. On the other hand, however, she wishes to foreground a womanist vision that articulates different perspectives and understandings of self and community—perspectives that not only dignify Black woman's embodiment and culture, but also highlight ways of knowing and being that are steeped in embodied experiences resulting from living under racially oppressive conditions. The fourth tenet of the definition of womanism is an attempt to seek a solution to this dilemma.

Walker pushes beyond the binaries characterizing Western thought by calling for a critical engagement of womanism with white feminism. She likens the relationship of the Black womanist and white feminist to the relationship of purple to lavender. The deeper shade of purple evokes a radicalization of feminism, one that connects with and absorbs women's culture that white feminism has independently undertaken, but that carries it to a deeper level. It is not a question of just adding black to lavender to get purple. Rather, it is an interrogation of what being Black and woman means as a constitutive element of Black women's identity, and of how Black women's identities inform more deeply or correct our understandings of all women's realities, ways of knowing, and feminist struggle. The color purple represents the developmental process of identity formation toward wholeness and the reconstruction of the meanings of the experiences of womanhood, now more amply investigated than the white feminist journey alone comprises.

This four-part definition that began a movement allowed new questions to be asked that could not be addressed by feminism or feminist theology, nor by normative (Black and male) theological sources departing from the Black Power movement. Some of the questions were: What validates the truths of Black women's lives in a society that denigrates, dehumanizes, and ultimately despises Black womanhood? What is the definition of what it means to be a woman? What does it mean for a Black woman to exercise virtue? How have Black women been marginalized from the position of the knower and how might we understand the world differently if we depart from the experiences and thought processes of Black women, their communities and their cultures?

Womanist Katie Cannon crystallizes these concerns when she states:

> The chief function of womanism is not merely to replace one set of elitist, hegemonic texts...with another set of Afrocentric texts.... Rather our objective is to use Walker's four-part definition as a critical, methodological framework for challenging inherited traditions for their collusion with androcentric patriarchy as well as a catalyst in overcoming oppressive situations through revolutionary acts of rebellion. (1996, 23)

Walker's definition has since served as a foundational event for Black women scholars who working within and in the interstices of the disciplines of Religion, Sociology, History, and Anthropology, seek to theorize the moral development as well as the political consciousness and praxis of Black women. The interdisciplinary scholarly production of womanist theologians and ethicists has produced a significant body of scholarship. Two generations of womanist scholars have drawn upon Walker's definition as a means to revise current disciplinary traditions and frameworks derived from normative ethics and theology, using it as the basis for constructing both a moral articulation of Black womanhood that does not divest embodied realities from spiritual yearnings, as well as a framework for charting ethical and political action.

While Black feminist cultural criticism represents efforts to bear witness to the resistance efforts of Black women as evidenced in cultural texts, womanist ethicists and theologians draw upon social texts and historical representations as they are embedded within Black women's literary traditions in order to make visible how Black women's moral agency formation has been shaped in the midst of oppression, and to indicate the ways in which Black women carve out constructive paradigms of moral wisdom. As womanist scholar of religion Joy Elizabeth Browne states:

> [T]he literary critic and theologian play roles that are at once complementary and circular. In a sense, they are working with the same material—African-American culture and society, with all the complexities and idiosyncrasies born of a peculiar history in the United States.... The African-American literary critic takes the "text" of the culture—be it literature, "orature," or event—and decodes the content encoded in language, structure, style, and context: What does this text really *say* to us? What does it *not* say? The theologian takes the same material and examines its content for issues of meaning and ultimate significance: What does this text really *mean* for my life? What does it imply about my humanity, as one made and formed in the image of God? (1995, 115)

Womanist ethicists use Walker's definition to articulate new ethical standards by which to determine what is right or wrong, according to the particular values and lived conditions of a community, thereby making evident the ethical frameworks used by Black women and their communities, within which judgments are made and actions taken. For their part, womanist theologians build on the foundation of womanist ethicists in their exploration of unstated assumptions about Black women that derive from white society.

Placing emphasis on Black women's worthiness as a subject of serious study, womanist theologians construct theological theories, using hermeneutics as a primary interpretive method for critically interrogating heteropatriarchal and white supremacist ideologies informing social institutions, values, traditions, language, ritual, history, statistics, and sacred scriptures. They use womanist theory as a tool to interpret Black women's lives in such a way as to contest negative valuations of Black women's understandings of their world—their relationships, community, theological perspectives, and themselves. The goal of womanist theologians is to investigate historically grounded approaches that Black women have used to name the sacred in their lives, and to develop new ways to listen to Black women as they speak about their meanings of their faith as resources for theological and ethical construction.

Womanist theologians and ethicists both emphasize the importance of communal and spiritual life. Working concurrently with each other, they employ the interdisciplinary tools of historical analysis, ethnography, literary criticism, folklore, sociological analysis, economics, and medicine in order to examine how Black women's texts and contexts define and give value to their experiences and faith (Mitchem 2002, 60–62). Their writings, moreover, highlight a causal dynamic within the lives of Black women, one that makes salient the link between human and divine justice.[13]

A WOMANIST READERLY APPROACH TO BLACK WOMEN'S WRITINGS: PERSPECTIVAL DISCOURSE

To undertake an analysis of Black women's writing following the critical foundations established by womanists working in the area of ethics and theology is first to understand that Walker's definition does not merely describe Black women's experiences but also makes visible identity-formation processes represented in narratives through the changed moral attitudes and politics of the characters (Cannon 1988, 14; Floyd-Thomas 2006a). However, beyond engendering a movement, Walker's definition as well as the work of womanist scholars, have triggered new modes of academic thought and discourse, or what Cannon refers to as a perspectival discourse, capable of infusing academic theoretical frameworks with new modes of interpretation, hermeneutical analysis, and knowledge validation processes about social and cultural realities.

Perspectival discourse is premised on the basic notion that what one describes about the events that occur in one's culture is never simply a straightforward description, but rather always dependent upon the social position of the scholar and the correlating perspective one is afforded from that position. The background against which features of an identity or cultural value are picked out is in fact the individual's own cultural context. It is this partial or located perspective that objectivist discourses, in the positivist sense, frequently fail to acknowledge (Chandler, Davidson, and Harootunian 1994). When wrestling with issues of cultural hegemony, moreover, there is often an unexamined assumption that culture is a set of interconnecting events and artifacts that preexist their composite description, when in fact, as Claudia Sálazar, points out, "culture is not a static object of analysis but a multiplicity of negotiated realities and identities within historically contextualized (and contested) communicative processes" (Sálazar, 1991, 98).

Descriptions of culture and identities are always perspectival social constructions, that is, they always depend upon a host of theoretical assumptions and not upon some guarantee of correspondence to a real world. Since our identities based on race, class, gender, and nation are always already taken up by and created in hegemonic systems and ideologies, it is imperative for us, as agents of change, to be particularly attentive not to unintentionally reproduce ideological discourses under the false assumptions of descriptive neutrality, but rather make salient the particular subjective theoretical assumptions informing our perceptions. Thus, as an example of such critical attentiveness, womanist theological ethicists cultivate a hermeneutical methodology. In their scriptural analyses, they implement a hermeneutics of suspicion toward historical commentaries of biblical texts and their normative interpretations, claiming that these serve white supremacist, androcentric functions.

A womanist hermeneutics posits a form of reading and listening that does not claim to be disinterested, detached, and objective. It claims instead a dynamic and engaged perspectival interaction in which the writer/reader or preacher/congregation can, through their capacity to identify the social contexts from which historical-critical interpretations are derived because they are embedded in that context, contest dialogically the dehumanizing representations and stereotypes that define Black women as well as produce new ones. The call-and-response traditions within the Black church exemplify perspectival discourse by making evident the power relations that have been obscured within normative historical-critical readings, but that inform the ongoing experiential realities of the reader or congregation. Cannon thus states:

> Womanist hermeneutics regards sociocultural context as an important component of the sermon. The preacher's testimonial function is necessarily looked at within a personal-existential framework. The utterances of the preacher must be examined in the situation in which they are produced and delivered to the hearers, that is, in terms of the preacher's and congregation's own experiences. Nothing prohibits us

from asking questions about the role of social factors in shaping sermonic texts and what part the preacher's gender plays in selecting the kinds of biblical stories and sayings that she or he uses in preaching. (Cannon 1996, 121)

Womanist M. Shawn Copeland succinctly underscores this epistemological struggle as the core of womanist method and movement, a struggle that she refers to as a "critical realist" praxis and way of knowing that has the ethical aim of enhancing the human flourishing of Black women:

> [B]lack women *know* (in mind and body) just what it means to be the object of relativized opinion or stereotype, what it means to be excluded from or be regarded as the conspicuous exception within the community of rational discourse. Rejecting knowledge grounded in empiricism and idealism, womanists advance a critical realist way of knowing, in which human experience can be interrogated and differentiated seriously; in which different and analogous experiences, questions, and judgments are engaged and weighed in the service of understanding reality and truth; and in which knowledge exists for the creation and development of the common human good as well as individual human liberation. (2006, 232)

From a postpositivist realist perspective, one's embodied identity is more than a subjective identity; it is also an objective social location. Because of the presence of racism and sexism, social identities often distort one's lived sense of oneself or even subsume one's own understanding of the self. Because there is not an exact correlation between these two versions, writing or performing one's identity becomes a mediated interpretative process that corrects not only the distorted interpretations of minority identity(ies) that are the result of racism and sexism, but also provides a more accurate rendering of our social world. Members of marginalized groups negotiate the dominant meanings of their ascribed identity(ies) and the social world in which they are played out, with an ultimate aim to achieve a coherence between the two domains. Ostensibly, all social beings undertake such processes. Yet those who routinely find their identities distorted due to social inequality are more likely to encounter conflicts between internal and external understandings of their identity. They are therefore more likely to engage such processes as a means to create a more accurate version of their self.

In her work *Visible Identities*, Linda Alcoff elaborates a framework for thinking about real identities that takes into account not only the subjective knowledge that is attained through the human subject's analysis of her lived experience, but also the objective knowledge that human subjects can provide about social reality, insofar as they exist within the social and natural world. Drawing upon philosophical hermeneutics as developed by Hans-Georg Gadamer, she offers a framework that resonates with womanist hermeneutics. She employs Gadamer's notion of 'interpretive horizon' to explain the relationship between identity and knowledge production. Gadamer defines interpretive horizon as everything that can be seen from the perspective of one's situatedness. As an open-ended temporal and spatial field, the horizon constitutes the range of cultural and social conditions in which the self moves and in which vision occurs, and includes both the seer as part of that locality, as well as what is seen, the content. Alcoff thus asserts:

> The horizon is a substantive perspectival location from which the interpreter looks out at the world, a perspective that is always present but that is open and dynamic, with a temporal as well as physical dimension, moving into the future and into new spaces as the subject moves. (2006, 95)

Following Gadamer, Alcoff states that human judgment, which entails the use of moral and practical reasoning, always involves an interpretation, and that interpretation—the process of trying to make sense of something—is going to depend upon one's embodied experiences within a particular location. Thus, experience informs the background, foreknowledge, or framing assumptions that are indexed to the location the individual occupies. The subject develops prejudgments from his or her situated experience that the self uses to make deliberations and build knowledge. Thus, reasoning is always dependent upon context, and is always changing since contexts are continually changing. The concept of horizon helps to illuminate the invisible framing assumptions that we bring to our perceptions of the world as well as the range of ideas and feelings (experiences) that we have available to us within our social location that we use to interpret our social environment. The concept of horizon also helps us understand the differing and often incompatible interpretations within and between social groups.[14]

Gadamer's philosophical hermeneutics resonates with and fleshes out a womanist hermeneutical approach to knowledge as it relates to identity. First, the notion of interpretive horizon facilitates a de-essentialized understanding of subject-centeredness. Within a hermeneutic tradition, subject-centeredness does not assume mastery of knowledge. Rather, it makes salient that the knowledge or consciousness that the subject has of social reality, derived from living in a specific social location, is directed toward a particular content, that is, a particular experience or event that also develops within that location (2006, 100). The notion of interpretive horizon highlights the interdynamic, dialectical relation of the self and the social world because the interpretive horizon encompasses the self as both the subject that sees and the object that is seen within that location.

In that we all share the same horizon—our social world—our interpretations must have some elements in common, and, therefore, some level of commensurability, even though we may be very differently situated and therefore have more perspectives that separate us than join us. Indeed, because of the enduring presence of racism and sexism, the interpretive horizon that Black women discover and articulate can render intelligible certain features of our social world. Secondly, the notion of interpretive horizon allows us to view interpretation not as arbitrary or exclusively subjective, but as objective as well. This is because the interpretation of one's experiences requires the subject's participation in and engagement with the entire social context of which he or she is a part. Such an engagement is, moreover, constrained by the physical/spatial and historical parameters of that context.

The hermeneutical process of identity re-negotiation, one that entails a reconstruction of the historical and spatial dimensions of one's lived experience through the introduction of perspectivalism, has been salient in African American cultural expressions. Vernacular signifying, for example, is an African American rhetorical device that engages a Black postmodernist aesthetic. It is characterized by an indirect and referential rhetorical style. It can be identified with the aforementioned interpretive struggles between private and public identities. As an intertextual intervention, signifying deconstructs Black identity as it is represented within public domains and/or within the pages of a literary text. As Wahmeena Lubiano states: "[S]ignifying is a mode of vernacular artistic production as well as a mechanism for 'on-site' metacommentary. Signifying redefines racial differences as cultural difference, with all of the complexities entailed in such a recategorization, and puts our notions of reality up for grabs" (1995, 96). These epistemological processes work toward a political end, to create texts and contexts that can shift consciousness with respect to history and one's place within it, a necessary step for personal and collective empowerment.

Black women's writing on culture and identity engages these intra- and intercultural processes, to the extent that it can be considered one of its defining elements. Cheryl Wall addresses the problematic relationship in Black women's writings between the world of art and the 'real' world Black women writers attempt to engage through imaginary constructs. Wall states there is a relationship between the verbal text and the social text, but this relation is rendered problematic in African American literature because hegemonic critiques of minority identity politics and the texts that articulate them often point to such relations as an example of the text as perceived mimetic representation. Wall eschews the notion of text as the mirror of reality. Yet at the same time notes that the politics informing Black women's texts is rendered ineffective if such a relation cannot be made: "[T]o read Black writing as if it has no relation to political reality is to vitiate its power" (1991, 9). African Americanist Claudia Tate notes that Black women writers do not just chronicle life, but actually use art as a mediating vehicle for reinterpreting, reorganizing, and revising reality: "In fact, art seldom mimics life. An intermediary process involving reflection, distillation, organization, and most of all, imagination, separates the two realms. The writer projects her understanding of life, her vision as it were, into an imaginary world" (1985, xvi–xvii). Drucilla Cornell expresses an analogous perspective when she states: "The recollection of oneself is always an act which imagines through the remembrance of its own claims of selfhood what can never be fully recollected but only forever reimagined and re-told." (1993, 42).

Finally, womanist Katie Cannon states: "Most of the writing by Black women captures the values of the Black community within a specific location, time and historical context" (Cannon 1988, 77). She also argues that we can find within Black women's writings a fidelity in communicating the Black experience in America, with all of its contradictions and complexities (Cannon 1996, 70). Cannon's womanist view considers the writing of race, gender, and culture as an act of faithful rendition, whereby the author serves as translator or scribe that captures a transparent 'truth'. Using a postpositivist realist approach, however, we might think of perspectival discourse as rendering an untold version of history. The perspective from which the author writes allows us to see certain aspects of an event from a perspective that had not otherwise been seen or told and that must be analyzed for its accuracy.

In her 1983 essay, "Beyond the Peacock: The Reconstruction of Flannery O'Connor," Walker exemplifes womanist perspectivalism.

Walker seemingly describes a visit down the memory lane that she made with her mother to her childhood home, a sharefarmer's shack in southern Georgia, as well as to Flannery O'Connor's home that was just a few miles away from her own. However, Walker retells the formation of their shared history from two dislocated perspectives in order to negotiate the meanings of that history as well as her social position: the externally ascribed reality that invisiblizes her sociohistorical reality within that historicized space and the subjective experience of those processes of erasure. Thus, as Walker finds herself bewildered by the care with which O'Connor's house had been maintained in contrast to her own, she considers that the former was built by slaves, and was probably the work of her own ancestors. As she reflects on O'Connor's visibility and her own invisibility, Walker explains how she finds herself still trapped in this historical moment that configures and prefigures her identity vis-à-vis O'Connor's privilege as a white woman:

> Whenever I visit antebellum homes in the South, with their spacious rooms, their grand staircases, their shaded back windows that, without the thickly planted trees, would look onto the now vanquished slave quarters in the back, this is unbearably my thought. I stand in the back yard gazing up at the windows, then stand at the windows inside looking down in the back yard, and between the me that is on the ground and the me that is at the windows, History is caught. (Walker 1983, 47)

In order to reinsert herself into that history of raced, classed, and gendered exploitation, Walker must splinter her consciousness and her agency. This splintering is reflected in the dual perspectives of herself: the one perspective brings into view Walker's identification with the slave on the ground and at the back who looks, and the other perspective brings into view Walker's looking at herself being looked at from the house above. As she embeds a vision of double-consciousness into the story that begins with her own subjective experiences, and then imagines that experience as felt by her ancestors, Walker facilitates a process of rendering visible and then re-negotiating a public identity of social invisibility—a process that indeed represents an act of moral agency in the form of a revolt and resistance against a condition of invisibility.

In effect, she makes salient a particular ongoing pattern of structured relations that occur along a continuum of spatial-temporal relations. First, she analyzes the effects of the marginalization of

Black women's writings from the literary canon on her own identity-formation processes as a university student and her creativity as a writer. She then analyzes, in company of her mother, the invisibility of exploitation in the antebellum South as the other side of accumulated white wealth and cultural visibility within historical relations. The juxtaposition of these two events, she concludes, have come to shape but not determine her identity. Through this theoretical mediation or reflection of her experience of canonical invisibility, Walker is able to achieve a more accurate and therefore 'realist' interpretation of her experiences as a Black woman. While her experience is not the same as that of her slave ancestors, or of her mother who never went to the university, there is a recognizable experience of invisibility that is recursive, that can be verified intergenerationally, and that can predict future experiences.[15]

Besides re-negotiating realities as posited within externally ascribed realities by members of the dominant culture, Black women writers also engage in critical, intra-communal dialogical reinterpretations of sociohistorial realities. This dialogic has been noted so extensively that it has been given a variety of rubrics within Black feminist and womanist thought. In conceptualizing the ways of knowing of Black women as the construction of partial and specific understandings of one's social realities, rather than universal ones, Patricia Hill Collins thus states: "Dialogue is critical to the success of this epistemological approach, the type of dialogue long extant in the Afrocentric call-and-response tradition whereby power dynamics are fluid, everyone has a voice, but everyone must listen and respond to other voices in order to be allowed to remain in the community" (1990, 236–37).

Black feminist literary critic Mae Gwendolyn Henderson helps shape a more nuanced understanding of the dialogical nature of Black women's writings. She uses the term "creative dialogue" in reference to Black female subjectivity, as "the expression of a multiple dialogic of differences based on this complex subjectivity." Henderson affirms: "Black women enter into a *dialectic of identity* with those aspects of self shared with others" (1991, 19). She argues that Black women writers enter into a relationship of fellowship with a tradition of thought by using the language of the Other. This allows the writer/speaker to understand what the Other who uses that language has to say about a shared identity and communalism. In the case of Black women writers, this language is not just a reflection of a language of consensus, but it is also one that articulates a challenge to hegemonic traditions of what identity is and how it is constituted. Indeed, it is a rereading and reinscription of identity within Black women's writings that facilitates the notion of shared identity and communalism:

> It is this notion of discursive difference and identity underlying the simultaneity of discourse which typically characterizes Black women's writing. Through the multiple voices that enunciate her complex subjectivity, the Black woman writer not only speaks familiarly in the discourse of the other(s), but as Other she is in contestorial dialogue with the hegemonic dominant and subdominant or "ambiguously (non)hegemonic" discourses. (1991, 20)

Another articulation of this particular mode of discursive relationality encountered in Black women's writings has been articulated by Ashraf H. A. Rushdy. This critic defines those texts authored by Black women that have a dialogical structure embedded in them as "palimpsest narratives" (2000). They are so labeled because they replace individualist conflicts with intersubjective ones that link the past experiences to the events occurring in a more contemporary period, but which she links to Black women's narratives published in the '70s:

> My primary argument is that the palimpsest narratives address the social problems, political issues, and cultural concerns of their moment of production by generating a narrative in which an African-American subject who lives in the 1970s is forced to adopt a bitemporal perspective that shows the continuities and discontinuities from the period of slavery. (2000, 5)

Womanist theologian and anthropologist Linda Thomas refers to the labor of the womanist religious scholar, in an analogous manner, as one that engages a hermeneutical undertaking to understand other Black women through the generations and their historical interconnections:

> The method of womanist theology validates the past lives of enslaved African women by remembering, affirming and glorifying their contributions. After excavating analytically and reflecting critically on the life stories of our foremothers, the methodology entails a construction and creation of a novel paradigm. We who are womanists concoct something new that makes sense for how we are living in complex gender, racial, and class social configurations. We use our foremothers' rituals and survival tools to live in hostile environments. (1998/99, 491)

Thomas concludes:

Ideally, the womanist religious scholar is an indigenous anthropologist —that is, one who reflects critically upon her own community of origin and brings a sensitivity to the political, economic, and cultural systems which impact poor and working class Black women being studied. At the same time, she gives priority to the life story of the subject in a way that underscores the narratives of a long line of subjugated voices from the past to the present. (1998/99, 498)

Similarly, womanist theologian Delores Williams speaks of the "multidialogical intent" as one of the major methods of the womanist scholar in religion, the purpose of which is to disrupt normative understandings of the sociopolitical status quo in both Black and white communities, underscoring the fact that the meaning of such intent is easily distorted or devalued outside of the intergroup context: "Multidialogical activities, may, like a jazz symphony, communicate some of its most important messages in what the harmony-driven conventional ear hears as discord, as disruption of the harmony in both the Black American and white American social, political, and religious status quo" (1987, 69).

Womanist theological ethicist Katie Cannon affirms that Black women writers, drawing from the legacy of folk cultural traditions encountered throughout the African diaspora, encode in their texts the moral processes that Black women undertake as they face a myriad of social oppressions, in such a manner as to make intersubjective communication-as-survival central to such texts:

Locked out of the real dynamics of human freedom in America, they implicitly pass on and receive from one generation to the next moral formulas for survival that allow them to stand over against the perversions of ethics and morality imposed on them by whites and males who support racial imperialism in a patriarchal social order. The Black woman's literary tradition documents the "living space" carved out of the intricate web of racism, sexism and poverty. The literary tradition parallels Black history. It conveys the assumed values in the Black oral tradition. And it capsulizes the insularity of the Black community. (1988, 7)

Cannon underscores here that Black values, embedded within African folkways and stories, become the author's departure point for projecting her understandings of her own sociohistorical realities as well as the moral vision that shapes her responses to such realities.

Given on the one hand the lack of access Black women and their communities have had and currently have to dominant cultural forms due to structural racism, resulting in their cultural insularity; and on the other, the ongoing pervasive continuity of African-based symbolic systems in the Black cultural imaginary, the meaning of such practices have been available as resources for those who belong to the collectivity that has inherited them. Indeed such practices are powerful forms of intra-cultural communication, providing a web of understanding within the context of sociopolitical relations in which a particular collectivity defines itself, functioning internally to combat dominant cultural forms and acts. Black women's participation in such communication practices should be understood as a deliberate and radical act of engaging with systems of thought that have imposed their social identities, and determined the extent of their moral agency within the larger society.

It is important to note, in this regard, that Black women's rewritings of the multiple experiences of Black women's moral identity formation do not only register radically subjective understandings of Black womanhood as a corrective to the parochial stereotypes that have denigrated them, that is, indicating that they remain in a defensive posture in relation to hegemonic discursive renderings of Black womanhood. Black women's rewritings of culture also draw on the oral-aural tradition as a resource for reinstantiating dialogically the moral counsel and value standards of Black women, embedded and codified within the folk tradition, for the purpose of 1) articulating the specificity of social situations and contexts in which Black women have found themselves historically; and 2) documenting the various ways in which Black women have acted as agents, as well as the values that have informed their actions. The texts of Black women's lives, in this regard, become the venue through which such linkages are constructed and tested out, at the intertextual and intersubjective levels.

When I refer above to the dialogical reinstantiation of Black values, moral standards, and historical accounts within Black women's writings, I do not mean to say that Black women register some universal or absolute 'truth.' Having access to such knowledge does not mean, as one sometimes gets the impression when reading womanist theological and ethical theory, having exclusive domain over the truth of the African American female experience. Instead, as Johnnella Butler suggests, it is the imperative of assimilation into white culture that causes Black women and their community to theorize their experiences, and attempt to verify the knowledge base received intersubjectively within their particular location and social context. Such an imperative impels them to an "encounter with others, the other, and the world and all it holds in a dialogical unfinalizable sense, where identity is spawned in the processes of theorizing experience" (Butler 2006, 176). Such is the attempt to gain a holistic perspective, and thus, wholeness (176–177). With regard to Black women's writings, Butler further argues that a character's dialogical engagement with social reality through the exploration of 'rememory,' that is, critical reflection on the Black experience in relation to a past history of enslavement, allows for a re-negotiation of past or present events that can lead to accurate knowledge or error. In this sense, she suggests, the dialogical is "tantamount to theorizing about reality, separating the legitimate from the illegitimate towards the end of a theory-mediated objectivity" (Butler 2006, 173).

Womanists and Black feminists provide the methodological procedures for engaging critical rememory of past and present experiences, using Black women's literary and cultural texts as their resources. In order to cull from narrativities of race and gender the constructive paradigms of moral wisdom or restitutive axiologies, the womanist critic starts with investigating cultural codes embedded within the characters' social contexts that point beyond the characters to conditions, events, meanings and values that have crystallized in the African American community around women's variegated activities and traditions (Thomas 1998, 491). In this regard, the remembering of experience is a humanizing gesture that elicits complexity and heterogeneity, as Wall underscores, drawing from Hortense Spillars:

> Appeals to experience need not be essentialist and ahistorical, because the experience of Afro-American women is unmistakably polyvalent. The simultaneity of oppressions in their lives resists essentialist conclusions. Black women are indeed "witnesses to and participants in [their] own experience, and in no way coincidentally, in the experience of those with whom [they] have come in contact." (1991, 10)

This methodological approach recognizes axiological restitution as constitutive of an ethics that undergirds Black identity formations and serves as a basis for the recovery from distortion or anthropological loss the values and aesthetics of Black bodily integrity, as well as foments psychic and bodily wholeness (Hesse 1993, 167). It also acknowledges that the process of moral restitution, embedded in Black women's writings, serves as a nexus between oral-aural values, passed on from one generation to the next, and the fabric of Black life today. Such a process is in turn resonant with the individual lives and realities of womanist scholars/interpreters who seek to understand the complexities of their own moral struggle with tripartite oppression outside of preestablished approaches to morality that have ignored their sociohistorical circumstances (Cannon 1988, 5–6).

This intra-cultural, intersubjective dialogics also demands a new model of reading Black women's writings, one that asks that the reader seek the generative sources and themes of Black women's writings, not for the purpose of establishing a canon of privileged texts or thought, but for understanding how such generative sources provide models for the encoding of a variegated contestorial and liberatory dialogics. A liberatory dialogics obliges the reader/critic to enter into and be a co-participant of a womanist consciousness by pivoting her attention from the writer as Other that enunciates her complex subjectivity in the discourse of the other(s) to the writer as Other "in contestorial dialogue with the hegemonic dominant and subdominant or 'ambiguously nonhegemonic' discourses" (Henderson 1991, 20). Here, Mae Henderson, following Rachel Blau DuPlessis, draws attention to the full range of discursive power that Black women must confront, including the more ambiguous discursive status pertaining to Black men and white women. The womanist critic further pivots her attention from social texts to biotexts, that is, to her own embodied history. The narrative re-articulation of self and group identities reflects a means to create a moral ground on which to rest Black women's identities and to imagine psychic healing and wholeness. In this regard, womanists turn their critical and deconstructive attention to those works authored by Black women writers that in turn are referential, that write or rewrite histories of racial exclusion and otherness, and insert in such histories racial, material, and historical specificity as a means to make visible Black women's cultural values, moral wisdom and political praxis.

The womanist critic, due to her own social location as member of a racially disenfranchised group, engages dialogically with the moral dilemmas that Black women's stories evoke. In this sense, to read and analyze Black women's writings as a womanist is to already be situated within histories of oppression and resistances, and to acknowledge and privilege Black women's perspectival knowledge about their sociality. Clearly, Black life in contemporary United States—a social context in which structural racism continues to prevail—affords Black women a set of experiences that allow them to accumulate interpretations of the way oppression works. From a realist perspective, Black women scholars are not masters of interpretation. Yet because their own lives are embedded within the traditions to which Black women's writings pertain and to which Black women's writings respond, the proximity of their social location and the extent of their participation in analogous social contexts allow them to achieve a more credible, and more valuable interpretive performance, that is, to act as more ideal epistemic agents.

Thus, by examining their own social locality against those that are constructed in cultural texts, womanist critics can use their heightened sensitivity to cull out the strategies deployed by Black women authors to recreate situations in which Black women, now symbolized by fictional protagonists, have historically wrestled with forced identities and struggled in various ways to form their unique identity positions within their communities. Womanist critics approach these texts with the collaborative intent to participate dialogically in the reconstruction of knowledge about Black women. They do so by remaining attentive to those aspects of culture embedded/encoded in them that have been cultivated by Black women for the sake of their survival and the survival of their community, including how to survive in white culture and how to survive in patriarchal and class structures; knowledge that has in early interactions been transmitted from grandmother to granddaughter and mother to daughter, during the maturation process. The transmission of excluded voices brings to life for womanist critics the hidden histories of oppressed people that now become Black women's privileged knowledge base, not just about their own lives but about other social groups and histories as disseminated through normative institutions through the written and recorded voices of the privileged.

Perspectival Discourse and the Cultural/Racial Outsider

Black women scholars' claim of privileged understandings of Black women writing has raised theoretical questions of cultural authenticity both within minority discourses as well as in mainstream academic discourses that address issues of cultural identity. These questions include, among others: What constitutes authentic Blackness, for example, in Black cultural values and expression? What counts for critical legitimacy, that is, who gets to define what authentic or "core Black values" are? What moral agency should Black people derive from a legitimized social identity? In other words, toward what political ends are such cultural idioms being used and with what effects on the agency of Black women and their communities?

These critical debates have been used within the academy to justify the belief that identity politics, a practice that assumes that there are 'cultural insiders' who can know and represent everything about their culture, does not provide a venue for eluding essentialist notions of identity. Postcolonial theorists have put into question the notion of authenticity as it relates to the notion of the 'native,' that is, the cultural insider. Arjun Appadurai critiques the underlying imperialist and ethnocentric assumptions in Anthropology's notion of the native, arguing that authenticity is in itself a mythical or fictive construct of the West, associated with more primitive modalities of identity: "Proper natives are somehow assumed to represent their selves and their history without distortion or residue" (1988, 37). Yet, he goes on to say, those in position to observe 'natives,' including anthropologists, are exempt from being authentic. What distinguishes them from the 'native' is their capacity to represent themselves in terms of complexity, diversity and ambiguity (37).

The critique that Appadurai levels at the concept of the native can also be extended to the native researcher, who supposedly carries a stamp of authenticity that the researcher of the dominant racial group does not. Such dismantlings raise doubts about the authority of the researcher as well as stability of identity on which such authority rests, either because they portray the insider/researcher as so far removed from her own culture (by virtue of physical location or education) that she would no longer see herself as an insider and therefore construct a false construct of the community studied as 'native'; or, conversely, a critic who has lived in close proximity with the community studied might be viewed as more of an insider, and thus be more a part of the fictive construct herself.

Rather than try to engage more deeply these ongoing debates over the authentic basis of identity within a number of disciplines, with polarizing arguments around foundationalism and identity surfacing between positivists and postmodernist/postcolonialists on the one hand; and between postmodernists/postcolonialists and Afrocentrists and womanists on the other, it might be more productive to foreground the fact that in our everyday contemporary realities, racism exists, and has provided a structure of domination as well as triggered resistances to domination since its inceptions in modernity (Winant 2004, 36–37). As Breinig and Lösch note in their discussion of multicultural societies, racism is both embedded and invisibilized in white America. Indeed, the civil rights movement began due to the realization of the ongoing and persistent reentrenchment of U.S. racism. This movement focused not only on carving out an agenda to promote equality, but also on fomenting a group culture that traced some of its significant roots back to Africa, an agenda that white America was to find threatening:

> Even among people who consider themselves free of the racism of earlier generations, basic elements of a racist society continue to shape their attitudes: a binary thinking along color lines—including the collectivizing "you" for all Blacks, past and present; an emphasis on economics as the bedrock of the social order; a competitive individualism bolstered by a sense of belonging to the white majority; an unwillingness to consider the consequences of a majority-minority situation, nay, of a hierarchy of power deriving from historical injustice...; and finally a distrust of the new claims to a specific culture of their own articulated by African-Americans (2002, 11).

As previously noted, the perspectival nature of discourse is more particularly problematic when it is obscured or denied by scholars who pertain to a racial group that has exploited or colonized the culture being written, scholars who rely on academic frameworks that claim to be universal and objectivist. This is because universal and objectivist discourses tend to fail to acknowledge that the background against which the critic selects and foregrounds determined cultural features is really partial. Indeed, hermeneutical processes are dependent upon the critic's own cultural context and purposes, which might indeed be ideologically at cross-purposes with the moral or political objectives of the community itself (Chandler, Davidson, and Harootunian 1994).

This does not mean, nonetheless, that cultural and racial outsiders cannot read and interpret Black women's writings. Yet it would be safe to say from the outset that because of the culturally and physically segregating practices that result from our current racist social structures, the cultural and biological outsider, generally speaking, is less able to understand and appreciate the nuances of marginalized cultural expressions or grasp their perspective from the location they occupy. And because outsiders are less able to understand, it is also more probable that they would draw upon, for compensatory legitimization, universal or objectivist methodological frameworks as a means to make claims of academic legitimacy when critiquing minority cultural work.[16]

As a cultural outsider who is also a member of the racially dominant group, I wish to make explicit the significance of acknowledging partial perspective, a partiality that has led me to focus my inquiry into the complexities of inequality on the lives of women of color, in order to have a more complete or more correct understanding of our social world. Such an acknowledgment allows the cultural outsider to take a first step in enacting racial justice by putting limits on her own power to privilege the interpretation that she develops from her location as a basis to define herself and her group against a cultural Other. Such a step allows for a tacit acknowledgment that one can only know and recognize/interpret what one has lived, what one has experienced, and can only know from a determined social locality.

Secondly, the cultural outsider ought to acknowledge that because of the perdurability of white supremacy, a more accurate interpretation of her own identity and of the social features of the world that she shares with others is dependent upon the perceptual practices, paradigms, and narratives developed and deployed by minoritarian women. This boundedness to other women's realities and experiences is akin to the liminal sensation Walker describes as experiencing in her narration of her visit to Flannery O'Connor's house, namely, of finding herself split between seeing (whiteness) and being seen (by whiteness), but in the inverse: in order to access more adequately the real features of our social world, the cultural outsider must engage the position of seer/reader, and engage the text in such a way so as to open herself up to everything in the text/context that would allow her to position herself differently—as being seen. In doing so, she can begin to assess the sustainability of her own perspectives, in light of the new information she can now access.

The cultural outsider should begin, I suggest, by reading Black women's writings using the perspective offered from their location as a means to see herself anew, to grasp what could not otherwise be understood by virtue of not occupying the same locality. Rather than eliminating the descriptors of 'insider' and 'outsider' as arbitrary and essentialist, in order to justify speaking for Black women's realities more adeptly than they can for themselves, the cultural outsider should foreground these rubrics as reader, to inform her efforts to make systems of racial dominance visible, that is, her own framing or background assumptions, as well her identification with racial dominance. No longer an impartial reader, the cultural 'outsider' can then work to critically engage the perspective of the Other. She can do so by consciously picking out the specific features of white dominance she enacts, and then reorganizing her dispersed feelings and experiences in order to create a more coherent interpretation of her identity and of her world, that is, the shared histories of domination and subjugation by which insiders and outsiders are defined and interconnected. Having achieved a more accurate and therefore realist identity schema, the cultural outsider can then make salient the resistance methodologies developed and implemented by Black women as a means to effect change, as well as determine how she can construct a feminist, anti-racist politics that is coherent with these newly fashioned identities.

With regard to her own social transformation, the cultural outsider enacts positive racial formation processes by working to create an identity for herself not founded on dominance. Her goal instead is to attain her own psychic need for healing and wholeness, jeopardized by her engagement with hegemonic perspectives and practices. Whether a self-named cultural/racial insider or outsider, womanist critics must already do this collective work of culling patterns of thought, values and attitudes from Black women's writings as a means to reinterpret and reframe what is already ostensibly 'known,' ultimately locating the newly learned particulars within larger cultural patterns, social relations, and historical shifts in ways that are socially transformative.

The Transnational Dimension of Womanist Identity Politics

There is so much that is ours that we've lost and, we don't even know that we're missing it: ancient Egypt, ancient Ethiopia, Eatonville, Florida! And yet there's no general sense that the spirit can be amputated, that a part of the soul can be cut off because of ignorance of its past development.

(Walker 1985, 183)

If womanist identity politics seeks to locate radical Black female subjectivities in the in-between of disciplines, movements, and periodizations within specific U.S. histories, it also seeks to locate Black female subjectivities across nationalisms and nations. Yet womanist articulation of postmodern Blackness as a resistance ethics becomes the target of ideological assaults within diasporan and transnational discourses in the '90s. Approaches in Cultural Studies during this time accentuate the inevitability of difference both in terms of identity and knowledge formations, prioritizing the overlapping, plural affiliations, and inter-identitarian states of being within lived realities. The realities of migrations and the theories that have surfaced to explain the effects of these realities, such as hybridity, *mestizaje*, and transculturation, have engendered more complex understandings of identities.

A new theoretical aim here is to understand such realities by emphasizing the nature of cultural grafting that is the consequence of geographical migration and the ensuing emergence of the 'multicultural' nation-state. Identity is now the site of struggle for all human beings, resulting in dislocations across the binary divide, in essence, canceling it out, and ultimately causing a disjuncture in what had been understood as an easy correlation between one's identity and one's (political) allegiances. The theoretical implications and critique of such globalizing and nomadic discourses is that hybridity, now seen as an endemic human feature, renders inoperative an identity politics that has been historically undergirded by a consciousness of oppression shared by a particular collectivity.

Once that correlation is disrupted, difference can be repackaged and hegemonically reinscribed for the purpose of optimal commodification and exchange in the global marketplace, actually giving the illusion of economic equality (Hutnyk 1997, 119). Nonetheless, it is important to remember that racial hierarchies continue to exist within geopolitical realities, and the embodiment of hybridity will have enormously different social effects, depending on one's location within dominant or subjugated racial groups and within specific geopolitical sites. New and changing social and cultural conditions do not alter the fact that people live out their realities in a given material location and within specific histories. In this regard, hybridity theories can actually mask how people derive and constitute their identities and political agency within specific historical locations, precisely due to the fact that they are located within relatively stable spatial-temporal relations with others to whom they feel accountable (Ahmad 1995, 13–16).

Nonetheless, scholarship developing in the terrain of the New Racial Studies foregrounds the attention that must be given to the ongoing racialization processes within the global terrain. Howard Winant cites a number of themes that deserve urgent attention: diaspora and globalism as racialized processes; micro-macro racial linkages; communication/media as racial phenomena; the legacies of conquest and slavery; race and revolution; race and capitalism; race and democracy; race/gender as co-constitutive in modernity; whiteness; and the race/ethnicity arguments (2004, 75–77).

Womanist scholarship has long been intentional about foregrounding just such political continuities and critiquing racial projects. As Black feminist Ann duCille states, while postcolonial discourses may be relatively new on the academic scene, the theorizing of power relations between colonizer and colonized has nonetheless been undertaken by scholars including W.E.B. DuBois, Pauline Hopkins, Anna Julia Cooper, Marcus Garvey, Frantz Fanon, Aime Cesaire, Cheikh Anta Diop, Stuart Hall, Paul Gilroy, Hazel Carby and many others of African American descent throughout the diaspora dating back to the late nineteenth century (1996). Moreover, insofar as womanist scholars are inheritors of this rich intellectual legacy, they are able to draw on the theoretical strands of Afrocentric and postcolonial theories in order to inform their analyses of power relations, and even enhance theories of colonization by making visible the particular forms of marginalization that Black women experience. In doing so, they develop a pluralistic identity politics that accounts for diverse hybrid enactments of Black female subjectivities.

While womanist scholars benefit from the modalities of postcolonial and Afrocentric discourses, they do not necessarily conform to the contours of their politics. Thus, while womanists adopt Afrocentric notions in order to focus on their African heritage, they also reject the erasure of Black women's experiences within that legacy. Similarly, womanist scholars draw upon the insights of postcolonial theory to theorize the colonizer-colonized relationships that have impacted their identities and agency, but at the same time critique how such theories problematize the diversity of Black subjectivities as a corrective to an innocent homogenizing Black politics to the extent that it is no longer possible to talk about a Black politics or a "collectivist spirit" across differences (Hutnyk 1997, 121).

Womanist scholars draw on both postcolonial and Afrocentric theories in order to allow for the enactment of a resistance politics that transcends the bounding of cultures by nationalist demands, including Black or white nationalisms within the United States, and nationalisms pertaining to other nations in the African diaspora. The forging of diasporic constellations of Black women's subjectivities obliges us to consider not just the common experiences of oppression among Black women and their communities, but also the historically and geographically variable forms of relationality among Black communities within and between different diasporic formations. Herein, it is possible to conceptualize analytically a confluent construction of Blackness that gives rise to a diasporic community unified in struggle, without falling into overgeneralizations that discount the diverse experiences of each Black culture's realities (Brah 1996, 91–92). Indeed, because so much of what Blackness is has been described through a hegemonic perspective, it is now more necessary than ever to understand Blackness through the lens of those marginalized voices that embody it. As Carol Boyce Davies states, Black should be provisionally used in the ongoing search to find the language to articulate the experiences of Black peoples' encounters with overwhelming whiteness and Eurocentricity (Boyce Davies 1994, 8).

Womanists turn and return to Black women's literary and cultural traditions as a primary repository of the Black communal experience because they are bound to Black people's historical context of struggle within specific locations, times, and experiences. Womanist Dianne Stewart reflects such a cultural return with her investigation and remembering of limbo dancing, an African-based tradition that is also indigenous to Jamaica, her ancestral home. Although later commodified and appropriated by the tourist sectors on the northern coast of Jamaica, the womanist aim is to liberate the tradition from such appropriations. By traveling back through family narratives, Stewart foregrounds what W.E.B. DuBois calls a "second sight"—a signifying practice that allows her to connect the various parts of herself an African American, and Caribbean—for the purpose of eradicating the manufactured shame associated with these cultural sites (2006, 87–89).

The identity formation of the "diasporic imagined community" is thus constituted at the crossroads of each society's everyday material life as it is lived and transformed through individual and collective memory and rememory, chronicled in the canon of Black women's writings (Brah 1996, 183). In other words, Black women's writings offer a snapshot of a Black diasporic political site, a site wherein "Black people redefine identity away from exclusion and marginality as they reconnect to and remember Black experiences that are otherwise dislocated and sequestered by the geopolitics of nation, space and time" (Floyd-Thomas and Gillman 2002, 532–33). Womanist analyses of such diasporic connections in Black women's writings not only compare texts that have been produced within different diasporic sites but also ones produced within the same geopolitical site, insofar as social identities are always already transnational. Diasporic scholarship thus highlights imperialist projects produced within the context of the expansion of European empires in the New World dating back to the African slave trade in order to determine how they have produced dislocations of Black women's identity and place over time (Levin 2003).

Womanist analyses of Black women's literary and cultural production across the diaspora implement a relational scrutiny of Blackness, an exploration into the diverse forms and experiences of subjugation (imperialism, enslavement, colonization, and apartheid) that Black women and their communities have faced. Rather than homogenizing

Black female subjectivities in the face of dominant colonizing practices, however, womanist scholars clarify the differently accommodated enactments of radical Black subjectivities and simultaneously affirm a persistence of the notion of Blackness as a provisional and problematic yet binding identity that transcends state and nationhood and functions in contestation to diverse encounters with whiteness and Eurocentrism.[17]

In spite of the analogous or parallel positions they may occupy, Black women's participation in a given collectivity means that they continue to have particular understandings and histories of race, gender, and economic oppression. Therefore the focus given to the multiplicity and fluidity of identity does not mean that the group identity or that the individual's membership within it disappears, as in the case of postmodern hybridity theories or other hegemonic forms of postmodernism. Rather, womanist analysis examines Black women's writings and the common cultural traditions from which they originate across cultures, nations, and continents, undertaking a type of method, espoused by Hill Collins, that assesses how Black women's various spatial and historical experiences with racial inequality broadens our knowledge of how mechanisms of institutional power can change according to the referent or situation within specific histories and locales and be responsive to it, while at the same time perpetuating the age-old inequalities based on race (Collins 2004, 248–49).

U.S. womanists' efforts to produce diasporic frameworks of racialized gender have, nonetheless, been met with resistance by Black women scholars working in the United States and abroad. British womanist Julia Sudbury, for example, claims that U.S. womanist scholars are divisive and essentialist insofar as they claim the uniqueness of their experiences and the theoretical perspectives emerging from them, in contrast to British Black feminists, who have focused on histories of resistance to colonialism that are common to women of color and a shared intersectional analysis of racist oppression (Sudbury 1998, 28). She further claims that due to different experiences of Black womanhood, it is not only probable that there can be internal contestations within the category of Black women, but it is highly probable that Black British women would dispute the characterization of Black women's perspectives as articulated by U.S. Black feminists and womanists (46–49).

Other Black feminists and Africana womanists add their voices to the discussion. Africana womanist Clenora Hudson-Weems, while affirming womanism's roots in the realities and origins of African culture, objects to the extent to which U.S. womanists have been influenced by white feminism's quest for gender emancipation (1993). According to Hudson-Weems, founder of Africana womanism, racism dictated that Black women and men assume unconventional gender roles, disallowing their conformity to more traditional roles within African kinship systems. African women do not view their possibilities for empowerment in terms of autonomy from Black men but rather from white supremacist structures. Indeed, for Hudson-Weems, the bonds between Black men and women are an integral aspect of the African worldview and are often considered the foundational element of continuity of Black culture (Alexander-Floyd and Simien 2006). For her part, legal education scholar Isabelle Gunning has critiqued Alice Walker's version of womanism, construing it as a diasporic construct that views the world from a first-world perspective, as noted by Walker's tendencies to act in the guise of savior when responding to the plight of women in the 'third world' (1998).[18]

Clearly, U.S. womanists are responding to such critiques, and in the process, further assessing their own identity formation in relation to other articulations of Blackness and femaleness. In the following chapter I chart Alice Walker's efforts to create a perspectival discourse that continues to be compelling in its acknowledgment of both the influences and continuity of African cultural and symbolic systems of thought that provided group identification to African Americans. I also examine Walker's investigation of U.S. Black women's negotiation and advancement of those systems in the specific spatial and temporal contexts of the legacy of enslavement that they have inherited.

CHAPTER 4

Storytelling as Embodied Knowledge: Womanist Praxis in Alice Walker's *The Color Purple*

[B]lack writers seem always involved in a moral and/or physical struggle, the result of which is expected to be some kind of larger freedom. Perhaps this is because our literary tradition is based on the slave narratives, where escape for the body and freedom for the soul went together.

Alice Walker (1983, 5)

INTRODUCTION

Central to womanist thought and mobilizations is the investigation of Black women's identity formation that is celebratory of Black women's moral struggles and achievements (Floyd-Thomas 2006a; and King 2004).[1] Toward this end, womanists have adopted and theoretically extended Alice Walker's four-part definition of womanism in order to gain an appreciation for and offer a positive reassessment of the complex experiences of being Black and female in a racist and patriarchal society. Womanists analyze Black women's literary texts in order to retrace the fictional characters' interrogations of the limits of their selfhood as well as their ultimate claiming of a full humanity as a lived praxis of social justice. They additionally portray the events shaping the characters' lives as manifestations of real-lived instances of oppression and resistance, shadowing, in effect, anonymous or documented historical figures. Following Walker's own assertion that her characters in *The Color Purple* wanted to speak *through* her (Walker 1983, 356), Katie Cannon affirms that the Black female literary tradition "cryptically records the specificity of the

Afro-American life" (1996, 60). Cannon also suggests an investigation of Black women's writings that will help facilitate an "understanding of some of the differences between ethics of life under oppression and established moral approaches that take for granted freedom and a wide range of choices" (Cannon 1996, 60–61).[2]

The major intent of this chapter is to move beyond a celebratory examination of Black women's moral identity formation struggles and resistances to an interrogation of the heuristic function of Black women's fiction, that is, its evocation of a struggle in the terrain of truth—how the truth might be best represented, who is entitled to speak for that past in the present, what narrative context and/or theory offers greater epistemic and ethical validity, and how and under what cultural or historical conditions such interpretations are later verified or contested.[3] The aim of this chapter is not exclusively to restore to history the excluded subjective experiences and understandings as well as acts of resistance in order to trigger a healing or liberatory effect on the character or reader. Nor is it even to focus on and resolve through the analyses of various fictional emplotments the "truth" versus "distortion" binary, thereby reproducing this binary as a model of historical authority or authenticity. Rather, a primary concern here is to situate womanist interrogations of identity formation in Black women's writings within a larger postpositivist cultural production. I thus attempt to relocate the multiple meanings of the past within the imaginary or theoretically mediated dimension of individual and collective social memory as a means to test out history's claims to facticity. In this regard, the embedding of events within Black women's fiction is significant in terms of the ways which the characters bring into play the cognitive component of historical experience.

The thematizing of truth about the past as a site of struggle in both private and public spheres finds its formal expression in Black women's fiction in the narrative device of storytelling. Storytelling is used as a heuristic device in Black women's writings in general and in Walker's fiction in particular, to mediate Black women's race-gender formation, allowing the author and reader to interpret identities and social realities on a trial-and-error basis through their characters' reflections on their own life stories as they remember and retell them to others (McKay 1990, 52–53; Pryse 1985, 12–24). A postpositivist realist mode of inquiry contributes additional intellectual resources to a womanist analysis of storytelling. Emphasizing the cognitive nature of experience, postpositivist realists claim that telling one's own story is the context and process for clarifying erroneous conceptions regarding the epistemic and political status of existing identities and social structures, and a means to resist social constructions of identity that serve oppressive ideological functions (Mohanty 2000, 38–41).

Indeed, there is a strong resonance here with womanist approaches to identity. Womanist theologian M. Shawn Copeland signals "cognitive praxis" as a core element of womanist thought. She defines "critical cognitive praxis," drawing on philosopher theologian Bernard Lonergan's work on cognitional structure, as a struggle to know through the reinterpretation of one's experience:

> The phrase *cognitive praxis* denotes the dynamic activity of knowing: questioning patterns and the sometimes jagged-edge of experience (including biological, psychological, social, religious, cultural, aesthetic); testing and probing possible answers; marshaling evidence and weighing it against cultural codes and signs, against imperious and subjugated truths; risking judgment; taking up the struggle. (2006, 227)

Copeland's womanist orientation of "struggle" advances the fostering of a perspectival discourse. Herein, the womanist locates knowledge about the self and society in an objective social location that surfaces as the Black female subject comes to know herself and the social world differently, by measuring her own interpretations about the unequal social arrangements that have defined her moral choices against those of others. Copeland acknowledges that such a critical praxis, one that poses an ethics of thinking that in turn exposes ethical bias and distortion, occurs through an exchange with others. She does not, however, explicitly label such a process as a different sort of 'objectivity,' nor does she reference storytelling as the context for this exchange:

> Rejecting knowledge grounded in empiricism and idealism, womanists advance a critical realist way of knowing, in which human experience can be interrogated and differentiated seriously; in which differing and analogous experiences, questions, and judgments are engaged and weighed in the service of understanding reality and truth; and in which knowledge exists for the creation and development of the common human good as well as individual human liberation. (2006, 232)

Storytelling, as I argue in this chapter, becomes the privileged means in Black women's writings through which the female characters achieve cognitive efficacy. I use the notion of storytelling more broadly here to refer to the different ways in which a character speaks and tells stories, constructs and deploys arguments and other rhetorical and linguistic devices, as well as performs emotional expressiveness, and embodied dialogue systems, systems which I will define and analyze in depth in the sections below. In their roles as storyteller and listener, the characters not only provide new theoretical frameworks for explaining the self under oppressive conditions, but also undertake public acts of moral agency with the aim of influencing the broader social and communal contexts in which they find themselves and their social position within them. As the characters (re)interpret themselves through listening to and telling stories, an objective process of gaining knowledge becomes illuminated. Herein, the storyteller both refers to those preexisting identities, constructions, and socio-political realities in which such identities are shaped. She also performs, through contestation and revision, the presumed objectivity of the social structures and institutional practices in which she finds herself caught, and from which moral conflict originates. The storyteller thus exposes the discontinuities, fissures, and contradictions of 'objective' reality.

Thus, the storyteller places herself not only inside of and inseparable from the context of history and its various constructions of realities, but also makes her locatedness within history central to the story/history. Through her discursive interventions, she makes palpable the moral silence and evasion of racism and sexism that has become constitutive of dominant Eurocentric literary and cultural discourses through which the history of our nation has been represented and through which her own identity has been constructed. It is through the public domain of storytelling that the character/teller attempts, as I will demonstrate through an analysis of cognitive realist practices within Alice Walker's *The Color Purple*, a re-articulation and recuperation of a past, present, and future self in relationship with others that is epistemically productive in that it allows the character a chance to arrive at a more accurate interpretation of the self and the world.

Walker's 1982 Pulitzer prize-winning historical novel has been deemed a classic or paradigmatic womanist text, moving the female characters from a state of crisis and alienation to conscientization and effective resistance. Walker uses the device of storytelling as a central motif through which characters and readers critically respond to an underlying moral question that the characters' lives pose: how does one assert oneself as a Black woman and reclaim one's cultural heritage and social identity in contemporary society, given the ongoing legacy of dehumanizing hatred, violence and injustice caused by the institution of chattel slavery and the penetration of its principles into the institutional and ideological foundations of U.S. society?

Rather than using the function of storytelling as a device to focus on the conflicts the main characters confront and the actions they must take to overcome them, Walker uses storytelling in her work as a set of cognitive critical practices that facilitate a remembering of the sociopsychological and historical circumstances of their social identities that need to be retold and heard again differently for the very sake of the teller's and the listener's survival. In what follows, I will first relate the issue of such narrative and performative processes of recuperation to the historical and neo-slave narrative traditions in which Walker and other Black women novelists worked, as well as link these traditions to the various other recuperative projects which were spawned in the wake of the civil rights and Black Power movements. Following that, I will define and analyze the specific cognitive practices embedded within Walker's novel with the aim of showing how Walker's characters retrieve human experiences from the past, render them intelligible, and evaluate them in the context of their own lives in order to assess their cognitive validity.

BLACK WOMEN WRITERS' INTERVENTION IN THE HISTORICAL AND NEO-SLAVE NARRATIVE TRADITIONS OF THE 1970S AND '80S

The focus of African American women writers of fiction in the '70s and '80s on an exploration of self and community through an interrogation of the historical circumstances of racism and sexism visited upon Black women during the periods of chattel slavery, Reconstruction, post-Reconstruction, and contemporary eras was intimately linked to new lines of scholarly and creative inquiry spawned in the decade of the '60s, ones that, nonetheless, privileged the concerns of Black men's historical experience of racial oppression. The civil rights and Black Power movement became the conduit for a revival of new historical discourses on slavery, including the historical novel and neo-slave narratives. These genres could best capture and rekindle the community's historical memory, and make it available as an interpretive tool for dissecting and contesting current political struggles, namely, the political enfranchisement of African Americans into American society.[4]

With white America's failure to meet civil rights demands to create an inclusive and integrated society, the Black Power movement generated new strategies for group empowerment by fashioning a new racial Black social subject. Calling for African Americans to assert their subjective personal and communal identities as a means to contest their objectification as African Americans, the appropriation of their culture and the erasure of their history, the Black Power movement began to produce new social histories that contested the ongoing racist assaults on African American culture. A principal site for examining the ongoing stigmatization of African Americans was a scholarly one, the historiography of slavery that cultivated between 1959 and 1968. Historian Stanley Elkin's pivotal work, *Slavery* (1968), focused predominantly on the Black male's experience as the means to understanding slave life and culture as a closed system that had wide-ranging effects on the personality of the Black slave. Elkins reproduced the male myth of the Sambo figure as a trope to explain slave personality development by affirming that the only role available to Black men was that of the 'perpetual child' in a closed system where power and authority is given to the slave master. The female slave, on the other hand, a figure given scant critical examination in this work, was, according to Elkin, able to find an alternative role as mother, allowing her to escape Samboism.

This argument of an infantile slave personality was taken up in public and political discourses of the '60s as a justification for blaming African Americans, rather than U.S. social structures that are in turn a product of chattel slavery, for their own social and economic marginalization. Thus, Senator Daniel Patrick Moynihan's "The Negro family: The Case for National Action," released in 1965, drew on Elkin's thesis to posit that a contemporary cycle of social and moral and economic deterioration of the Black family was traceable to a slave tradition of domineering women (matriarchy) and emasculated men (symbolized by the Sambo figure) and was, moreover, responsible for welfare dependency, illegitimacy, crime, and Black male unemployment. William Styron's *The Confessions of Nat Turner* (1967) represented another site for the mythologization of slave culture. Influenced as well by Elkin's controversial interpretation of slave community and character, Styron used the genre of historical fiction to construct Nat Turner's slave's revolt against Virginia slavocrats as an isolated and atypical event, given the personality development of the African slave. Using the slave/narrator as spokesperson of Elkin's Sambo thesis concerning the personality structure of slaves, Styron depicts the slaves' character throughout the novel as divested of moral responsibility and manhood.[5]

Throughout the '60s, '70s, and '80s, the intellectual labor of literary critics, writers, progressive and Black Power historians intersected with that of Black Power activists, producing a revised understanding of American history and of the Black experience within it. Within the publications of the new social histories of slavery, Black racial subjects articulated racial subjectivity, using their own language, and life stories for the purpose not only of refuting the assumption of Black cultural inferiority or historical absence but also of asserting the dignity and continuity of African cultural forms. George Rawick brought to light the nineteen volumes of the WPA narratives in the 1970s, thereby helping to launch a mode of inquiry that aimed at illuminating the subjective historical experience of enslavement. John Blassingame's *The Slave Community* and Rawick's *From Sundown to Sunup,* published in 1979 and 1973 respectively, were crucial in correcting stereotypical histories of slaves, and legitimizing slave testimony as primary source material for historians; Robert Fogel and Stanley Engerman's *Time on the Cross* (1974), Eugene Genovese's *Roll, Jordan Roll* (1974), and Herbert Gutman's *The Black Family in Slavery and Freedom, 1750–1925* (1977) are some notable examples of revisionist historiographies from the "bottom up," ones, nonetheless, that continued to focus on the male slave experience.

Black women writers, scholars, and activists who had either participated in the civil rights and Black Power movements in the '60s, or who attempted to interpret their experiences of Blackness and femaleness through the context and ideological lens of the Black nationalist movement and a developing Black aesthetic that stressed racial solidarity, were becoming increasingly aware in the late '60s and '70s of the ways in which their agency and critical expression within these social and intellectual projects were delimited due to a "philosophy of masculinism" (Beaulieu 1999, 1–27; Davis 2005; Giddings 1984, 311–24; and Roth 2004, 82–76). Deeply ambivalent as well toward the feminist movement for its insufficient attention to the significance of race and class oppression in Black women's lives, Black women activists and intellectuals began to form a politically distinct agenda that concentrated on recovering the specific historical legacy and contemporary manifestations of tripartite oppression in Black women's lives.

Angela Davis' 1971 "Reflections on the Black Women's Roles in the Communities of Slaves" was a pioneering study that attempted to fill the void regarding the lives of Black women during slavery in male-authored histories produced in the '70s. The new fields of Cultural History and Cultural Studies as well as of feminist and womanist thought in the '70s and '80s caused historians to begin to emphasize personal experience as the means by which categories of identity such as race and gender are constructed and evolve over time and space. As knowledge about the relationship between race and gender grew as a result of the influence of these modes of inquiry, historians began to change their ways of studying chattel slavery, giving greater attention to the ways in which these categories were shaped through historical processes in mutually constitutive ways. Such historical revisions ultimately led to the coming into being of a different understanding of race and gender as part of historical processes of slavery itself. A groundbreaking historical essay reflecting and advancing these changes was Barbara Fields' 1982 essay, "Ideology and Race in American History," in which she articulates race as historically constructed rather than a biologically established fact, forged in social and political struggles. Race became articulated ideologically in the context of slavery, providing "the means of explaining slavery to people whose terrain was a republic founded on radical doctrines of liberty and natural rights (112).[6]

The evolving nature of historical analysis of slavery as it relates to race and gender became evident with the publication in the '80s of a number of works that brought Black women's history into the center of analysis. The publication in 1985 of both Jacqueline Jones' *Labor of Love, Labor of Sorrow: Black Women, Work and the Family, from Slavery to the Present* and Deborah Gray White's *Ar'n't I a Woman? Female Slaves in the Plantation South* increased attention to women while historicizing and differentiating racial identities. Harriet Jacobs' autobiography *Incidents in the Life of a Slave Girl, Written by Herself* (1861) was authenticated in 1985 by Jean Fagan Yellin. In the realm of literary criticism and history, Mary Helen Washington and Henry Louis Gates, Jr. collected the writings of nineteenth-century Black women writers of the 1970s and '80s, causing a tradition of Black women's autobiography to be better known to the broader public (Beaulieu 1999, 1–27; and Mitchell 2002, 1–21).

Within this politically and intellectually evolving milieu, Black women writers of the '70s and '80s, such as Toni Morrison, Sherley Ann Williams, Octavia Butler, Alice Walker, Toni Cade Bambara, and Gayl Jones, in tandem with Black feminist and womanist theorists, activists, and scholars, began to re-situate Black women's lives and culture at the center of African American history and cultural production as well as at the center of the Black Power movement, the Black community more generally, and at the center of the second wave feminist movement. In cultivating the genres of historical fiction and neo-slave narratives during this period, Black women writers attempted to explore in greater depth the complexities of the historical, material, and discursive processes through which race and gender as historically evolving and mutually constitutive categories of identity were shaped (Christian 1985, 242–48).

Their emphasis on everyday experience fomented an alternate site of consciousness wherein the interior thoughts and embodied testimonies of the characters allowed for the construction of a perspectival discourse, capable of challenging and resisting the "truth" of race-gender identity formations of Black women, conceived in the historical trajectories of the slave trade, slavery and subsequent historical junctures, including Reconstruction, post-Reconstruction and contemporary eras, each of which had, in different ways, plunged Blacks into a state of 'neo-slavery.' In the section that follows, I will discuss such re-articulations of identity through the concepts of memory and *rememory* informing Black women's writings, as womanist scholars and women writers of the neo-slave narratives interrogated these concepts. I will then define the cognitive practices by which memories of historical events can be not only established and verified but also brought to bear as political strategies for evaluating and transforming current social realities.

History, Memory, and Embodied Cognitive Practices in The Color Purple

All water has a perfect memory and is forever trying to get back to where it was. Writers are like that: remembering where we were, what valley we ran through, what the banks were like, the light that was there and the route back to our original place. It is emotional memory—what the nerves and the skin remember as well as how it appeared. And a rush of imagination is our "flooding."

Toni Morrison (1987, 119)

My contention is that responsible, critical inquiry can take place, and that effective forms of cognitive agency will take place, when each of us ask ourselves, what are the ancient memories that lay dormant in our souls? Where are the religious archaeological sites in our own life journeys that provide us with sources and resources to resist domination? What are the rememberings and memories that tell us that we cannot love, that we will not love, and in turn, we, too, have become desperate people who do desperate things?

Katie G. Cannon (1998, 12)

Black women writers engage the genres of the historical novel and neo-slave narratives dialogically to effect a critical reconciliation of the literary (imaginary) treatment to the historical subject, a reconciliation which is designed to fill in the missing pieces of Black women's experiences of psychic and bodily dispossession that change the contours of our understanding. Intervening in these historical discourses from a site that is 'close up' to the historical subject by virtue of a shared social location, based on race and gender, they make salient the epistemological and ontological tensions between textuality, the privileged mode of communication in the antebellum slave narrative and orality, the privileged mode in the contemporary neo-slave narrative.

As noted in Toni Morrison's quote above, the neo-slave narrative of the late twentieth century is explicitly and self-consciously written with the historical slave narrative as its referent and historical antecedent. Yet, these two narrative forms were underpinned by very different philosophical and political motivations. Authors of the antebellum slave narrative strove to acquire and deploy literacy and literary modes as a means to record and authenticate the atrocities of life in bondage, thereby transmitting deeply imbricated value patterns of literacy, individual identity, and freedom that were morally compatible with a white abolitionist readership who could aid them in their cause (Olney 1985, 156). On the contrary, the authors of the late-twentieth-century neo-slave narratives as well as those of historical narratives, attempted to recuperate the past lives of enslaved Black women through an imaginative reinstantiation of the oral/aural storytelling community of the slave quarters, and, along with it, the invisibilized oppositional knowledge systems and practices emerging from that location.

Within these contemporary revisions, there is an explicit rejection of empirical veracity, or what Toni Morrison refers to as "publicly verifiable fact" (1987, 112). Instead, these works foreground the authors' struggle to use acts of the imagination to 1) critically reassess the cognitive practices associated with literacy and the life of the mind that were used as a source of achieving public identity and freedom; and 2) offer, simultaneously, alternative cognitive practices located in the emotions and in embodied interventions, suppressed by the Enlightenment legacy, as a means to recover not empirical facts but a greater truth about the real-lived experience of living under oppressive conditions. The reliability of these alternative embodied practices as a source of knowledge that can get us to a better sense of that experience is premised on the notion that knowledge of the self and the world are shaped and mediated by the material conditions and experiences of the embodied subject, experiences that can in turn be used to reinterpret/retell the self and the world.

These two literary modes are equated with two different sets of psychosocial motivations for writing. As noted by James Olney in his classic study of slave narratives as literature, " 'I Was Born': Slave Narratives, Their Status as Autobiography and as Literature," the writers of the antebellum slave narrative, given the necessity to attain assistance in the quest for abolition, were obliged to limit their narrative to a neutral recording of "slavery as it is." They therefore labored to construct a story that retold a linear and apparently objective, chronological narrative of historical events. Any deviation from such neutrality could be construed as "lying." (150). On the other hand, autobiography corresponds to a "configurational" dimension. The autobiographer uses his or her own memory to create an emplotment of events that gives form or patterned significance to the past according to the configuration of a present in which the author is placed. In order to effect such a reordering of historical events, the writer must abandon the role of neutral recorder and draw instead on his or her memory to effect a significant reinterpretation and reshaping of past and present realities (Olney 1985, 148–151).

Commenting on the connection between history, memory, and writing, and the shift of consciousness that she attempts to effect as a writer at the end of the twentieth century, Toni Morrison takes such distinctions one step further. She distinguishes the neo-slave narrative from the earlier slave narratives as well as autobiography. Morrison identifies the literary or fictional recuperation of the slave experience as one that is akin to certain autobiographical strategies insofar as it depends on the author's capacity to draw on information from the past, and through the narrative act, reorder events in order to reflect how the past has led to the present state of being. Yet it is distinct from autobiography in its attempt to recuperate that past through the imaginary act, an act that also involves the use of memory. The fiction writer must trust her recollections from her own life and also from those of others to *imagine* the 'remains,' that is, the feelings and thoughts that are the effects of the events, as a means to construe a sequence of patterned significance. The reordered sequence evokes a truth that is more valuable than historical sequencing in that it is rendered by human intelligence, while facts deriving from historical realities are random. She calls this critical process of uncovering and reordering a "rememory." Rememory is achieved thanks to a 'literary archaeology,' whereby "on the basis of some information and a little bit of guesswork you journey to a site to see what remains were left behind and to reconstruct the world that these remains imply" (1987, 112).

This process, facilitated by human intelligence and yielding a greater objectivity than the historical document, entails the writer's dialogical engagement with history, through embodied memories. Johnella Butler affirms that dialogical engagement of the individual to life events is "tantamount to theorizing about reality, separating the legitimate from the illegitimate toward the end of a theory-mediated objectivity" (Butler 2006, 173). Dialogical engagement through rememory is pervasive not only in the works of Morrison, but also in African American literature as a whole, as a necessary framework for theorizing African American literature and experience within the context of Western hegemony (171–72).

Morrison's preoccupation with memory as a site of a more accurate historical recovery of meaning and identity resonates with works of cultural critics such as Pierre Nora and Paul Connerton, who pioneered in the last decades of the twentieth century a field that merges History and Cultural Studies, that of Memory Studies. In turn an offshoot of oral history, a branch of historical research that surfaced in the '60s, Memory Studies attempts to recover history 'from the bottom up' in order to better investigate the processes by which individuals accord significance and react to the social forces that inform current realities (Hutton 2000). In his classic essay, "Between History and Memory," Nora highlights the epistemological tensions between the collective commemorations or versions of the past that derive from state-sanctioned history, ones that came into being under the forces of modernity, and those sites of memory produced through living or self-actualizing memory. The sites of memory, Nora argues, challenge the so-called truth of these authoritative discourses—ones that ultimately cause one to disremember or forget one's own cultural identity and heritage.

Nora finds meaning not only in the disjunctures between different sources and formats of these two forms, but also in the expression of these two forms of the past. Nora views history as static and unchanging. In contradistinction, memory is constantly redefining its versions of the past and of its own tasks. Its evolving nature is due to the fact that memory becomes manifest in the spatial dimension. Unlike history, memory embraces material spaces, including material objects and bodies that can physicalize and condense memory, functioning as a dynamic interconnector of the present and the future. Through such sites or locations, memory, attached to human subjects, is always in a state of permanent evolution, always actualized in the present.

A critical awareness of the rift between memory and history, and the privileging of the latter by dominant society, engendered a reactive deployment of 'memory strategies' on the part of social and oral historians and minority groups, whose heritage has been forgotten or disremembered by means of the textualization of history. These strategies effect what Nora calls a "memorial consciousness" (1989, 12). In this regard, to re-retrieve forgotten, unarchived meanings is an act of memorial consciousness or rememory, linked to orality and oral traditions. These memory interventions introduce doubt into textual orderings of events by transferring the locus of memory from the historical message to its psychological and embodied or material "rememoration" (Nora 1989, 15). The site of memory thus enacts a commemorative function, in effect, drawing on the affective life and material conditions of the body, including the sensorial dimensions, such as smell, sound, and touch to interact with, contest and take the place of the historical "archive"—documents, speeches, and the written word as a site of truth (18–21).

The self-actualizing and subjective component of producing knowledge through embodied acts suggests, furthermore, that the site of memory allows for the interrogation of the cognitive not just through textuality but also and primarily through performative acts, both nonverbal and verbal ones. Performance Studies and Cultural Studies theorist Diana Taylor thus links and correlates Nora's notion of the site of memory and history to the "repertoire" and the "archive" respectively. Taylor affirms that the repertoire is that which can be drawn upon to enact embodied memory. The repertoire includes performances, bodily gestures and habits, orality, movement, dance, and singing—acts that cannot be reproducible in mimetic form. She equates the repertoire, that which contains memories, not only with praxis or process, but also views it as a form of transmission that privileges orality (telling, singing, reciting, cursing, and gesticulating) over textuality. This is because the memories that are stored in or inscribed on the body are communicated or performed 'live' and in the presence of others who dialogically engage with the meanings of the performance. In this regard, embodied practices are extra-textual cognitive systems, ones, nonetheless, that are always in a constant state of interaction with the textual and archival as well as other methods of knowledge transmission, layering the memories that constitute community (Taylor 2003, 22–26).

Taylor's analysis of the performative nature of cognition derives from or coincides with cultural historian Paul Connerton's analysis of memory as embodied cognitive practice. Focusing on that which is forgotten from history, Connerton examines the practice of oral history and performance as the mechanism for rescuing the culture of subordinate groups from silence and social invisibility. For Connerton, following Maurice Halbwachs, memory is always a social project, shared by members of a group, never a private endeavor. He affirms that it is within one's membership in a social group that individuals are able to acquire, locate, and remember their memories (1990, 36). In this sense, memories are situated in, and reactivated in the spaces that social groups occupy through bodily practices (36–37).

Connerton's theory focuses on the commemorative performance as the privileged site for the "act of transfer," that is, the process by which memories are transmitted from one generation to another in order to produce a shared group memory (38–39). He foregrounds two embodied performances of commemoration: inscribing practices and incorporating practices. Inscribing practices are transmitted by symbolic systems of writing, and therefore are more formalized and unalterable. Connerton gives the example of the alphabet as an inscribing practice. Here, the act of transfer occurs as the voice speaks, formulating temporally the spatial properties of the inscribed marks. This form is formalized, repeatable, and unalterable in its process and practice. The second form, that is, the incorporating practices, is less formalized and more flexible in the processes of expression and in their social meanings. While inscribing practices inform the privileged story, often in the form of written text, incorporating practices constitute the neglected story of human experience. Bodily practices as a way of knowing are backgrounded, lost from view. These include tones, gestures, bodily habits, and emotional expressions, all of which depend upon performance as a means by which the evidence of a will to be remembered can be left behind (100–02).

Womanist scholars have critically engaged with the work of creative writers and cultural critics in order to investigate the processes of historical recovery through memory. Womanist theologian Katie Cannon espouses "human archaeology" as a method of womanist investigation that calls the materiality of the body into being as a resource for disremembered knowledge. Archaeology is a process of remembering that uses the body as a site of forgotten or textually unarticulated memories. As Cannon states, the body represents both a site of inscribed patriarchal white supremacy and a new consciousness that resists it:

> This theme of embodiment as rememory, and rememory as re-incarnation, is the basic motif. Flesh houses memories—the color of flesh, the reproductive character of flesh, and the manifold ways that the flesh of African women is the text on which androcentric patriarchy is written. (Cannon 1996, 75).

Cannon affirms that the implications of embodiment as a site of alternative knowledge is that in having no language to carry the memory, African Americans must draw upon affective and sensorial responses registered in the body that comprise the memory trace, and in doing so, use bodily practices as cognitive resources. In this regard, cognitive practices are not just symbolic and discursive, but also extra-textual, material, and enacted through bodily practices, including individual verbal performances, such as reciting or singing, and tell-ing stories to others, but also through bodily acts, such as gestures and habits. Womanist theories indeed foreground a cognitivist critical praxis that is achieved through the triggering of analytical/mental, affective, and somatic capacities that provide knowledge of the self, and that have immediate implications on others within the commu-nity who share those experiences.

For her part, womanist linguist Geneva Smitherman notes that the evolving linguistic patterns that capture the somatic/kinesthetic con-texts of the African American community intergenerationally can be found in the call-and-response tradition. Derived from the Black church and intrinsic to a Black folk tradition, the call-response com-munication process includes phenomena such as antiphony, function, improvisation, and audience performance (1977, 104–11). Smitherman highlights both the analytical affective, and sensorial (visual) compo-nents of the call-and-response tradition, initiated through the prac-tice of "testifyin"— "a ritualized form of Black communication in which the speaker gives verbal witness to the efficacy, truth and power of some experience in which all Blacks have shared" (Smitherman 1977, 58). She further emphasizes that the telling of one's story or "testifyin," one that asks for a response in the form of the affirmation of the teller's truth-telling, is an attempt to re-articulate one's own self and group identity through the retelling. She thus states that testifying is not "plain and simple commentary but a dramatic narra-tion and a communal reenactment of one's feelings and experiences" (150). The testifying utterance is a story or chronicle that bears "wit-ness" and provides evidence of one's embodied experience and one's emotions that, due to the directness and rawness of the communica-tion, causes interactants (readers or spectators) to be drawn in to the experience, make it their own, and therefore be better equipped to respond to that experience. The testimony is never just to express a thought, but rather to achieve an objective, just as if it were a physical action. In this regard, words become gestures and acts.

According to multiracial feminist Maggie Sale, the call-and-response aesthetic is interactive, process-oriented and concerned with innovation, rather than mimetic, product-oriented, or static. It depends upon audience performance and improvisation for the purpose of creating spontaneous interpretations or perspectives about history and systems of critical inquiry. Indeed, according to Sale, the call-and-response aesthetic foregrounds the power and problematics of perspective itself. It suggests a complex method of interpretation that values multiplicity. It uses embodied performance as a site for testing out master versions of history, ones that pass themselves off as transparent renderings of the past (Sale 1992, 42). The interactive component, then, is pushed to the level of complexity that makes it co-participatory, both at the level of the physical or somatic, and at the level of the imagination.

Womanist performative artist and theorist Freda Scott Giles articulates a poetics of womanist drama that draws upon space and time as the defining features of the African theatrical event. The theatrical unfolding or presentation of the event is not linear, but rather circular or spiral, so that the past is included and co-exists with the present. Moreover knowledge derived from the performance of an event is derived not just from the intellect but also from the emotions. Indeed, rhythm, an element pertaining to oral folk traditions derived from the Black church, rather than words, are the most significant component of the theatrical event, allowing for improvisation as well as audience interaction and co-participation (1997, 179–80).

Giles defines his ritualized theatrical form as "methexis," and distinguishes it from the mimetic forms found in Eurocentric-based theater, derived from Aristotelian theory. She uses the term methexis to draw attention to this nonlinear, communal, and improvisational form that characterizes an Afrocentric ritualized theater. The womanist dramatist that works within this tradition returns to the past, to the dramatist's foremothers, to reinterpret past events in terms of her and her community's struggles, and to bring to consciousness the community's identity through the remembering and reordering of "history, myth, culture, symbols, dreams, and inspirations, for the creation of the dramatic event" (180). The womanist performance of methexis brings to the fore the interior terrain of Black women's lives while at the same time pointing to the external social factors that map out and shape that terrain (181).

The interactive and performative elements in the call-and-response tradition have also been noted by performance theorists Antoinette Lafarge and Roger Allen. Lafarge compares the call-and-response tradition to the embodied dialogue system of "kinesthetic relatedness," a phenomenon that she views as fundamental to interactive theater. She also notes that it is manifest as well in digital game-playing. Kinesthesia refers to the body's spontaneous response to motion that occurs outside of oneself. The kinesthetic response can be small, often imperceptible—a subtle movement that lives in the joints and muscles. Palpable enough to generate an emotional response, this small movement allows the interactant to relate and find authentic the embodied experience of the actor/speaker (Allen and Lafarge 2006). It is through the bodily movement and the feelings related to that movement that the actor translates and transfers her experiences and feelings to the audience.

In the kinesthetic performance, the embodied self that the actor/speaker remembers and calls self-consciously into being allows for an evolving re-negotiation of who one is or who one imagines oneself/or one's body to be in relation to the Other. In this regard, kinesthetic relatedness is both imaginary/psychological and physical. In the act of exchange between the imaginary and the physical, it becomes possible to conceptualize a changed understanding of what is *real* or *true* about our selves and our social reality, as Allen and Lafarge state in relation to digital interactivity and theater:

> We might formulate the relationship between kinesthesia and imagination as an infinite loop: if sensory experience is rendered intelligible through the imagination—as images and emotions, for example—then these constructs are in fact both subtle biophysical responses and impulses that lead to further responses in the body. If there is any reality in "virtual reality" it rests on the relationship between sensory experience and fantasy. In theater the vitality of this relationship is understood as the essential element that validates a performance, and insofar as it is orchestrated by the creative imagination, it can extend and modify what we accept as real (2006).

The above-referenced embodied cognitive practices, when taken collectively, form a repository of knowledge that, while not always visible and/or acknowledged in public history, has been consistently deployed throughout history as a corrective to accepted notions of truth, meaning, and identity. In the next two sections, I explore the ways in which Walker interweaves in her narrative a complex interplay of interpretive frameworks for examining and representing the past, imbuing her characters with an impetus to control and/or contest the current hegemonic histories in which they are caught and defined. Indeed, the novelistic tension is brought to fruition in a struggle between history and memory, between written or inscribing practices and the oral/dialogical incorporating practices that contest them.

Disremembered Memories in The Color Purple

While critics of *The Color Purple* have linked Walker's novel to a number of literary genres, including the Christian parable, Shakespearean romance, the eighteenth-century epistolary novel and the *Bildungsroman*, Walker herself has situated her work within the genres of historical fiction and the slave narrative tradition, rewriting these modes so as to put memory and history into dialectical tension.[7] Set between the two world wars in the post-Reconstruction south, Walker brings to life and memorializes the myriad disremembered lives of her Black female forbears and would-be literary mothers who, due to the more pressing exigencies of economic survival and the threat of physical violence in a white supremacist patriarchal culture, were delimited in their opportunities to record their histories, accumulate knowledge of the social forces impacting their reality, and endow themselves with a creative interior life that would help them use their understanding to dismantle the ideological grasp of those 'realities' on their bodies and psyches.

The protagonist, Celie, is indeed a reembodiment of Walker's great great-grandmother who was raped at the age of twelve by her slaveholding master. Walker also uses the lives of her female characters more broadly to point to and pay tribute to her mother, quilter and gardener, and to the lives of other Black women as well, whose struggles, while not recorded in writing, had been preserved orally and transmitted intergenerationally within kinship and communal systems. Walker's selection of an autobiographical epistolary narrative form serves as an appropriate structure for recording in Black vernacular the differentiated and relatively unmediated folk expressions of the value patterns of forgotten Black womanhood. The narrative is comprised of ninety-four letters, which, taken collectively, chart the liberatory struggles of four Black women and their community as they struggle with the social realities of the sharecropping economy, as well as racial violence in the form of lynching and rape that functioned to enforce economic and social segregation, and their attending ripple effects within the privatized sphere of family, extended kinship systems, and broader U.S. institutions.

Walker situates the plot action within a recent past, the first half of the twentieth century. This recent past, however, is a pivotal point, reflecting back on the more remote past of enslavement that left a legacy of memorialized scripts of Blackness and femaleness, as well as on the future, that is, on the vicissitudes of race-gender oppression that Black women faced in the '80s intercommunally but also intracommunally, within Black nationalist circles and the Black community more generally. As such, Walker's work is a palimpsest, a text or set of texts on the lives of Black women, partially erased and written over, but that become exposed in the process of writing and telling. Or, alternately, we can conceive of her work as constructed within a tradition of methexis. Walker presents contemporary female characters who discover and animate some aspects of the past that still need to be told, in a new patterned sequence, that is, remembered—so that they can be better understood.

Through her letters to God and her dialogic exchanges, Celie begins the process of both arresting the individual and collective cultural amnesia that has distorted her self-understanding and caused her to internalize self-hatred, and renegotiating who she is or who she imagines her embodied self/body to be. Walker creates the new textual circumstances of her characters' lives with the motifs and themes of the slave narrative tradition to 1) explore and expose the invisibilized systemic and ideological processes of racism, sexism, classism that early on legitimized the dehumanized treatment of Black women and constrained their agency; and 2) to mobilize, through her characters' rescriptings of the self, the countless practices that Black women have deployed to contest and resist such processes in order to reinterpret their experiences through a changed perception, thereby cleansing themselves of self and collective hatred.

The myriad conventions associated with the slave narrative tradition are notably manifest in *The Color Purple*. The description of an individual's birth and induction into the brutalities of slavery is developed in Walker's text, as Celie is turned into chattel by Pa and then sold to Mr.__. A skeletal account of parentage is relayed in the opening pages of the tale, when Celie explains the brutalities and drudgery of domestic life in her paternal home. A description of the cruelties and dangers associated with bondage is offered when Celie writes about the beatings endured by Celie, Sofia, and Squeak; the rape of Celie and Squeak; the coerced domestic servitude of Celie; and the coerced indentured servitude of Sofia. We also have in the figure of Sofia, as evidenced in her exchanges with her husband Harpo and then with the white mayor, the representation of an exceptionally strong and hardworking 'slave' who refuses to be beaten.

The theme of literacy is developed, both in terms of the barriers raised against the achievement of literacy and the difficulties of overcoming them. Celie's beatings, rape, and impregnation, the threat of being married off to Mr.__, as well as her domestic subjugation as caretaker and indentured domestic, produce in Celie physical fatigue and distraction as well as mental apathy, and depression. In spite of the passion that she has for school and her sister Nettie's dedication to teach her, it is clear that such obstacles make it difficult for her to retain the information that Nettie attempts to teach her: "But look like nothing she say can git in my brain and stay" (1982, 11).

The thematization of women's dehumanization finds expression in the economic and sexual dispossession of the female 'slave' as well as of slave children. An account of a 'slave auction' is rendered when Pa brings Celie before Mr.___ for his consideration in marriage. Celie is forced to turn full circle, thereby putting her body on display from the rear. The erosion of the slave's humanity is manifested as well in the work patterns of everyday life. In her domestic life, Celie performs the drudgery of household chores—cooking, sewing, washing, cleaning house, and raising the children. She also labors outside in the fields, along with her stepson Harpo. When Mr.___ is home and unable to pursue his long-time mistress, Shug Avery, he fulfills his instinctual urges with his 'property.' As was the case with Pa, his reduction of Celie to a biological being through sexual assault functions not only to satisfy his sexual needs but also to break her spirit through bodily dispossession, thereby warding off from the start Celie's nurturing of a desire to fight.[8] As in the slave narratives, the representation of stolen babies becomes manifest. Celie's babies are taken away from her and 'sold' to another family.

The motif of the white mistress engaged in acts of betrayal and/or cruelty is engaged here as well, in the figures of Miz Millie, the mayor's wife, and Eleanor Jane, her daughter. There is an inclusion of the motif of the escape of the slave and the slaveholder's attempt at pursuit and capture. In the case of Sofia, escape is impossible, and she is first jailed, and then remains as an indentured servant in the house of the mayor for twenty years. In the case of Nettie and Celie, the escape is successful, with Nettie fleeing the sexual onslaughts of Pa, and then those of Mr.___, ultimately becoming a missionary in Africa under the tutelage of Samuel and Corrine. Celie, decades later, flees the marital home to join Shug, the blues singer, her lover and the estranged mistress of Mr.___.[9]

In adopting thus the conventions, gestures, motifs, and voice of the slave narrative tradition, Walker does not aim to produce an official historical record of either the period of Reconstruction or of the earlier period of enslavement, told from the perspectives of the dominant, that is, "the taking of lands, or the births, battles, and deaths of Great men" (Walker 1983, 356). Rather, her aim is to implode official versions of history in order to expose the suppressed feelings and voices of living Black women, whose subjective and historically variable identities and embodied realities have been invisiblized or distorted. In essence, Walker obliges the reader to compare past renderings of the genre and the present set of events she is presenting in order to explore the causal linkages between generic conventions of the tradition and the social formations of Black women's identity that was partially birthed by such textual conventions.[10] In doing so, she creates a perspectival discourse that allows her readers to critically examine the continuities and discontinuities in race-gender formations brought about by events and practices in different historical periods, spaces, and nations in tandem with the ongoing implacability of the original slave identity in contemporary society.

The Color Purple thus begins with sexual dispossession, the rape of Celie by Pa, and along with it the suppression of the voice of protest, that is, of the ability to memorialize the event itself: "*You better not never tell nobody but God. It'd kill your mammy*" (1982, 1). Pa's initial erasure of the rape and later his narrative portrayal of the controlling images of 'Black woman as whore' or 'spoiled goods' and 'Black woman as liar' that legitimized the white slaveowner's sexual assault and subjugation of Black women allow him to cover-up his sexual exploitation to her future husband to whom she might potentially confess his crime. He thus inserts himself into and rememorializes a preexisting story. His story is historically resonant with an American national identity narrative dating back to enslavement—one that legitimizes white heteropatriarchal interests through the control of women as property, land wealth, and entrepreneurial activities. His story also naturalizes such interests through the enactment of religious ideologies and practices.

No longer denied easy access to Black female sexuality as his male ancestors, Pa is free to exercise white dominance, now manifested in its manufactured form of male supremacy. Celie not only takes the place of her deranged, physically debilitated, and finally deceased mother in the marital bed, but also replaces her as maid and surrogate mother to her siblings. Through her hard work, cleanliness, and filial obedience, she abides by the religious ideologies that the virtuous woman should embody in homage to a white patriarchal God. It is the site of the church moreover, that Pa uses, following the white slave master, as the context in which Celie as a Black woman must learn to internalize an understanding of the self as essentially lacking in moral virtue. He portrays her as temptress, accusing, and then beating her for apparently having winked at a boy in church. Pa aims thus to call attention to her covert seductions, as well as punish and suppress her uncontrolled bodily desires.

Pa's sexual possession, impregnation, and silencing of Celie result in a traumatic rupture and repression of subjectivity. His acts circumscribe not only Celie's ability to feel, but also her self-expression and self-understanding. Thus, for example, in her letters to God, she does not initially attempt to confront the reality of her crisis of subjectivity in the face of such violence. Instead, she uses normative theological frameworks that legitimate absolute filial authority to define what her exemplary identity as a Black woman should be. And she does this in spite of the irreconcilable moral conflict in which she finds herself— that of attempting to abide by filial authority even though doing so leads not only to a loss of her chastity but also to her apparent participation in acts of incest. Her literal partial erasure of her assertion of virtue reveals her cognitive dissonance, manifested by her attempt to defend herself to God: "Dear God, I am fourteen years old. I am I have always been a good girl" (1).

Pa's sexual violence, a manufactured variant of white supremacy, corresponds to and reinforces the disremembered memory of racialized sexual violence in Celie's family that occurred some twelve years earlier. In a letter that Celie reads at least two decades following the rape, she comes to know the story as narrated by Nettie. She reveals that Pa is not their biological father as they had long believed, but their stepfather. Their real father was a prosperous farmer who had used his earnings to open a dry-goods stores and blacksmith shop. He and two of his brothers had been lynched by white storeowners for having taken away the white storeowners' business. The lynching not only left Celie fatherless, Nettie explains in her letter, but also deprived her of maternal nurturance. Her mother, pregnant with Nettie at the time of the lynching, became both widowed and mentally deranged at the sight of the burnt and mutilated body of her husband.

What Nettie and Celie come to learn through this story is that Pa had interpolated himself into this identity narrative of lynching, one that tells the story of white dominance, in an effort to identify and then implement mechanisms for garnering economic success while avoiding persecution. Lynching was deployed as a real method of terror and as a trope or story throughout the last decades of the nineteenth century and the first decades of the twentieth, with particular persistence in the decades of the '20s. It ostensibly served as a method of white vigilante 'justice,' aimed at deterring Black men from raping white women. In reality, lynching perpetuated a narrative that facilitated the reassertion of white male control over white womanhood. The creation of the story of the moral degeneracy of the Black male who, no longer under the master's control had regressed to a primitive and criminal state that was indicative of the "African type," mitigated the sexual threat of interracial marriage. It also mitigated the economic threat of the loss of land wealth, insofar as the Black male, in his roles of entrepreneur and landowner, could potentially attempt to achieve social equality through property ownership as well as in the marketplace (Giddings 1984, 27–28).

Pa refashions the narrative of moral degeneracy in order to protect his own interests, by reinventing a narrative of individual economic success which he protagonizes as token. Celie's biological father failed to achieve economic gain because he literally believed in the ideal of economic and political freedom, as evidenced in his individual agricultural and business efforts, only to find that marketplace gains were 'for whites only.' Pa, in contradistinction, acts on his economic aspirations by overtly acknowledging his assigned subjugated status and capitulating to the entrenched resistance of southern whites to giving up the 'negro' as a source of income. He turns one-third of his earnings over to the white storeowners and employs a white boy to serve in his store. His acquiescence to a subservient status, to the myth of Black male degeneracy, has its benefits: it allows him the boon of performing the role of the white master as usurper of the bed and lands of Celie's Ma.

Pa erases the history of his pillage, however. Just like the white storeowners who inscribed marks of moral degeneracy on the bodies of three Black men for the purpose of their own economic gain, and then erased the memory of their strategy for economic gain by condemning the lynched victims to be buried in unmarked graves, Pa inscribes marks of moral inferiority on the bodies of Celie's Ma, and Celie by sexually subjugating them. His burial of Ma, the secondary victim of that original lynching, in an unmarked grave, moreover, allows him to simultaneously erase his own strategy for garnering an identity based on land ownership and sexual dominance, and the white storeowners' strategy for economic control with which he colluded. His co-optation of white supremacist practices are represented through the presence of inscribing practices following his death. The epitaph on his tombstone covers up the memory of his role as race traitor, and memorializes his public identity in such a manner that embeds him within the myth of an American national identity based on the promise of prosperity through individual efforts and moral action: "Leading businessman and farmer. Upright husband and father. Kind to the poor and the helpless" (252).

The dismemory of memory expands within various proliferating narratives that Walker braids together as the characters become active co-participants in reproducing histories that take the place of their own memories. As was the case with Pa, Celie's Ma as well as Samuel and Corrine, collude with dominant stories of identity, practicing their own versions of exceptionalism. Accordingly, these figures live out their identities as instances of individual social, economic, and/or moral success while at the same time denying their internalization of and resulting cooperation with systemic and structural processes of race, class, and gender oppression. And, like Pa, their individual successes in turn erase the systemic and structural processes that they have internalized for their own social benefit.

Notably, the cooperation of Celie's Ma with narratives of dominance did not cause her to enjoy the same success that her second husband enjoyed. Her willingness to believe in and be co-participant of the rags-to-riches schema of both of her husbands led to the dispossession of her own body and psyche, as well as of her lands. It also made her equally responsible for the ensuing perpetuation of poverty and economic disenfranchisement of her neighbors. Her derangement or psychic dissociation symbolically represents her social dissociation from her community. It is thus revealed in Nettie's narrative of paternal origins that in her deranged state following the lynching, Ma retold her and Pa's rags-to-riches aspirations on a daily basis to her neighbors. The neighbors perceived *their* class pretensions not only to be anomalous to the Black experience, but also, in its egocentricity, hostile to the plights of those who had on the one hand made *their* upward mobility a potential reality due to the community's patronage of their business, but on the other did not themselves have the wherewithal or 'degeneracy' to achieve such lofty goals. In response to their caste disposition, Ma's neighbors ultimately turned their backs on her, shunning her, and, in the process, disremembering her and her husband as co-architects of internalized, racially divisive caste hierarchies.

However, the parental suppression of memories of economic and sexual dispossession in Celie's family and community does not die with Ma's passing, but is reproduced through an intergenerational act of transfer by Corrine and Samuel as well as Celie. In effecting the transfer, they collaborate in the production of a shared set of memories of origins, identity, and communal/social relations—memories that function to legitimize their own personal social and economic aspirations. Samuel becomes complicit with Pa's attempt to cover up the fact that he begun raping Celie from the time she was fourteen years old and had impregnated her twice. He takes into his home Adam and Olivia, the offspring produced by Pa's violent acts, without asking any questions. Giving priority to Pa's interests, Samuel takes the opportunity of Nettie's appearance at his doorstep in search of work to take her in as maid and teacher to his children. He interpolates his own actions and hers into a preexisting narrative of moral superiority and moral degeneracy. Noting her resemblance to the children, he casts himself as the kind and charitable Christian missionary who is simply affording a mother out of wedlock the opportunity to follow her children. Decades later, he admits to Nettie that he suppressed his own memory of his running buddy as 'scamp.' He conveniently remembers the dismemory only after decades of allowing Nettie, who he assumes to be the real mother of his adopted children, to journey to Africa as part of his missionary household in the subjugated capacity of servant and teacher to the children, which then permitted his own wife, an educated, middle-class Black woman, to act in the capacity of real mother.

Correspondingly, Corinne participates in the suppression of the origin story of Olivia and Adam, claiming that she has no previous knowledge of their parentage. In this manner, she works toward her own interests. Materially, she is able to keep the children and justify this action by willfully believing that they are Samuel's offspring, the product of a tryst between her husband and Nettie. On moral grounds, she is able to construct herself, in contradistinction to Nettie, outside of normative understandings of Black womanhood. Her erroneous belief in this narrative of her victimization, caused by Nettie's lack of moral virtue, not only tormented Corrine in her illness and dying moments as well as throughout her life, but also further victimized Nettie. Indeed, Corrine ostracizes Nettie and her children both from her and her husband's home and presence because of her willingness to believe the dominant storyline of Black womanhood. Moreover, Corinne, in her belief, converts herself into perpetrator, as she is one who stole and/or bought the children. Rather than exposing the history of her collusion with the narrative of white female virtue, however, she constructs another story which she protagonizes as charitable and generous Christian woman. In this narrative, Corinne covers up her own victimization and her husband's sin of adultery in order to maintain the destiny that she imagined for herself: her privileged social status as a Religious Studies graduate, wife of preeminent minister, teacher of the Olinka tribe, and upstanding African American assimilated into the dominant social and religious structures.

The act of transfer of disremembered memories is further perpetuated by Celie herself. Not only does she become, like her mother, willing believer and victim of the narrative of her deserved dispossession, submitting first to her father's and then her husband's abuse, but she also becomes the willing perpetrator to her daughter-in-law, Sofia. Sofia's body is the site of convergence on which the intergenerational act of transfer of race, class, and gendered violence at both systemic and interpersonal levels is committed. Indeed, Celie builds on and colludes with other figures in the narrative, as well as with the broader U.S. institutions, represented within this narrative by the criminal justice system. Celie inscribes marks of inferiority on Sofia's body when she urges her stepson Harpo to beat her into domestic submission. This act of discursive violence allows Celie to believe that her own submissiveness is natural and therefore inevitable. Blinding herself to the dissonances, she acts as if human experiences have self-evident meanings, rather than tied to preexisting theoretical accounts, narratives, or paradigms that are in turn susceptible to varying degrees of accuracy or error.

Celie fails to ask what Sofia's refusal to acquiesce to submissiveness signifies not only in terms of confirming or discounting the accuracy or spuriousness of her own self-description but also in terms of the concepts of identity and meaning as hermeneutical constructs that require our critical engagement for their epistemic accuracy. Bereft of such a critical lens, Celie patterns her own behavior on dominant inscribing practices and therefore enables them, as manifested in the police beating of Sofia for 'sassing the mayor's wife' when she hostilely refuses Miz Millie's request to be her maid. Sofia's near-death beating as well as her indentured servitude resonates with the supremacist and patriarchal logic of the act of lynching at the submerged and disremembered root of Celie's family history. Thus, lynching was designed to benefit white southern farmers' ongoing exclusive control and inheritance of economic power through accumulation of wealth and property, situating Black men and women in a subjugated, and economically disenfranchised position within the sharecropping economy. The beating, incarceration, and domestic servitude of women, manifested in the novel through the character of Sofia, was analogously designed to relocate the Black woman into an economically subjugated role with respect to white women within the domestic quarters, and to provide the white woman with her rightful inheritance, that of the female 'slave' (Carby 1987, 20–39; Hine 1979, 123).

In her 'slave' identity, Sofia is portrayed as being in a dichotomous Other to white women. Notably, white women have had to submit to the patriarch in order to enjoy their pedestalized position of white womanhood, accrued through wifehood and motherhood, as well as the accompanying assets, privileges, and protection derived from home, family, and a masculine protector. In contrast, Black women must be deprived of wifehood and motherhood, as well as privileges and assets associated with these domains. She cannot, like Sofia, as Walker's narrator affirms, "clam out on the street, looking like somebody" (90). Instead, the Black woman must take on the flattened identity of 'mammy,' caretaker and maid, an identity that serves to reproduce white women's pedestalization (Carby 1987, 35).

In the case of Sofia, her robust constitution and her outspoken behavior present in the white cultural imaginary external evidence of an overt sexuality that is denied white womanhood—a sexuality that legitimized her physical containment within the white family, her subjugation to heavy labor, and the injunction of silent and acquiescent obedience. In her commemorative performance of the female slave identity, upon which her very survival depended, as it had for Celie, the purpose of Sofia's enforced acquiescence was to serve to remind her and her community that they were not to aim for or give the appearance of having achieved economic enfranchisement, and to preclude her from using her own voice to constitute her subjectivity.

Squeak represents yet another variant of the exploitation of Black women's sexuality and as such represents another side of Sofia's struggle to maintain agency in her sexuality and moral agency. She is second wife to Harpo and later the caretaker of Sofia's children. Although in many ways the opposite of Sofia—light-skinned, small-bodied, and obedient—her rape at the hands of her jail guard 'kin' and her ensuing struggle to come to voice places her in an analogous position of servitude and resistance against white institutional power. Her mission to visit the prison guard for the purpose of compelling her 'kin' to lessen the severity of Sofia's imprisonment does achieve its desired results but also an unintended consequence: her rape. The sexual violence of the rape serves here, as do the indentured servitude and the lynching, to memorialize gendered and raced relations based on dominance and subjugation. In this case, the rape mitigates the sexual threat that Squeak's mother posed through her 'relationship' with the warden's brother, as well as the attending economic and/or political power that can be presumed, as Squeak's act implied, when, dressed up as a white woman, she assumed equal status within interracial kinship systems. Indeed, Squeak's experience of rape speaks to the patterns of sexual violence suffered by enslaved women as well as points to the experiences of Black women in today's society, where white on Black rape continues to be employed as a mechanism of social control and subjugation (Carby 1985; Clinton 1994; Hine 1979).

Remembering Disremembered Memories in The Color Purple

The inscribing practices that foreground Black women's cultural identity in its subhumanity, and that become manifest intra-communally in their internalized forms as self-hatred and horizontal violence, are gradually substituted within Walker's narrative by incorporating practices, as the female protagonists move out of their imposed silences to give voice to and evaluate their experiences in dialogue with one another. In the process, they come to acknowledge the need of a community of engaged female listeners who can use their affective exchanges to bring about epistemic transformation. Celie's unanswered letters to God that begin the narrative reflect her willingness to understand her historical life as a life reported on and narrated, that is, as a set of empirical facts, albeit with pieces of information included that might not be known through previous reports. In this regard, her narrative form can be likened to the narrative tradition of the antebellum slave narrative.

As the narrative progresses, however, and Celie becomes located in close relationship with and also in opposition to other Black women within hierarchical patrifocal family arrangements, she begins to discover her physical and emotional identity. She also demonstrates a willingness to memorialize her identity through another form of communication that the letters incorporate, that of oral storytelling and embodied cognitive practices—one that allows her to begin to construct her identity, rather than assume a preexisting identity.

Celie begins to piece together the story of her own family and national history with the help of Shug and Sofia, just as they pieced together their quilt, in a manner that allows her to render salient the cracks and fissures of the official version of those histories. Drawing upon a call-and-response cultural tradition as a means to come to voice, Celie transforms the historical message of social relations, that of her raced and gendered inferiority, to its psychological and embodied rememoration. Sofia becomes, for Celie, not just someone with whom she speaks about marital love and sexuality in both its successful and failed forms. Rather, Sofia and Celie are literally the other side of each other's life story. Both of their fathers give birth to twelve children. Both have mothers who are under their husband's patriarchal 'foot' to the extent that they leave their daughters vulnerable to abusive fathers and/or brothers. Both find solace and solidarity in their female siblings. What sets these two figures apart, however, are their respective responses to their upbringings.

Celie's embodied reality is in antiphonal relationship with Sofia's. Celie survives by negating the body, repressing all feeling, even rage, and submitting to filial authority. Sofia, on the other hand, acts purely on feeling, living in the body, and using her body as a tool of subjective resistance. Celie hands Mr.___ the whip when he wants to beat her; Sofia, as Celie tells Harpo, can't be beat (66). Early on, Sofia is the antiphonal expression of Celie's marital plight. Her testimony functions to communicate the enactment of radical subjectivity within the marital and family sphere. Unlike Celie, Sofia demands a nontraditional division of labor, and remains free to undertake domestic functions of her choosing. Drawing on her strengths and interests, Sofia is therefore able to continue to develop a sense of unfettered selfhood and sexuality in her marriage. However, in trying to make sense of herself and her world through her experiences as her father's daughter, Harpo's wife, and later as indentured servant, Sofia gradually begins to understand, as Celie had, that her identity is indexed to a social location from which she must define herself and act.

And it is through that understanding that Sofia begins to realize that she has more in common with Celie than she may have originally believed. Thus, Sofia becomes increasingly identified with Celie as she notes that Harpo begins to take cues from his external social environment regarding historicized patterns of social relations and demands that she act 'like a wife,' or 'mammy,' that is, like Celie. As Harpo gradually demands that their marriage be patterned on socially scripted hierarchical gendered relations, Sofia becomes incapable of responding emotionally or sexually to Harpo. Sofia now shares with Celie the experience of sexual exploitation. However, unlike Celie, who accepts her lot, Sofia responds first through resistance, and then by leaving Harpo.

We again see a realignment between the two women when Sofia becomes the victim of white institutional power first in jail, and then in the mayor's house. In this social context, however, Sofia undergoes a shift of identity, assuming a position that is similar to that of Celie's, as she becomes subjected to physical beatings. At the same time, Celie, upon witnessing Sofia's subjection as a result of physical force, begins to undertake an epistemic shift with respect to her own identity. In the encounter between Sofia and Celie during the prison visit, their mutual identification develops as a form of kinesthetic relatedness, one that triggers a subtle but significant change in Celie. In her conversation with Celie, Sofia admits to 'acting' as if she were Celie following her detainment. However, in relaying this information, the narrator reveals Sofia's dissent in bodily expression in general as well as in her eyes: "Every time they ast me to do something, Miss Celie, I act like I'm you. I jump right up and do just what they say. She look wild when she say that, and her bad eye wander round the room" (93). Her "wild look" reveals that she experiences her identification with Celie's submissiveness as self-loathing. In turn, Celie's recognition of herself in Sofia's eyes catalyzes a kinesthetic response. Herein, she tries, albeit unsuccessfully, the narrator informs us, to move the muscles in her mouth to begin to give voice to this growing awareness of who she is in the eyes of the oppositional seer: "I can't fix my mouth to say how I feel" (93).

When Sofia admits to 'acting' as if she were Celie, she reveals that though she shares the same embodied reality as Celie, she nevertheless experiences and responds to that experience differently. The experience of acquiescence to oppression evokes in Sofia the emotion of 'wildness' that we could interpret as terror of unimaginable subjection, objectification, and self-hatred. Celie gives to understand, on the other hand, that by attempting to set her muscles in her mouth so that she can speak, that she not only recognizes Sofia's rage as an appropriate response to injustice, but also as an emotional praxis that disallows Sofia's captors to claim ownership over her being and moral agency. The wild look, in effect, becomes the hermeneutical lens through which Celie begins to discover that only by fighting for one's selfhood can one begin to claim oneself morally and politically.

The antiphonal dimension of their relationship develops throughout the narrative. While Celie sacrifices subjectivity and subsumes the self to a hegemonic identity of Blackness and femaleness, Sofia disregards her imposed identity as "Black" and relies absolutely on her subjective identity, to the extent that it eclipses her moral agency. As Linda Martin Alcoff argues with regard to the relation of Black identity politics, following Robert Gooding-Williams, it is not only necessary to be racially classified as Black to have the public Black identity of being a Black person; rather, it is necessary to begin to identify oneself as Black in order to begin to make choices, develop plans, and express one's political interests (2000, 339). In this regard, Sofia can only begin to enact a liberatory identity politics when she becomes aware of the preexistence of an imposed Black identity.

Sofia's imprisonment and ensuing servitude for a total of twelve years in the house of the mayor is the living laboratory in which not only Sofia, but also Celie, Squeak, Shug, Harpo, Mr.___, Grady, Odessa, and Jack all work to recognize their preexisting identities as Black men and women, understand their moral and political relationship to a historical community, and renegotiate that identity through their reinterpretations as well as their actions. Sofia's story is a testimony as articulated within the call-response tradition—a chronicle of her embodied experience that to some degree all members of the community undergo, and, as such, draws the others into it, so that they may make it their own, and thus be better equipped to negotiate the meaning of that experience (Smitherman 1977, 150).

In the case of Sofia, what she learns is that one must fight for one's identity not through physical resistance, as such a choice would only re-inscribe her within public definitions of Blackness as brute physicality only. Instead, she must renegotiate discursively her public identity to make it cohere with her lived experience of the self. In her exchange with the mayor and Miz Millie's daughter, Eleanor Jane, decades following her imprisonment, Sofia begins to combat discursively the intergenerational effects of the performance of white femininity as pedestalization. With Celie as witness, Sofia lets the young white mother know that she is unwilling to suffer the intergenerational effects of the performance of white femininity as pedestalization, enacted by Miz Millie on the day she asked her to be her maid—a performance that functioned to oblige Sofia to enact a public performance of her identity as mammy. When Eleanor Jane unrelentlessly demands that Sofia confess that Stanley Earl is sweet, smart, and worthy of her love, indicating her expectation that Sofia love her unconditionally, Sofia refuses to accommodate her. In the ensuing dialogue, Sofia signals an understanding of her race-gender identity as indexed to a social location while at the same time contests it.

Sofia begins by calling attention to a past of hierarchical race relations that mediates their relationship, a past that they cannot change. The social fact of their identities is such, she asserts, that Eleanor Jane's son can grow up to persecute her and her community, in spite of Eleanor Jane's stated promise to raise him to behave differently to her and her people: " You and whose army? . . . The first word he likely to speak won't be nothing he learn from you" (273). Interwoven into this dialogue as part of Eleanor Jane's justification for such demands of affection from Sofia is the fact that Eleanor Jane is bereft of love. She demands that Sofia serve the role of mammy as she had done in the past, compensating her (and by extension her child) for the love and attention that her parents and her husband have not given and/ or do not give her.

Refusing to pedestalize Eleanor Jane at the cost of her own further subjugation, Sofia uses her subjectivity, together with an enhanced understanding of her objective location, in a final exchange with Eleanor Jane. Not having the benefit, as Celie will later through Nettie's letters, of learning about the history of hierarchical race relations, she is obliged to rely upon her real-lived experiences with structural racism as the social context for learning about difference, and use that self-discovery to seek a balance between her own experience of the self and the racial parameters that structure her identity. And she does so at the same time that she recognizes through her engagement with white womanhood/feminism that racial identity is imbricated with and mutually constitutive of gender and class as well. Sofia at once mobilizes the four liberatory stages of Walker's womanist agenda as she interacts with Eleanor Jane: subjectivity, traditional communalism and capability, redemptive self-love, and critical engagement.

Her critical engagement with white women/feminism becomes manifest first when she counsels Eleanor Jane to consider leaving her husband and becoming employed as a means to address her problems with her husband and parents, a piece of advice that Eleanor Jane initially rejects. Sofia enacts the only moral agency possible from her social location, one that is intimately linked to the ongoing condition of slavery that casts her alternately as mammy and matriarch. Dislocated from her own children and unable to oversee their upbringing, provide them resources, nurture them, or protect them from violence, Sofia's advice reflects a refusal to stand in as mammy and pedestalize Eleanor Jane or to mobilize her own rage. Instead, Sofia calls upon Eleanor Jane to free herself from her own victim status and to work to gain an active understanding of what it means to be white and female in her culture. She in effect asks her to claim ownership of the moral and political implications (e.g., of power and powerlessness, of perpetratorship and victimhood) of that identity rather than continuing to be a victim that needs to reassert herself, like Miz Millie, who placed Sofia in the role of the mammy so that Sofia could mirror back to her the illusive projection of her exalted status as a white woman.

Eleanor Jane ultimately takes Sofia's advice. By doing so, she remembers the disremembered memories of her family and of the institution of justice that her family represents. In effect, Eleanor Jane becomes the justice agent that her father was to embody as mayor when it occurs to her to finally ask her mother how it was that Sofia came to work for them in the first place. In acknowledging that her willful ignorance (dismemory) is complicit with the perpetrator role, she is able to achieve a measure of redemption. As cultural 'outsider,' she is the other side of Sofia. She must work consciously to pick out the specific social features of her objective location, that of white womanhood, and analyze them in light of those of cultural insiders and outsiders in order create more integrated understandings of the shared histories of domination and subjugation by which insiders and outsiders are objectively defined.

Seeing herself from the perspective of the Other through a remembering of the disremembered memory of her family history, Eleanor Jane ultimately becomes capable of effecting a perspectival shift that allows her to recognize her social position within relations of racial power. Toward the end of the novel, she begins to cultivate resistance practices through critical engagement not based on her dominance over Black women but rather through a re-negotiation of her identity. She effects a redemption of her own multidimensional humanity when, from her subjective understanding of an identity and interaction based on reciprocity and mutuality, she works as caretaker of Sofia's ill daughter, Henrietta.

Eleanor Jane's changed choices free Sofia to work in Celie's store, alongside the white boy Alphonso had employed. Because Sofia has recognized her racial location as a social fact, she can now begin to act not just on behalf of her own subjective understandings and desires, but also to use an objective understanding of her community on behalf of her community. She starts to serve her community in the capacity of storekeeper. She is thus able to put her moral agency to use to enact redemptive self and communal love through the public restitution of their dignity, as Celie underscores: "[P]ut Sofia in there to wait on colored cause they never had nobody in a store to wait on 'em before and nobody in a store to treat 'em nice" (287).

Celie's enactment of radical subjectivity through the prism of Sofia's embodied practices of the self follows the same womanist path of liberation as that of Sofia. However, because of her traumatic past, her journey is more laborious and in need of ongoing critical elaboration of her experiences. Shug and Nettie indeed embody for and enact with Celie two stages of womanist stages of liberation, as prescribed in Walker's four-part definition, those of subjectivity and redemptive self-love, respectively. In her engagement with these two stages of womanist liberation through processes of embodied rememory, Celie extricates herself from her roles as drudge and mammy to a person capable of trust and love.

The repression of memories of the pain of abuse, sexual violence, and bodily loss caused by the dominant narrative of her family history manifests itself on Celie's body and psyche as numbness—the lack of emotionality and feeling. Thus, she confesses early on to Sofia the actual process of repression. She states that not only did she not remember the last time she got angry, but she admits to feeling that it is socially inappropriate to feel anger toward her father or her husband's abuses since the Bible mandates her to simply obey. Moreover, the initial responses she had to Pa's sexual abuse and beatings were so terrible and caused her so much illness that she ended up blocking them out. Indeed, pretending she is like a tree or a piece of wood is her method for surviving sexual violence and the beatings at the hands of Pa and later Mr.___. She also admits to Shug that she feels absolutely nothing in her sexual relations with Mr.___.

Celie's ability to fulfill a project of redemptive self-love calls upon her not only to negotiate dialogically her public identity as her exchanges with Sofia have taught her, but also to negotiate the epistemic struggle of identity between externally imposed (public) and internal (subjective) perspectives within embodied dialogic systems, through her relationship with Shug. In kinesthetic terms, Celie gradually engages in an embodied dialogical process of *somaesthesis*. I define somaesthesis as the experience of remembering and/or of a reawakening of the body's feeling. Somaesthesis can take two forms. An individual can experience the body subjectively, as when one feels and sees one's own body from one's particular perspective. This is referred to as *proprioception*. Or, one can attempt to know, feel, or view one's body by experiencing or feeling it from the perspective of another object or body with which it comes into contact. This is referred to in the literature on kinesthesia as *exteroception*. Often these two tactile experiences of the body go together (Gibson 1975).

In Celie's initial narration of her feelings for Shug, she reflects an inability to interpret her bodily experience of desire, manifested overtly in her shaking hands and shortness of breath. With Shug's insistence that she should claim herself as a sexual being, however, Celie begins a process of knowing herself as a desiring subject. Her ensuing actions, including identifying her desire and claiming agency over her own desire, exercising the right to love another woman, and leaving her marriage, make salient that in order to fight for something, one has to know what one is fighting for, and what is being taken away. In her self-examination, Celie takes a mirror and examines her sexual anatomy by both looking at and touching her vagina, vulva, clitoris, and breasts, searching for the source of her own erotic being. By doing so, she replaces the exteroceptive perspective (seeing herself from the eyes of the other) with proprioception (the subjective perspective). Looking at herself, she perceives her sexual being not as an empty hole to be plunged into, as she says her Pa and Mr.___ perceived her, but the site from which to negotiate the value, meaning, and representation of Black womanhood and sexuality.

Celie's self-selected image of the "wet rose" to describe her sexuality and her embodied identity more generally transforms Celie's body from its states of absence and degradation respectively. Celie experiences her embodiment subjectively, and then defines and attributes value to her embodied self. Through the process, Celie reshapes her self-perception. The image of the rose, with its multilayered petals, as well as that of the "button" and "black pussy lips" focalizes female erotic power on the multiple sites of female desire, outside of and beyond the site of male penetration that she has experienced with her stepfather and husband—those of the vulva and clitoris, feelings that prepare her for her sexual encounter with Shug.

The particularity of the Black women's vagina (color, texture, fragrance), moreover, is interrogated through Celie's self-examination as a means to counteract assumptions generally held by white women that Black women do not have vaginas, that is, their own legitimate desire, gendered understandings, and experiences, as manifested by Miz Millie's interactions with Sofia. As Alice Walker explains in her essay, "One Child of One's Own," the white woman does not want to know that Black women have vaginas because to do so would make them feel guilty about their supremacy:

> She fears knowing that Black women want the best for their children just as she does. But she also knows Black children are to have less in this world so that her children, white children, will have more (in some countries, all). Better then to deny that the Black woman has a vagina. Is capable of motherhood. Is a woman. (1983, 384)

The image of Celie's wet rose thus offers a poignant rememorialization of the erased history of Sofia's identity as mother and as sexual being. Through the metaphor, the official history of Sofia's criminal deviance gives way to the disremembered memory of Black women's legitimized sexuality and maternal desire, not only repressed by Pa, Mr.___, Harpo, and finally, Celie, but now by the mayor and his wife, who forbid her to have familial or sexual contact, as Sofia asserts: "I'm at they beck and call all day and all night. They won't let me see my children and they won't let me see no mens" (108). The reaffirming incorporation of the wet rose, and the alternate colloquial description, that of the 'button' and the 'pussy lips,' function to replace the inscribing practices, linked to Sofia and Celie, with incorporating practices. This substitution foregrounds unapologetically Black women's embodiment and the knowledge associated with bodily desire, ultimately allowing Celie to fully realize her attempts to move beyond the crisis of subjectivity that began the narrative, as well as beyond her first attempt to come to voice in her encounter with Sofia in jail.

Celie's sexual awakening, first through self-discovery and then in her ensuing sexual and amorous relationship with Shug, solidifies her subjective self-understanding and redemptive self-love. With Shug's empathy, Celie is able to retell the story of her rape and in doing so feels safe enough to remember the disremembered memory of embodied feelings—fear, confusion, pain, and loss. In the embrace between Shug and Celie, and later, with the sexual consummation of their love, Celie remembers and releases the repressed emotions caused not only by the trauma of the rape, but the secondary and interrelated trauma of having her babies stolen. Celie's sexual expressivity begins as Shug licks her nipples, an act that triggers both a feeling and attending emotion that causes her to remember the emotional and physical knowledge of maternal love: "Then I feels something real soft and wet on my breast, feel like one of my little lost babies mouth" (118). In effect, Celie's breast becomes a palimpsest, the site at which she knows herself/her body as a desiring subject. Celie's breast also becomes the site of awakening of disremembered memories of her children. In claiming her body as a feeling body, she releases the pain caused by violence and loss. In trusting herself to tell her story and to feel her feelings, Celie undertakes a human archaeology, using her body as a resource—a site of forgotten or textually unarticulated memories.

Celie's changed self-perception allows her to begin to intervene proactively in the social milieu to initiate womanist liberatory action. Whereas before she was incapable of anger, now, trusting her own perceptions and judgments, she allows herself to react with rage when she discovers, shortly following her sexual encounter with Shug, that Mr.___ has hidden Nettie's letters from her. Indeed, her murderous rage is incited by a deep knowledge, emerging from the body, that the stolen letters are also a palimpsest. In effect, Mr.___'s act of stealing the letters, the textual body of Nettie, erases and ultimately reveals his earlier act of stealing Nettie from Celie when he forced Nettie to leave.[11]

Celie's rage is not only an indicator of her newfound consciousness of the self but also the tool that allows her to exercise her moral agency to gain an understanding of the global dimensions of oppression that the letters reference—the variously differentiated modes of Black experience, both in the urban centers of the United States and in Africa. Celie's rage allows her, with the help of Shug, to retrieve the letters as well as physically retrieve Nettie and her children. Equally importantly, Celie's rage allows her to critically engage, through the reading of Nettie's letters, the social parameters constraining and defining her own family history as well as the broader historical and transational raced and gendered systems by which other Black communities had been asymetrically structured, fragmented, and put in opposition to one another. In effect, through her rememory of the lost and stolen babies, Celie is capable now of also remembering the body politic, the forgotten knowledge of her peoples' social and cultural contributions to Western and world cultures, and the universal dimensions of the struggle of Black women and their communities against oppressive social structures, dominant theological and ethical ideologies and practices. Indeed, it is through Celie's process of acquiring of such knowledge, that she is able to leave her husband and take the necessary steps, in community with others, to transform herself, her family, and her community.

CONCLUSION

Through the deployment of alternative and transformative mnemonic systems located in embodied cognitive practices, Celie, along with Shug, Nettie, and Sofia, undertake willful acts of collective imagination to evaluate comparatively their experiences. In doing so, they reconstruct a shared historical experience, recreate the past, deepen their understanding of the social and historical dimensions of their individual selves, and ultimately reclaim their selves and their community. In piecing together through storytelling a reexamination of their diverse and particular experiences that form the different parts of their shared cultural history, they ultimately construct a more accurate coherent narrative, 'story' or 'theory' that is causally relevant, that is, that refers to social facts, such as gender, race, sexuality and nation, that have informed their identities. Moreover, in coming to analyze the contexts of their own lives, they develop a more fully actualized sense of moral character that allows them to wrest their agency from the forces of oppression and in turn use their experiences of resistance as the context to inform normative ethical inquiry as well as future agendas for social justice. This is the enactment of a womanist cognitive realist or postpositivist realist identity politics.

CHAPTER 5

Latina/o *Mestizaje/Mulatez:* Vexed Histories, Ambivalent Symbolisms, and Radical Revisions

INTRODUCTION

In the previous two chapters, I argued that Black women's writings are informed by an intersubjective dialogics that draws upon narratives of rememory to contest hegemonic histories. While both womanism and the tradition of feminist *mestizaje/mulatez* cultivate a perspectival discourse that allows Black and Latina women writers to take their congealed experiences and translate them into developed knowledge, I argue in this chapter that feminists working within the *mestizaje/mulatez* traditions draw more centrally on the concepts of space and place as a lens through which to interpret their lived experiences. I use the term 'place' to indicate an analytical construct that challenges the notion of space as univocal in meaning, conditioned by merely physical parameters. From the lens of Human Geography, a subfield of Geography that draws upon and merges the philosophical camps of phenomenology and hermeneutics, the notion of place makes explicit the social construction of space by the people who inhabit it, and, who, through their lived experiences, endow it with meaning and value (Peet 1998, 48). Place is both a product of the often contentious and politicized concerns and interests of diverse people inhabiting a given space, and a mnemonics—encapsulated in folk traditions, narratives, and other cultural forms of expression (Mesa-Bains 2003, 306–08).

The aim of this chapter is to examine spatialized experience in the cultural work of *mestiza* feminists. *Mestiza* feminists consider the complexities of place and space as the privileged context within which to understand identity. Place and identity are ineluctably linked for all people. However, place is a construct that is particularly illuminating for interpreting the identities of peoples who, due to imperialistic processes, have had to inhabit different places, crossing borders as immigrants or exiles, or having the border cross them. *Mestiza* feminists articulate the embodied dimensions of race-gender formation at the crossroads of cultures, races, and nations, in order to construct knowledge of place and identity along multiple perspectival axes.

The implications of my analyses throughout this chapter are that the labels *mestizaje* and *mulatez,* along with the national origin labels, such as *Boricua/mestiza, Cubana mulatez,* as well as other nomenclatures that indicate newly claimed or newly created diasporan identity formations, such as *Nuyorican,* Afro-Puerto Rican, *Boricua* Black, and *Xicanisma,* call into being the complex factors that make up one's spatialized "sociality," a concept that Africana philosopher Lewis Gordon defines as "the processes by which people define themselves relationally or intersubjectively with others that are similarly situated, thereby achieving the status of 'community'" (Gordon 2002, 111).

Importantly, community depends upon what Africana philosopher Lewis Gordon calls the "irreplaceability of others" in similar social positions so that within a community "social relations...heighten each member's understanding of every other member's value and uniqueness" (111). Sociality is achieved through an interpretive process that takes into account the intersubjective negotiations over identity, meaning, and perspectives that members of a community test out as they navigate their social world from a particular place or their imagined sense of that place when they no longer occupy it. The concept of sociality helps us to think about place not just as a random site that people arbitrarily or coincidentally inhabit, but as one that acquires meaning as people create a collective definition of their community. In doing so, they create a space of co-implication and/or of opposition.

Throughout this chapter, I develop a framework that conceptualizes a diasporan identity formation and politics of *mestizaje/mulatez* as derived from embodied, spatialized experiences. Notably, it is through the construction of spatial metaphors that *mestiza* feminists discover and develop alternative perspectival discourses. Metaphors of hybridized, embodied space, such as 'border woman' or of space conceived as mobile, such as the metaphor of '*acá y allá*' ('here and there'), make visible the relationships of dominance and subjugation between multiply situated identities (*mestizaje/mulatez*) and multiple diasporic histories of conquest, colonization, and enslavement.[1]

These developed metaphors serve, notably, two political aims. First, they critique the global macroprocesses and practices responsible for the reproduction of subjugated identities. These processes include both colonizing histories as well as contemporary market forces and media images. I examine metaphors highlighting these processes in order to explore how they enrich our understanding of the discursive and extradiscursive struggles over raced, gendered, and classed identities, and how such identities evolve in confrontation with the racial and gendered projects of colonization and globalization. Second, spatial metaphors serve as constructive paradigms that feminists working within the tradition of *mestizaje/mulatez* use to develop new identities and new publics that will be recognizable as integral but not assimilated to the U.S. nation-state or to other nation-states (Mignolo 2000). I do not undertake an exhaustive critique of these metaphors, but rather examine selected texts informed by *mestizaje/mulatez* traditions in order to suggest how spatial metaphors facilitate epistemic reorientation. I now turn to a review of phenomenology and hermeneutics as particular orientations in Human Geography, comparing their approaches to identity with postpositivist realist understandings of identity.

Conceptualizing Feminist Mestizaje/Mulatez as an Oppositional Spatial Identity: Social/ Human Geography, the Body Schema, and Poetic Language

Through the lens of Human Geography, it becomes possible to determine how place constrains and enables social conduct and interactions, the types of experiences one will have and the choices one can make. The invocation of metaphors and other symbolic representations by peoples that have been dislocated and relocated by processes of colonization or globalization helps us to understand identities not only in relation to embodied histories, but also in relation to embodied spaces. Embodied space, as defined by Setha Low and Denise Lawrence-Zuñiga, is "the location where human experience and consciousness take on material and spatial form" (2003, 3). As social and human geographers have noted, analysis of the movement of bodies as a result of global and diasporic histories is crucial not only to our understanding of the (re)creation and (re)conceptualization of space, but also to an understanding of the located body as a site of knowledge. The body, in relation to space, is conceived not as a mere container but rather as organic, in motion within a determined space (Pandya 1990); Human geographer Sally R. Munt describes the body as a symbolic nexus of relations produced out of interactions between bodily actors and terrestial spaces (1996, 449).

The fields of phenomenology and hermeneutics have been of interest to human geographers because they help to uncover the complex reciprocal relationships between identity, subjectivity, history, and space/place from the subjective perspective of individual actors. Human Geography developed in the late '60s as a critical reaction against logical positivist forms of knowledge that prevailed in the discipline to reconcile the objectivity of social science with human subjectivity, as well as to reconcile the materialism of space/place with idealism, that is, with the meanings given to space. These meanings include one's emotional responses to a given space, ethical judgments, social interactions, and understandings of historical practices. Phenomenologists examine the conditions of human existence, describe the phenomena of things as one experiences them, including seeing, hearing and other sensory experiences, as well as one's beliefs, memories, imagination, judgments, and feeling. They also examine physical phenomena as well as the feeling of the physical (Peet 1998, 37).

Maurice Merleau-Ponty's *Phenomenology of Perception* (1962) is an important work for human geographers because it presents a sustained critique of empiricism and rational understandings of the human experience in relation to the physical and social environment from the point of view of existential phenomenology. For Merleau-Ponty, the task of phenomenology is to describe rather than explain scientifically, in order to get at the real through mental and interpretive processes that involve the imagination. The world people perceive is not 'objective' in the empirical sense, but rather consists of objects in a world with unspecified properties, relations of meaning, and reciprocal expression. Because ambiguity is a pervasive component of the lived world, the interpretation one constructs about one's experience is going to be crucial in assigning meaning (Peet 1998, 43).

Merleau-Ponty does not view the human body as just another object in the world, but rather acknowledges the intentional nature of human subjects, that is, their active responses to relevant features in the social world that define people. The body grasps relationships, senses how things should be done, acquires habits, and feels what new movements would be like. The body can acquire new skills or habits, that is, a new understanding of the embodied self through conscious analysis and mental imagery. Intentionality belongs not to the mind but to the body, providing the basic connection between humans and the world. This body that reacts and grasps knowledge is not an empirical body, but rather a "body schema," that is, the locus of intentionality where conscious experience and the external world encounter or are opened up for each other (1962, 206).

Following Merleau-Ponty, social geographer Nancy Munn highlights both the indexical and subjectivist nature of space. Space, Munn argues, is "defined by reference to an actor, it's organizing center" (2003, 94). Thus, the spatial field extends from the 'actor'—a situated body—that moves within and across different social environments, interacting with and registering these spaces through its tactile and sensorial capacities. Munn further underscores the dynamic interconnection between space and the actors inhabiting a given space by drawing on Lefebvre's notion of the 'field of action.' She affirms that "the body is thus understood as a spatial field and the spatial field as a bodily field" (2003, 94). Within the context of Human Geography, the body is not just the material body as it is subjectively captured by the actor, but is often portrayed as embodied space that becomes visible as people consciously reflect on their lived experiences. Soja and Hooper view the spatial field as a counter-hegemonic practice which, combined with materialism, that is, the lived experience of space, idealism, and the conceptual, creates a radical standpoint (2002, 387). Social geographers Elizabeth Dyck and Pamela Moss define embodiment as "*lived* spaces where people are constitutively located conceptually and corporeally, metaphorically and concretely, discursively and materially, being simultaneously part of material forms and their social constructions" (2002, 49).

The notion of the habitual body, that is, those taken-for-granted habits and knowledge of our everyday comportments, lodged in our bodies, are of interest to human and social geographers as well as other scholars investigating the social world because habitual comportments become manifest not only in physical behaviors, such as walking or eating, but also, as noted by the work of the aforementioned scholars, in our social behaviors. Because habitual social behaviors, that is, preconscious raced and gendered codes that bodies internalize and reproduce, are just that—habitual—it is difficult to have consciousness of them. In her phenomenological study of the *chicana* lesbian experience, Jacqueline Martínez thus affirms that by focusing attention on the phenomenon of imposed or subjugated identities, it becomes possible to access the social and discursive patterns that we take up habitually through bodily interactions, and also achieve epistemic reorientation (2000, 7).

Although phenomenology is often thought of as nontheoretical, that is, as a process that relies on the suspension of assumptions about causality and focuses instead on describing the givenness of things, this does not mean that the observation of one's givenness is neutral. Rather, the description of a phenomenon that one constructs from his or her location simply implies that all interpretation is derived from some perspective (Merleau-Ponty 1962). Moreover, as philosopher William W. Wilkerson underscores, when one reflects on an experience, which entails examining the entire context in which the experience occurs, one engages a process that presumes from the start that our experiences are never self-evident nor, subsequently, can they be immediately apprehended. We only grasp the meaning of experiences as we reflect on their occurrence within a broader context (Wilkerson 2000, 260).

When we examine relationally our experiences against the range of elements constituting the context, we are able to discover patterns that provide a coherent meaning. It is through the experiencing subject's efforts to identify these patterns that knowledge is discovered. However, as Wilkerson underscores, neither the process nor the discovered knowledge are arbitrary. Rather, it is as if the patterns of meaning were always there, under the surface, as "latent" or "unrealized meaning" until one undertakes the effort to illuminate them. Then, their presence is made salient (264). Herein, the process of reflection and interpretation changes the character of the experiences one has, potentially allowing one to piece experiences together in new patterns of signification in order to achieve an interpretation that has greater coherence than those that arrive from a distant elsewhere (265).

In this sense, phenomenological reflection is an approach to experience that shares an affinity with postpositivist realist claims regarding the epistemic, theory-mediated nature of experience. Indeed, phenomenology provides resources to the implementation of a postpositivist realist praxis, insofar as it highlights the mediated nature of knowledge. Phenomenology acknowledges the need for attentiveness to the context in which we as experiencing subjects wrestle to make meanings of our lives. The struggle to understand as an embodied process includes the use of our emotions, our expectations, and our lived histories that inform that context, all of which facilitates our ability to achieve a coherent explanation of the self (Wilkerson 2000, 260–261). Phenomenological reflection also provides a process of interpretation that can be of use to a postpositivist realist analysis. Wilkerson cogently exemplifies this socially mediated process in terms of his own experience not only of coming out, but also of understanding contextually his own homosexuality. In doing so, he exemplifies the quintessential maxim of postpositivist realism, namely, that all knowledge is socially mediated, whether we are talking about accurate knowledge or error (276–77).

In her phenomenological analysis of the *Chicana* experience, one that includes critical reflection on her own life history, Communications scholar Jacqueline Martínez points to another distinctive feature of phenomenological reflection: its resistance to serving as a formula for achieving objective knowledge. This resistance occurs, Martínez argues, not only because conscious reflection is often fraught with potential contradictions arising from the great potential for error of interpretation, but also because of the unextrapolable nature of individual experience. For example, given that people internalize different aspects of a racist, sexist, homophobic, or xenophobic culture, the struggle for understanding and overcoming these social ills will be different for each person (Martínez 2000, 94). Yet it is for this very reason that phenomenological reflection is useful. She thus affirms that the cultural legacies informing *mestiza* identities cannot be investigated using "generalized theorization" but rather must begin with "a self-reflexive engagement with the facticity of our very lives" (113). Such individual projects are not to be deemed arbitrary nor socially irrelevant, however, that is, as individual journeys of consciousness, which would ultimately cause phenomenological critique to default into a support for the political status quo. This is because phenomenological descriptions necessarily interrogate the historical, social, and spatial circumstances of their own analyses (95).

Martínez thus emphasizes the fact that ways of seeing, feeling, and knowing are always tied to time and place of social relations and therefore get taken up into phenomenological reflection whether consciously or not. However, when consciously linking experience to the specificities of our historical and social-spatial environment, as she exemplifies in her own reflection on her lived experience as a *Chicana* lesbian, it is possible to make visible the latent political significance of lived experience comprising our social identity, thereby making transformation and personal empowerment possible. At the same time, conscious experience allows us to recognize the limitation of lived experience. Precisely because lived experience is situated in time and space, it is not always possible to elaborate generalizable meaning and value from it (Martínez 2000, 92–97). The implication here is that theories must, over time, be discarded, as the spatial field changes, to more adequately explain and ultimately theorize one's new context and one's identity within it.

Given the ways in which experiences of embodiment are necessarily constrained by specific historical practices within the spatial field, as noted above, the field of hermeneutics is also important to humanistic and social geographers, as a means to clarify the historical background assumptions through which people theorize their embodied experiences and interpret their perceptual practices. Together, phenomenology and hermeneutics offer a substantive alternative to positivistic geography (Peet 1998, 47). They also offer a substantive alternative to positivist forms of thought within Western philosophy (Alcoff 2006, 103). Following a trajectory that began with biblical interpretation, hermeneutics evolved in the nineteenth century with the works of such philosophers as Schleiermacher, Dilthey, and Heidegger, culminating in the twentieth century in the work of Hans-George Gadamer's philosophical hermeneutics.

In chapter 3 I have defined Gadamer's philosophical hermeneutics and suggested its reasonances with and utility for womanist thought. Here, I further expand on those definitions as I locate hermeneutics alongside phenomenology, following scholars of Human Geography and philosophy, in order to further advance a postpositivist conception of knowledge. In his *Truth and Method*, Gadamer emphasizes that interpretation is already conditioned by a 'tradition' in which we do our thinking, including our background assumptions, and the repository of concepts that we can draw from, from which reason can never be abstracted. Therefore, Gadamer argues, what is conceived as 'reason' is best understood as a philosophical construction or a tradition of thought that shapes our attitudes, behavior, values, and assumptions about what is true or false (1993, 280).

Because reason operates within a historical tradition, concrete temporal and spatial conditions and relations as well as individual experience become the context in and through which people create assumptions or prejudgments about the self and the social world (Alcoff 2006, 95). In this regard, reason or truth is contained in what Gadamer calls an 'interpretive horizon,' a term that indicates that people are never outside of their historical situation and therefore never able to fully grasp its meaning (Gadamer 1993, 302). As embodied beings, we are part of or located within the tradition, and always at the task of apprehending the social world and ourselves within it. Hermeneutics is thus concerned with ascertaining a rational and objective justification for a person's interpretation or perspective. Multiple perspectives on any given event are obviously possible, since people occupy different perspectival locations. The primary task of hermeneutics, however, is not to affirm the relativism of knowledge. The objective, rather, is to make visible the substantive content that exists in the social world within different perspectival locations, in order to obtain a more adequate vision of the horizon that forms our social world (Gadamer 1993, 302). This often requires an interrogation of the background assumptions that one inherits as participant of a 'tradition.' Such an interrogation is triggered by a sense of doubt or disbelief with regard to those assumptions. The sense of doubt is spurred by life experiences that seem to render such assumptions inconsistent with one's own understanding (Alcoff 2006, 96).

The coupling of the concept of the interpretive horizon and Merleau-Ponty's phenomenology of embodiment offers an alternative to the positivist practice of understanding or knowing ahistorically. Through conscious hermeneutical phenomenological engagement with taken–for-granted perceptual practices—constructed, imposed and reproduced through historical, and, often, hegemonic structures and practices—it becomes possible for the interpreter to modify inherited prejudgments in order to more adequately explain the social world in which he or she is located. In this regard, the engagement of the interpreter is not just subjective, but also objective, insofar as the interpreter is inserted in the social world, and can potentially provide more accurate knowledge about social reality in a given context.

Thus far I have suggested ways of thinking about identity as a series of interpretive practices, located in the body. Before analyzing how Latina feminists construct narratives of their embodied experiences through the practices of *mestizaje/mulatez*, I examine the concept of metaphor as the nodal point at which language and embodied practices intersect. I also explore the evocative capacity of aesthetic expression in order to illuminate its hermeneutical phenomenological function, namely, to call the phenomenon or the problem into being at the bodily or experiential level so that it can be shared and examined by the reader. Let me begin with an analysis of metaphor. Metaphor is defined within poetic discourse as the identification and linking of objects or ideas. It is viewed by Merleau-Ponty as a cognitive tool. The cross-referencing that develops between two terms creates relationships as well as makes new experiences and their interpretations possible. As Clive Cazeaux demonstrates in his work, *Metaphor and Continental Philosophy*, Merleau-Ponty's detailed considerations of "originating speech" or creative expression, as well as his analysis of language as an embodied practice impacting perception, makes his work easily translatable into a theory of metaphor as well as a theory of aesthetic linguistic expression (2007, 69). I retrace, in what follows, Merleau-Ponty's views of creative expression, drawing upon his own descriptions as well as Cazeaux's analysis.

For Merleau-Ponty, language, as well as the concepts and ideas transmitted by language, are not abstract entities but rather components of our locatedness in the world and therefore tied to embodied experience. Creative expression is like the embodied practice of intentionality. It is "that paradoxical operation through which, by using words of a given sense, and already available meanings, we try to follow an intention which necessarily outstrips, modifies, and itself, in the last analysis, stabilizes the meanings of the words which translate it" (1962, 389).[2] In this regard, metaphorical or conceptual pliability is fundamentally interconnected to bodily acuity or openness (Cazeaux 2007, 70).

The body schema is itself a metaphor, because, as a schema of cognitive articulation, it is the site in which consciousness and our lived experiences of the world are conceived and organized. The body is not just another object in the world—it is "the schema responsible for the disclosure of a world" (72). In other words, the body schema as metaphor is the context and site of the crisscrossing of domains, whereby the domain of generalized understandings or ideas is oriented toward or opens onto particular lived experience. The body schema is conceived as metaphorical in its operation. Cazeaux thus affirms that language, as an integral part of bodily acuity, does not simply draw a connection between objects or ideas, but rather serves as the very structure of human experience, indeed, as the very condition by which the body schema is able to construct reality. Metaphor is assigned ontological meaning and status because people perceive likenesses between things by virtue of their existence as an embodied presence in the world.

But in widening the scope of metaphor to embrace the ways in which we organize the world through embodied cognitive practices, it could quite easily be argued that metaphor takes on a new ontological dimension—the practice by which people habitually create likenesses as a fact of being located in the world. Accordingly, we could view metaphor as a simple fact of cognitive organization. If this were true, then the bodily gesture as well as the phonetic gesticulation would lose their interpretive and transgressive potential. Merleau-Ponty disallows such judgments. He states that while it is true that people create likenesses and connections among objects in the world as a matter of course of being in the world, there are also particular types of metaphors that transfigure or transcend current understandings, effecting what Cazeaux calls "ontological transposition," by reorganizing objects and ideas in new and surprising ways in order to achieve new meanings (2007, 72–73).

The occurrence of ontological transposition also happens as a normal occurrence, but we are not always aware of it. We become aware of its presence, Merleau-Ponty explains, on those occasions when "a system of definite powers is suddenly decentralized, broken up and reorganized under a fresh law unknown to the subject or to the external witness, and one which reveals itself to them at the very moment at which the process occurs" (Merleau-Ponty 1962, 193–94). Although Merleau-Ponty does not say when awareness occurs, he does affirm that its occurrence is a result or function of one's locatedness in the world at a given moment of temporal-spatial relations, and therefore cannot be determined in advance. Brought about at an unspecified moment in spatial-temporal relations, the deployment of metaphors of ontological transposition allows for the transformation of the self and the social world: "We must therefore recognize as an ultimate fact this open and indefinite power of giving significance—that is, both of apprehending and conveying a meaning—by which man transcends himself towards a new form of behavior, or towards other people, or towards his own thought, through his body and his speech" (1962, 194).

Merleau-Ponty makes metaphors of ontological transposition central to creative expression. He argues that it is through creative expression that systems and domains of meanings are broken apart and reconfigured (1962, 193–94). I would also like to suggest that the deployment of metaphors of ontological transposition are resonant as well with postpositivist realist processes of theory-mediated knowledge. Metaphors of ontological transposition are the culminating moment in a trajectory of radical reflection, shedding light on the dialectical relationship between the knower and the known. The notion of the metaphor of ontological transposition rejects the dualisms between body and world, subject and object, and past and present, as well as exemplifies an openness to the ongoing efforts of the human subject to verify and revise truth-claims.

The creative writer expresses his or her dynamic engagement with lived experience not only through metaphorical expression but also through vocative or mantic expression. Education scholar Max Van Manen has used hermeneutical phenomenology to develop innovative pedagogical theory around the notion of the "mantic," that is, how the text addresses or speaks to us, "how the text divines and inspirits our understanding" (1997, 346). He affirms that it is the expressive-mantic elements that infuse creative writing with its captivating quality, triggering our thoughtful reflection (Van Manen 1997, 353–68). Van Manen argues that much like metaphor, mantic-expressive components, which are intrinsic to poetic expression, are also cognitive in the 'felt' or embodied sense. They allow for the bracketing of everyday reality, which in turn allows the writer and reader of the text to examine one's 'felt sense' of it—how one finds oneself in the world. Such an examination can in turn trigger metaphors of ontological transposition. While these components are related to the body's felt sense or prophetic (mantic) knowledge, they are intrinsically related to the semantics of the text, insofar as they bring the world as we experience and interpret it closer, where we can examine the accuracy of our own understandings of it. The poetic dimensions of language prompt our knowing through the senses, enjoining readers to engage experientially and viscerally with the text (Nicol 2008).

These expressive or vocative elements include, Van Manen affirms, five textual/poetic features: concreteness, evocation, intensification, tone, and epiphany.[3] Concreteness or "lived throughness" is the process by which the writer examines and anchors the reader's given understanding of the phenomena so that the reader may gain experiential understanding of it. It is the researched phenomenon. Evocation illuminates lived meanings through a descriptive process. Description makes a lived experience present; it can reintroduce an object or event as was understood before current meanings were assigned to it, and creates images and associations that trigger critical reflection and reorientation. Descriptions can take the form of official myths or stories, as well as personal anecdotes. Intensification is the process whereby word images or gestures are brought together with other words, to the extent that they cross-fertilize one another. This crisscrossing of domains of meaning is itself a metaphorical process, one that intensifies the meanings of words as well as the relations of the word with other words with which it stands in repetitive relation. Intensification thus serves the function of saturating the reader with the meanings of the experience. Tone is comprised of the various ways in which the text addresses the readers in a stirring or feeling manner. These can include the repetitive, even musical elements of language that appeal to embodied or felt knowing, so that you can "hear the phenomenon in your own life" (Nicol 2008, 323). Van Manen states that felt knowing is related to the audible, the tasteable and the tactile, sensorial experiences that in turn cause words to exceed their originally intended meanings (1997, 361–33). Finally, the epiphany enjoins the reader to be transformed by this new apprehension of meaning or changed understanding as part of the overarching process the writer undertakes to understand the self through engagement with the reader or audience.

In what remains of this chapter, I analyze feminist texts pertaining to traditions of *mestizaje/mulatez*, highlighting the authors' practices of conscious reflection on racialized gender, as manifested through developed spatial metaphors and attending vocative expressive devices. I have selected the works of three writers: *Chicana/mestiza* feminist poet and theorist, Gloria Anzaldúa, *Nuyorican* poet Sandra María Estéves, and Puerto Rican diasporan scholar, Miriam Jiménez Román. I analyze their works in two separate sections. In the first, I explore *Chicana mestizaje* and attending metaphors of spatialized identity in the work of Anzaldúa. In the second section, I examine metaphors of *mestizaje/mulatez* as examples of how women pertaining to the Puerto Rican diaspora mediate their identities. Before examining their works, I provide some preliminary definitions of *mestizaje/mulatez*. I complement these initial definitions with further explanation of specific manifestations of *mestizaje/mulatez* within each section.

Feminist Mestizaje/Mulatez as Ontological Transposition: Metaphors, Symbolisms, and Paradoxes of Identity and Place

Feminists working within the *mestizaje/mulatez* traditions foreground their mixed race gender identity not as a deterritorialized "Latina" identity, detached from the specificities of space (in its temporal dimension) and assimilable to a U.S. identity, but as a nexus of raced, classed, and gendered relations produced out of interactions between themselves as embodied actors and the specific territorialized/spaces of sociality in which they are located. In their attempts to understand the different, often contradictory and fragmented categories comprising their identity in order to achieve a more coherent self, feminists working within traditions of *mestizaje/mulatez* have developed a set of spatial metaphors or paradoxes. They deploy these metaphors to articulate the bodily schema as a disclosure of the social world as it is hierarchically constructed. In the process of their critical reflection, they are able to reorganize their identities through the production of ontological transpositions. The linguistic and embodied reference point—feminist *mestizaje/mulatez*, unlike "Latina," reflects the bodily schema's openness to the world, to its locatedness, embedded within their texts through vocative mantic-expressive features.

I define the binomial *mestizaje/mulatez,* following Latina ethicist Ada María Isasi-Díaz, as a relational term, reflecting the full range of bodily manifestations of race-gender identity formation across the distinct Latina/o ethnicities. In this sense, it is analogous to the label "Latina/o." Yet, unlike "Latina/o," the *"new" mestizaje/mulatez* is a praxis of intentionality that exposes the raced, classed, and gendered meanings of Latina identity formation derived out of historical/material realities of conquest, colonial domination, and violent *mestizaje.* *Mestizaje/mulatez* reconceptualizes difference through a praxis that entails self-reflection, revision, and remembering differently the past, that is, the historical tradition in which Latina women's identities have been defined, in order to achieve self and communal transformation (Isasi-Díaz 2004b, 69–91). Conceived in this manner, feminist *mestizaje/mulatez* exposes the whole host of given and available meanings of *mestizae/mulatez,* following the intentionality of discursive and extradiscursive practices.

A mnemonics of *mestizaje/mulatez* is a purposeful reflection and retention of the past, or *a priori* experience. By purposeful, I mean feminists working within this tradition hold on to the historical tradition of *mestizaje,* that is, violence, genocide, and invisibility, as a spatial-temporal field that structures but does not absolutely determine their experiences and understanding. Thus conceived, a mnemonics of embodied space informing *mestiza* feminist writing is a dialectical arena where the meaning of embodied space is reflected upon, and, in the process, struggled over, imagined, and constructed anew. In this regard, *mestizaje/mulatez* is not reduced to its tragic dimension, but is used herein as a perspectival axis or interpretive horizon that allows new knowledge to surface. In what follows, I examine a series of central metaphors of feminism pertaining to traditions of *mestizaje/mulatez,* as exemplified in the work of Gloria Anzaldúa's *Borderlands/La frontera: The new mestiza*: "border woman," *"encrucijadas"* (crossroads), *"travesías"* (crossings), and *"la facultad"* (sleight-of-hand/capacity). I also examine a series of metaphors pertaining to Puerto Rican/ *Nuyorican* feminism through an analysis of the metaphors that inform the work of Sandra María Estéves and Miriam Jiménez Román: *"vaivén"* (to and fro or back and forth), *"acá y allá"* (here and there), *"cruzando el charco"* (crossing the pond, and mainland/island).

I. Chicana *Feminism*

The central theme and metaphor of *mestiza* identities as a spatialized concept, captured in the term "borderlands," reflects the idea of lived experience in the spaces of the *intersticios* (in-between) of cultures. *Mestiza* feminists use this term to describe their lived experience as an encounter or clashing of cultures. In the aftermath of the *chicano* movement, *Chicana/mestiza* cultural workers and writers engaged this experience as a hermeneutics, foregrounding their horizon or range of vision both as that which they could see before them and as that which lay beyond it. They thus sought to achieve a more adequate horizon of inquiry that could serve them in their collision with their culture's traditions. They cultivated narratives as well as other aesthetic modes of representation around the notion of "borderlands consciousness" and *"mestizaje"* to reevaluate and reshape *Chicana/mestiza* identity as it was conceptualized in the 1960s and '70s within *Chicano* nationalist and feminist discourses, U.S. marketing culture, and within various pivotal historical junctures of their culture. These writers and artists include, among others, Gloria Anzaldúa, Norma Cantú, Ana Castillo, Lorna Dee Cervantes, Denise Chávez, Sandra Cisneros, Alicia Gaspar de Alba, Pat Mora, Cherríe Moraga, and Helena Viramontes.

Primary Metaphor of Spatialized Identity: The Border Woman
In her work, *Borderlands/La Frontera: The New Mestiza,* Gloria Anzaldúa constructs the metaphor of 'border woman' in order to gain understanding of space and place as the organizing center that has structured her experience of *mestizaje.* But 'border woman' is also a metaphor of ontological transposition. It is a metaphor that allows Anzaldúa to become 'the new *mestiza.*' The notion of 'border woman' is interconnected to Anzaldúa's notion of *nepantla*, which, as AnaLouise Keating states, is a state and a space of transitional consciousness in Anzaldúa's work (2006, 9). Anzaldúa develops the metaphor of border woman through the deployment of the vocative expressions of concreteness, evocation, intensification, and epiphany. By deploying these devices, she is able to 'show' experientially rather than tell rationally the work of the body schema. She uses concreteness as a device in her work through her researched description of the phenomena of dislocatedness. She thus constructs a human geography that charts the entire range of her evolving understanding of self and community in its raced, classed, and gendered dimensions, causing the reader to understand through cognitive and noncognitive (felt) sensibilities related to the body.[4]

Anzaldúa begins with a reexamination of the history of the annexation of Texas and the U.S. southwest, viewed from the perspective of her own lived experience as well as the perspectives of her family, through six generations. She reconstructs *Aztlán,* once the center of Aztec culture and now the southwest of the United States, and the various migrations of its inhabitants from pre-Columbian times to the present, with focused attention on the Texan border in the lower Rio Grande Valley. Her historical reconstruction of the formation of the *mestiza,* hybrid identity brings to light the background assumptions or interpretive horizon under which the ruling metaphor 'border woman' or '*mestiza*' came into being. She retraces the social relations that developed within various historical contexts in order to understand how people located within specific spatio-temporal relations form prejudgments as they attempt to apprehend their locatedness. Because of the racial variability that resulted from miscegenation among Spaniards, Anglos, Africans, and indigenous peoples since the Conquest, Anzaldúa points to skin color as one factor among a host of others that result from inhabiting a particular site and inheriting a particular identity legacy that constitutes the given meanings of the '*mestiza-india*': "For 300 years she has been a slave, a force of cheap labor, colonized by the Spaniard, the Anglo, by her own people (and in Mesoamerica her lot under the Indian patriarchs was not free of wounding" (44–45).

Anzaldúa links *mestizaje* to a historically variable set of borders and geographies that in turn has produced for the *mestiza* an ongoing crisis of home, identity, place, and culture. It is a geography that extends south to Latin America and north to the two Mexicos, one to the south of the border and one to the north, that of *Aztlán,* the southwest of the United States. The Cochise, the parent culture of the Aztecs, suffered the violence of conquest at the beginning of the sixteenth century, when Hernán Cortés invaded Mexico, and exercised domination in the form of 1) military rule, including genocide, rape, and miscegenation; and 2) colonial rule, through cultural suppression and coerced cultural assimilation that was to last three hundred years. Through these two forms of colonial rule, a new hybrid people of mixed Indian and Spanish blood came into being—the *mestizo/a* (26–27).

Anzaldúa then etches out a series of historical moments that developed the new hybrid identity in racialized terms within a more recent history. The Battle of the Álamo, (1836), resulted when native *tejanos,* Texans of Mexican descent, refused to cede their lands to the Anglos. The victory of the *tejanos* was shortlived just as the lifespan of the ensuing independent Republic of Texas. The United States waged war with Mexico in 1846. Actions taken by the American government were not only economically but also racially motivated: the goal of economic expansion made the United States seek out territories that were relatively uninhabited by people that were also considered intrinsically inferior by virtue of their indigenous blood (28). The border fence that henceforth was to divide the Mexican people came into being on February 2, 1848, with the Treaty of Guadalupe-Hidalgo, a treaty that resulted in Mexico's ceding of Texas, New Mexico, Arizona, Colorado, and California to the United States. Anzaldúa describes the racialized underpinnings of this new embodied geography as a violation, an assault, a dispossession of the embodied self, a racialized and gendered act:

> The *Gringo*, locked into the fiction of white superiority, seized complete political power, stripping Indians and Mexicans of their land while their feet were still rooted in it. *Con el destierro y el exilio fuimos desuñados, destroncados, destripados*—we were jerked out by the roots, truncated disemboweled, dispossessed, and separated from our identity and our history. (29–30)

In ensuing decades, the new hybrid, the *Chicano* or American *mestiza/o*, became represented not just as a racialized Other, a 'foreigner' in his or her own land, but also classed as Other. The *mestizo/a* was able to eke out an impoverished existence by sharecropping, while enduring a variety of forms of Anglo terrorism, including lynching. Anzaldúa notes that her father's co-participation in the sharecropping economy obliged him to pay forty percent of his earnings to the Anglo farmers who allowed him to work the land he once owned for their economic gain. Anzaldúa traces Anglo economic gain up to her own lifetime. The increased dependency of Mexico's economy on the United States is the inevitable result of the migration of entire Mexican towns to the North in search of economic survival, only to encounter white racism and exploitation (28–35).

Finally, the evolving *mestizo/a* identity formation was also gendered. To elicit and apprehend the meaning of gendered identity, Anzaldúa places in the text not just historical but also historico-mythical accounts of *mestiza* identity formation, where they can be examined. The *mestiza* identity formed to fulfil the very condition of an imagined or mythical national unity, representing the pivotal possibility of the loss or retention of the nation. Within the context of the Spanish Conquest, *mestizaje* was both a racial and gendered social practice. First, its major function was to unify a racially/culturally heterogeneous population, creating a single national unity under the Spanish crown. But it was also gendered, because the lynchpin of this unity was the Indian woman, the dark woman, *Malinali Tenepal* or *Malintzín, Malinche,* also known as *la Chingada,* the fucked one (50–52). She was Cortés' whore. In her role as his interpreter, the one who learned the Conqueror's language, she became the sell-out, creating the entry point for the Spanish invasion. The only social role available that would allow the *mestiza* to escape her perdition and that of her people was the alternate mythical paradigm, modeled by the brown saint, the Virgin of *Guadalupe.*

La Virgen de Guadalupe is a syncretic figure. Anzaldúa explains that her name is homologous with the Mesoamerican fertility goddess *Coatlalopeuh.* In Aztec mythological history, *Coatlalopeuh* was a complex goddess, representing the upper or light aspects, but also the underworld or dark aspects, associated with *Coatlicue,* the Serpent goddess. *Coatlalopeuh* or *Tonantsi,* ultimately became split from her dark guise, *Coatlicue* (49–52). Following the Conquest, the Spaniards split *Guadalupe,* removing the serpent/sexuality from her. She was henceforth considered to be synonymous with the Virgin Mary, who also in turn became the Euro-Iberian woman's positive alternative to the fallen woman, Eve, the ultimate traitor to mankind. Guadalupe was named Mother of God by the Catholic Church in 1660 (51).

As patron saint of Mexico, the dark *Virgen de Guadalupe* came to be viewed by both Mexicans and *Chicanos/as* as the defender of the *mestiza* race and symbol of insurgency "against the "subjugation of the poor and the *indio*" (52). She completes the virgin/whore dichotomy. The virgin/mother has not abandoned her people. She is 'docile and enduring" (53) as well as domestically contained, unlike *La Malinche* or her contemporary counterpart, *la Jila.* Thanks to the enduring presence of this oppressive binary today, informing contemporary *Chicano* cultural nationalist discourse, the *Chicana/mestiza* who identifies with any aspect of Anglo-feminism is considered a *malinche,* including those who cultivate relationships, activities and roles outside of marriage, family, and the maternal or who do not conform absolutely to the imperatives of female subservience as stipulated by *Chicano* culture and the Church: the queer, the young woman who leaves the community to go to college or to have a career, in order to become "self-autonomous persons" (39).

In effect, the contemporary race-gender formation of the *mestiza-india* represents a symbolic and material convergence of hegemonic social relations, as encountered in Euro-Iberian, Anglo, Mexican, and *Chicano* cultural traditions, which locate the *mestiza-india* on the outside. The metaphor 'border woman' exposes the split body schema as an inhabited site of a stratified and bounded social world. Anzaldúa's 'border woman' is a cognitive articulation of the *mestiza-india* body schema as constitutive outside of social relations, located at the *intersticios*, the spaces of the in-between. *Coatlicue*, the dark, Indian *creatrix* figure and sexed woman is thus suppressed.

Metaphors of Place and Mobility: La Encrucijada (Crossroads); Travesías (Crossings); and la Facultad (Sleight-of-Hand) Importantly, Anzaldúa does not cultivate the metaphor of "border woman" at first as a creative expression. Anzaldúa simply uses concreteness as an expressive device that helps her to redraw the link between metaphorical language, lived experience, and the interpretation of social reality by laying bare the historical tradition in which interpretation develops and is experienced by people who form part of that tradition. Within the spatial field of action, the *mestiza-india* body, experienced as "border woman" is a body schema or interpretive horizon that illuminates the world by revealing how the social world in its various cultural/societal manifestations has created likenesses—structuring and organizing *la mestiza* as the outside, as bounded, and how that is uniquely experienced: "Blocked, immobilized, we can't move forward, can't move backwards. That writhing serpent movement, the very movement of life, swifter than lightning, frozen" (43).

But that metaphor changes its modulation as Anzaldúa now incorporates the vocative device of anecdote, through her introduction of two autobiographical narratives. Her reflection on these stories culminates in an epiphany, whereby she is able to transform the given meanings of her race-gender formation. She also draws upon the device of intensification in order to call upon the reader to share in the experience by coupling the original metaphor, border woman, with new metaphors, thereby sparking sensory knowing. These include: *encrucijadas* ('crossroads,') *travesías* ('crossings') and *facultad*, ('capacity,' 'sleight-of-hand psychical movement'). Anzaldúa describes the *facultad* as "anything that breaks into one's everyday mode of perception, that causes a break in one's defenses and resistance, anything that takes one from one's habitual grounding, causes the depths to open up, causes a shift in perception" (61). The *facultad* is linked to what Merleau-Ponty refers to as a metaphor of ontological transposition. In other words, the seer does not just apprehend or internalize meaning as a habitual mode of operating in the world, but also, by virtue of seeing herself being seen, is able to achieve a new seeing (61).

Anzaldúa begins to exercise the *facultad* as she consciously reflects on how she has internalized her own body schema, a schema patterned after the figure of the suppressed embodied, darker, underworld aspect of *Guadalupe—Coatlicue*. She follows the phenomena of raced-gendered meanings of *Coatlicue*, the Indian woman in herself, throughout the chapters entitled "Entering the Serpent" and "The Coatlicue State." I will focus here on two personal anecdotes, one childhood event, a nocturnal visit to the *escusado* or outhouse; and one adult event, a depressive bout, thirty years later.

The description of the nocturnal visit to the *escusado* is an apprehending of the bodily schema of raced, classed, and gendered border woman. Life on the border as the daughter of a sharecropper means no running water. *La Prieta*, the little dark one, must go out of the house to urinate, an exercise in fear and self-loathing. Her mother indoctrinates her with regard to the dominant social paradigms governing womanhood as a devouring sexuality, as filth, and stigmatization. The outhouse is the embodied space where sexuality appears as a dangerous, devouring black hole: "I can see my legs fly up to my face as my body falls through the round hole into the sheen of swarming maggots below" (47). At night the *escusado* is a particularly dangerous place. Snakes can bite you, kill you. The animalistic quality of the snake portrays the perverse female sexuality that devours, and that must be suppressed. Her mother warns *"No vayas al escusado en lo oscuro.* Don't go to the outhouse at night, Prieta." *"No se le vaya a meter algo por allá.* A snake will crawl into your *nalgas,* make you pregnant" (47). Through the mother's internalization of the dehumanized image of the *mestiza-india*, the dark child learns to fear the darkness, the snakes, and her own sexed and raced body all at the same time. She steps on a big black snake when she comes back into the house, slithering across the kitchen floor. Even the domestic space—that space that encloses the *mestiza*—is not free of danger, of the dark, that which defines womanhood.

In Chapter 4, entitled *"La herencia de Coatlicue/*The Coatlicue State," Anzaldúa examines her adult self, "Gloria," now in a depressive state, a psychical escusado, a place of fear and denial, of *susto* (fear) that she must transform. In facing the *susto* rather than suppressing it, she begins to experience the wounding of *Coatlicue* differently—as the soul or self that must wound itself in order to heal. Wounding, darkness, and death allow for the creation of new knowledge, and pave the way for the *travesía,* the transgressing of boundaries. Gloria fears her own depressive inactivity because it can easily be correlated with the controlling images of Mexicans as lazy. But it is through stasis—physical and mental apathy or listlessness—that her bodily schema responds to the world. Here, her struggle for a new consciousness takes on embodied dimensions. Gloria experiences a range of attributes associated with *susto,* as defined within *Chicano/a* culture: she has sweats and headaches. She is jolted by fear of sudden noises. She is reticent to communicate with others.[5] All of this is an attempt to close her self off, to keep the wounding from fully taking place.

But in that dark, fecund place, in the maternal arms of *Coatlicue,* Gloria begins to make sense of things. *Coatlicue* is the other guise of the mother—the one who wants the child to make her own felt sense of things, to face the fear, survive it, and use it transformatively. This is the moment of epiphany, brought about by the intensification of spatial metaphors. Gloria adds to the spatial tropes of boundedness (border woman and *encrucijada*) a trope of mobility, that of *travesía* (crossing). At this juncture, Anzaldúa's body schema becomes the site of a clashing encounter between the given meanings of the *mestiza,* associated with the monolithic snake identity of *Coatlicue,* and her lived experience, one that brings forth the multiple identities of *Coatlicue,* associated with *Cihuacuatal, Coatlicue,* and *Tonantsi.* These Aztec earth goddesses represented the underworld and the heavenly, the sexual and creative powers, as well loving motherhood/womanhood. No longer remaining at the crossroads, Anzaldúa undertakes a *travesía.* She discovers a new 'territory,' struggling all the way to give birth to the self that must inhabit it. In doing so, she further discovers that the darkness, the representation of the feminine and the *mestiza-india,* is really a repressed sexual and creative energy, what Jennifer Browdy de Hernandez defines as the "lesbian sublime" (1998, 250); and what AnaLouise Keating, following Anzaldúa, refers to as *conocimiento* (knowledge). *Conocimiento* is, as Keating indicates, an epistemology that is born in oppressive contexts, and uses processes linked to the body, including the emotions, sensorial experience, memories, and dreams, in order to nuance and transform one's perspective (Keating 2006, 10*). Conocimiento* facilitates a new consciousness that takes the place of the old disembodied, self-loathing Prieta: "Suddenly the repressed energy rises, makes decisions, connects with conscious energy and a new life begins" (Anzaldúa 1987, 71). In this new life, fear and self-loathing have been decentralized, and a new possession and knowledge of the self, felt tenuously, annihilates fear:

> Something pulsates in my body, a luminous thin thing that grows thicker every day. Its presence never leaves me. I am never alone. That which abides: my vigilance, my thousand sleepless serpent eyes blinking in the night, forever open. And I am not afraid. (73)

II. Boricuas and Mestizaje/Mulatez

Puerto Ricans became a divided and diasporic people as a result of a long and multi-layered history of enslavement, colonialism, and massive migration (Flores 1993). This history has produced a particular spatial field of translocality and transculturalism in which Puerto Rican women and their communities move and against which they push, characterized by both a material and metaphorical circularity. Puerto Ricans migrants first left the island to settle in New York at the beginning of the century, following the Spanish American War, a war that resulted in the U.S. acquisition of Puerto Rico. Migration continued throughout the first half of the twentieth century as a result of the U.S. government's ongoing policymaking and interventions. Significant migration occurred between the two world wars, and then peaked in the period between the 1950s and 1970. This was due to the U.S. government's establishment of a de-industrialization program known as Operation Bootstrap, a program that ultimately led to the collapse of the agricultural economy and provoked a massive exodus to the mainland, as Puerto Ricans searched for work. Finally, from the 1970s to the present, the migration patterns have taken a bi-directional turn. As the U.S. economy has in turn undergone restructuring, fluctuation, and recession, Puerto Ricans have relocated either to the island or the mainland in order to find the best economic opportunity. Migration has thus become circular and more dispersed (Whalen 2005). The persistence of Puerto Rican mobility is due precisely to the fact that they hold an American passport. Yet their citizenship status is fraught with ambiguity. While granted citizenship in 1917, their territory is still non-incorporated. To this day, it is not considered a state, nor an independent nation. Puerto Ricans cannot vote in U.S. national elections, nor do they have voting representation in the Congress. The United States retains authority over the military, the federal judiciary, and foreign affairs of the island.

Africana and Puerto Rican Studies scholar Juan Flores highlights the significant relation of migration to colonialism, stating that "as long as Puerto Rico remains in direct colonial bondage to the United States, Puerto Rican cultural expression in the United States evokes the relation, above all, between Puerto Rican people *here and there*, between the expressive life of the migrant population and the long-standing traditions of struggle and articulation of the Island culture" (1993, 14) (emphasis is mine). Clearly, the colonialist history of Puerto Ricans has made spatial identity, articulated as a mediation between mainland and island scholars, cultural workers and writers, a crucial component of Puerto Rican cultural expression and identity politics. While colonialism has resulted in the loss of national autonomy, it has also triggered popular expressions of national identity that convey the Puerto Rican experience as a series of mobile survival practices, manifested as an ongoing circular movement or migration between island and mainland.

Metaphors of Spatial Identity and Mobility:
Vaivén ('Back and Forth'), Acá y Allá ('Here and There'),
la Guagua Aérea ('the Air Bridge' or 'the Airbus'), and
Cruzando el Charco ('Crossing the Pond' or 'Crossing the Puddle')
Anthropologist Jorge Duany draws upon the concept of *vaivén*, a word used to connote a back-and-forth or to-and-fro movement, as a metaphor that makes explicit the shifting and mobile identities of Puerto Ricans. A number of other metaphors have surfaced to capture the experience of mobile identity. The *guagua aérea*, (air bus/air bridge) refers not only to the daily movement of airplanes and passengers circulating through space between island and mainland, but also conceptualizes a border identity. The metaphorical expressions of *cruzar el charco* ('crossing the pond' or 'crossing the puddle'), *acá y allá* ('here and there'), as well as the reference to two territories 'U.S. mainland/island' are also used to express the experience of living in the space of the 'in-between.'

With the rise of cultural nationalism emerging on the island subsequent to the approval of the Constitution in 1952, a unique nationalist cultural iconography developed among Puerto Rican cultural workers and writers that flourished on the U.S. mainland. Serving as a mnemonics of spatialized identity at the crossroads of cultures and nations, this iconography brought together the disparate elements that go into being *Boricua*, that is, Puerto Rican, including the use of Spanish and Spanglish, the public exhibition of symbols such as the Puerto Rican flag or image of the *jíbaro*—the field or agricultural worker who has come to embody the authentic Puerto Rican—as well as objects and activities associated with this figure (Duany 2007, 53). It further included icons, artifacts, and myths derived from the Taino Indian culture, as well as the folk art of carving *santos*, small wooden sculptures of Catholic saints derived from Spanish culture (Duany 2007, 57). Cultural workers and writers who have found themselves in constant dislocation represent these objects and cultural practices associated with them in order to reclaim the terrestrial space of Puerto Rico, while reaffirming simultaneously a distinct Puerto Rican diasporic formation, now connected to lived experiences on the mainland.

Since the '80s onward, a growing number of Puerto Rican women writers and cultural workers/artists, including Monica Brown, Sandra María Estéves, Esmeralda Santiago, Miriam Jiménez Román, Hilda Lloréns, Maritza Quiñones Rivera, Celina Romany, and Bibiana Suárez, have drawn upon this repository of cultural icons, along with embodied spatial metaphors conveying mobility and boundedness, in order to critique the idea of the Puerto Rican nation as a monolithic entity that has achieved unification as a result of island nationalism. These writers and artists link gendered *mestizaje/mulatez* not just to the historical and spatial realities of the Puerto Rican diaspora with its indigenous roots, but to the African diaspora as well, the one circular, and the other forever dispersed.[6] They infuse metaphors of spatial mobility with a critique of *mestizaje*, portraying it as the racial ideology that serves as the lynchpin of nationalist unification. In the works of these writers, the lived experiences of the *vaivén* facilitate conscious reflection on their everyday multiply embodied spatial and historical contexts, and on how they are defined within them. Upon reflecting on the invisibility of their raced gendered identity, resulting from a masculinist hegemonic *mestizaje* embodied in the *jíbaro*, they transpose their self-understandings. The *allá* ('there') of the island that is exalted over the *acá* ('here') of the mainland is replaced by new spatial metaphors: *ni allá ni acá* ('not there nor here') and *tanto allá como acá* ('there just as much as here'). In doing so, they boldly intervene in Puerto Rican debates around the nationalist identity.

Puerto Ricans have held a nationalist view of their identity ever since they were subordinated to Spanish rule in the sixteenth century, and have embraced *mestizaje*, the racial practice by which Spain was able to unify its people as a central strategy of their own national unification. Herein, the *jíbaro*, who varied in skin color from brown to black, was considered the icon of a nascent Puerto Rican identity and culture. Although *mestizaje* referred to the Spanish-indigenous mixing of blood and culture, the privileged entity was the Spanish component, while African blood and culture remained the invisibilized component. In this manner, national unification, which was only apparently achieved, masked the hierarchalized and divided nation. The U.S. acquisition of Puerto Rico and ensuing military rule over the island further divided and hierarchalized the nation through imposed segregation. U.S. racial practices reinforced the internalized ideology of *mestizaje,* in particular, its white, European component, which was disseminated through the ideology of whitening or *blanqueamiento* Ironically, this racial ideology led to a general conception that racial integration had been achieved. Whitening or *blanqueamiento,* in effect, "accepts the implicit hegemonic rhetoric of the United States with regards to 'white supremacy,' and often blames those people classed as 'Black' and 'indigenous' for the worsening of the nation" (Torres and Whitten 1998, 9).[7]

I now turn to the works of poet Sandra María Estéves and diasporic scholar Miriam Jiménez Román. These two women writers form part of the *Nuyorican* community. The term *Nuyorican* refers to those communities pertaining to the Puerto Rican diaspora that are located in the New York metropolitan area. I have selected their works for analysis because they exemplify a tendency within recent Puerto Rican women's writings to critique and revise spatial metaphors of *acá y allá* ('here and there') as exemplars of a unified Euro-Iberian-based Puerto Rican national identity.

In her poem "Not Neither" (1994, 60), Sandra María Estéves converts the metaphorical concept *acá y allá* from its construction as a hybrid spatial identity to *ni acá ni allá*, a construction that signifies first her bounded identity, and finally, through an antiphonal call-and-response technique to her African diasporic identity. She uses tone and intensification as the mantic-expressive features that reinforce these various conversions. She establishes tone by saturating her poetic constructions with conjunctions that work in tandem with affirming or negating words. She plays with correlating conjunctions ('neither/nor' or 'both/and'), juxtaposing them with coordinating conjunctions in order to accentuate her lived experiences of self as a series of continuities ('and,' 'yet') and discontinuities ('but,' 'not yet,' 'nor') as well as an affirmation, a reclaiming ('but,' 'yet'). These repetitive tonal features cause the reader to share the felt experience of mobile fluctuations of the poet. They also function, ultimately, to break down the binaries (American/Puerto Rican; Dominican/ Puerto Rican; Puerto Rican/African; and African/American) that these grammatical units instantiate, hierachalize, and reify.

The title "Not Neither" at once suggests that Estéves is negating her bounded identity by saying "*not* neither" (emphasis is mine). She thus affirms her hybridity: "Being *Puertorriqueña Dominicana/*Born in the Bronx." The beginning verses suggest that she also means that she knows herself through how she is seen by both Puerto Ricans and white Americans as an excluded racialized Other. She is, accordingly, not *jíbara*, that is, a true Puerto Rican, because she is half Dominican and Black in a nation that avidly practices *blanqueamiento*, and therefore denies its affiliations with Dominicans: "*not* really *jíbara* ... *Ni Potorra pero si Potorra* too," that is, "not Puerto Rican but yes Puerto Rican." Nor is she considered to be from the United States because within the American racial classification system of binaries, she is the perpetual foreigner—she speaks Spanish as well as English with an accent, and she is Black: "*Not* really *hablando bien/But yet, not Gringa either.*"

In the remaining verses of the stanza, Estéves further elaborates the paradox of 'not neither,' and ultimately transposes it as she foregrounds her African identity that had previously been invisibilized by the U.S. mainland/island referencing. Using English and Spanish, she affirms that what infuses her expressivity, what gives her voice and moves her lips are neither solely the Latino or Anglo linguistic systems but another language, expressed through African rhythms. She evokes the *bomba*, a Puerto Rican genre derived from West Africa through the importation of slaves to the island. This genre is characterized by its mixture of music, such as the *conga* drum and percussion instruments, with dance and song. As an expression of spiritual resistance against the system of slavery, the *bomba* draws upon the call-and-response tradition.

Estéves further evokes a visual image of her African and *Taino* self—the authentic Puerto Rican—as she personifies the rosa wood, a tropical wood that is between light brown, pink/red and yellow in color. By arranging the adverb 'here' so that it is juxtaposed with the rosa wood image of her self dancing, she brings the 'there' of Africa nearer, to the 'here' of Puerto Rico and the U.S. mainland: "Rhythms of Rosa wood feet dancing Bomba/*Not even* here, *but* here, *y Conga*" (emphasis is mine). At this juncture it becomes clear that the entire poem is an antiphonal response, achieved through the repetitive conjunctions of 'but' and 'and' that deny the 'not': 'but,' 'but yet,' 'but here,' 'but I am,' 'but yes,' and 'and we are.' The call and response culminates in the poet's transfiguration into a plural identity (*somos* or 'we are'), thereby claiming to all of those who locate her on the outside that she is constituted by multiple identities: "Yet not being, *pero soy,* and not really/*Y somos, y cómo somos?*"

Nuyorican scholar Miriam Jiménez Román pluralizes Puerto Rican women's identities in a manner that resonates with Sandra María Estéves' negation of her bounded identity and affirmation of her African identity as integral to *mestizaje*. In her partially autobiographical essay "*Allá y Acá*: Locating Puerto Ricans in the Diaspora(s)," this diasporan scholar draws upon the devices of personal anecdote and concreteness (the researched phenomenon) as well as the vocative device of tone as the principal vehicles for critiquing dominant versions of Puerto Rican *mestizaje/mulatez*. Jiménez Román begins with the description of her meeting with the director of a women's organization on the island. Jiménez Román states when she wanted to share her research on race and racism, the director dismissed her work, assuring her that *"aquí eso no es un problema"*: "this is not a problem *here*" (emphasis is mine), and that she should not impose *"las cosas de allá acá"*: "the things from *there here*" (my emphasis). She goes on to state the dissonance she experiences as she notes that the director has used research on women from the U.S. mainland, based on white women's experiences, and that women of color on the island had been obliged to form their own organizations.

Jiménez Román then turns from personal anecdote to the use of concreteness through an articulation of what she calls her dismissed research. She affirms that the entrenchment of Latin American exceptionalism that Puerto Ricans have pervasively disseminated has led to the alignment of their identity with nationalism, Hispanicity, and Eurocentrism, manifested as both denial and silence about the fact that "over ninety-five percent of the diaspora from Africa ended up in Latin America and the Caribbean" (2002). With these facts, she dispels the widely touted beliefs that Puerto Ricans learn about racism "there," that is, "Nuyoricans were 'infected' with las ideas de *allá*" since on the island, racial unification or *mestizaje* has been achieved. Miriam Jiménéz Román further uses her racial-ethnic boundedness to critique the bipolar system of race on the U.S. mainland that funnels Puerto Ricans into the categories of white or Black. For this scholar, racial identity cannot be conceived as a trading on the two monolithic national identities of *acá y allá*, that is, of being Puerto Rican or being a white American. She conceives her own racial identity instead as the experience of dissonance and of boundedness *"tanto acá como allá"* (both here and there), with expressions such as "good hair, bad hair" being heard in both Spanish and English in both places. As Jiménez Román gives to understand, the colonized has become the colonizer.

In the last part of the essay, Jiménez Román uses tone as the primary poetic/mantic device for fracturing the spatial identity of Puerto Ricans further. Turning from scholarly researched analysis to poetic language, she reframes her life and enjoins others on the island to do the same. She enjoins Puerto Ricans on the mainland and on the island to read the rubric of *mestizaje/mulatez* not as white and American, but as Black and African. She states: "Whether or not we are identifiably carriers of the content's genes, Africa is part of us-individually and as a nation." In the poem that closes the essay, Jiménez Román relocates the 'there' of Africa to the 'here' of Latin America, emphasizing the embeddedness of Africa in the island of

Puerto Rico. Through the alliterative emphasis on the word "Africa," she intensifies the changed experience of identity. In what follows, I cite some of these closing verses:

> Africa lives among Bolivia's Aymara-speaking Blacks, descendents of the Potosí miners who enriched the Spanish coffers during the earliest years of the colonial Conquest.
> Africa lives in the tango—born in the Black ghettos of Buenos Aires.
> And "Africa, of course, lives in Puerto Rico—*este pedacito de tierra* which, proportionately, received one thousand times as many Africans as did the United States!"

CONCLUSION

I began this chapter by developing an analytical framework of spatial identity, derived from humanistic geography, in order to illustrate the embodied and praxis-oriented component of knowledge and identity. An analysis of spatial identities makes clear that identities are never straightforward or transparent. Our lived experiences help us to form an interpretation of our selves and our social world. But the knowledge derived from these experiences is subject to error, because we are limited by our very situatedness. Nonetheless, the organization and reorganization of identity and meaning are the principal acts that human beings carry out. We do so through our metaphorical pliability, our openness to the world that we engage at the level of the gestural body and at the level of the word gesture. When examining relationally embodied (emotional) experiences against the range of elements constituting the context, the authors examined here were able to discover salient patterns of meaning that disrupted their previous understandings and perspectives. The relational analysis of contextual elements included, for example, viewing family histories in the light of national histories and myths, or examining social interactions, beliefs, and ideologies in the context of a variety of interconnected historicalities and spatialities. In the process, they also created the potential for seeking and locating themselves within new communities of accountability.

By analyzing how these scholars, theorists, and cultural workers interweave their researched colonialist histories of *mestizaje/mulatez* with their hermeneutical phenomenological descriptions of lived *mestizaje/mulatez*, I hope to have illuminated the dialectical processes that the work of discovering identities entails. I also hope to have shown that by virtue of their particular location, feminists working within the traditions of *mestizaje/mulatez* have been forced into situations of boundedness—a fearful event, a dire physical/psychical illness, a physical dislocation necessary for survival—that afforded them the opportunity to examine anew the habitual and taken for granted identity and perceptual practices by which they have been defined. Their conscious experience subsequently allowed them to produce word gestures, not as arbitrary inventions, but rather as metaphorical organic expressions of their locatedness in the world. Their cultural expressions, moreover, facilitated their reconfiguration of the postural body.

From a postpositivist realist perspective, it is pertinent to consider if the reconfigured identities of Anzaldúa, Estéves, and Jiménez Román should be deemed more accurate interpretations than those they had previously internalized. It is also worthwhile questioning if these authors were justified in dismantling previously held identities, insofar as they subsequently came to view them as byproducts of processes of structural power related to nation-building. To the extent that their newly developed interpretations continue to provide for each writer a coherent explanation of their future experiences across the course of their lives, the answer will be in the affirmative (Wilkerson 2000, 265). It would also be in the affirmative if their new interpretations can mesh with explanations of others similarly situated within a historical tradition. Judging from the cohesiveness of thought among these writers and other feminists writers and artists working within the *nuyorican* and *chicana* traditions throughout the last decades of the twentieth century, the spatial identities these writers have constructed through the cultivation of spatial metaphors have facilitated their achievement of a more coherent identity. It has also allowed them to achieve their sociality—their capacity to develop their own meanings of place. Their labor to reconstruct their identities has in turn afforded them a shared understanding of the structural and causal linkages between imposed identities and unequal access to power and resources, the first step in the forging of a collective identity politics.

CHAPTER 6

Constructing Identity(ies) through *lo Cotidiano* ('Everyday Practice'): A Postpositivist Realist Approach to Popular Spatial Traditions in Amalia Mesa-Bains' *Domesticana* Aesthetic, Ada María Isasi-Díaz's *Mujerista* Theology, and Ana Castillo's *So Far from God*[1]

INTRODUCTION

In the previous chapter, I examined *mestizaje/mulatez* as ambivalent and hybrid spatialized embodied configurations. Through radical, embodied reflection, Anzaldúa, Estéves, and Jiménez Román discover that their race-gendered identities have been articulated as socio-symbolic spatial sites, reflective of social anxieties around contact and dispersion that are constitutive of the practices of nation building. In this chapter, I explore social practices of Latina *mestizaje* that pertain to Latina popular geography, a subfield of Human Geography that attends to the reproduction of social identity through the cultural and social activities that people undertake in everyday life.[2] I examine manifestations of popularized space in the theories of Amalia Mesa-Bains (1998, 2003) and Ada María Isasi-Díaz (2004a; 2004b), as well in Ana Castillo's novel *So Far from God* (1994). I argue that these scholars and writers draw upon popularized conceptions of spatial identity in order to interrogate normative perceptions of Latinas and the social world of which they form a part as well as the effects of such perceptions on their life chances and opportunities.

Given the condition of enforced migration that has relocated Latinas/
os within U.S. boundaries, popular conceptualizations of spaces of identity are not rooted in particular places. Rather, space is conceived as fluid
and non-identical, as are the identities that people conceptualize as they
become mobilized within space. Herein, popular representations of spatialized *mestizaje/mulatez* focus on space as a materialization of the
embodied self, imbued with memory, value, and meaning, that evolves
as those that migrate come into contact with new cultural spatial practices. I argue that feminists of *mestizaje/mulatez* interrogate, through
embodied practices of the popular spatial, their understandings of rationality, grounded in Western modernity, that have proven to be contradictory with regard to its emancipatory hegemony.

I begin my analysis below with a somewhat protracted discussion
of cultural relativism. I thus hope to anticipate possible objections to
my attempt to develop a postpositivist realist analysis of texts ani-
mated by traditions that mix a linear progression of events, characteristic of literary realism, with elements pertaining to the supernatural
and the magico-religious. An initial aim here is to call attention to
how cultural incommensurability locates the Western (feminist)
reader problematically as reader of these texts. It is worthwhile underscoring here, as I did in chapter 2 of this study with respect to womanist theories and texts, that the epistemological resources that
identities provide are potentially threatened when they are examined
by scholars that pertain to a racial group that has exploited or colonized the culture under examination (51).

Careful consideration of the reader's own taken for granted assumptions with regards to rational deliberation—and that would include the
explanations of the social and natural world as well as relevant evidence—are always grounded in a particular historical and spatial context. This task of careful consideration poses particular challenges,
given that our assumptions are masked behind the façade of what 'we'
deem to be universal or objective truth in the current historical moment.
It is this context of our own Eurocentric normative assumptions that
the academy has as its legacy and practice with regard to rationality—
understood as knowledge achieved from a distance—that I bring to
center stage, in order to examine it for the validity of its application.
Such a task is necessary, that is, if we are to be serious about engaging
social/cultural identity, with its whole range of attachments to the particularities of cultural traditions, beliefs, and practices, as a legitimate
source and locus of both particular and generalizable knowledge.

In my discussion, I locate postpositivist realist interrogations of
cultural difference within broader debates taking place among

postcolonial feminist and transnational feminist scholars around the disjunctures between social and cultural practices pertaining to traditional and modern societies. I argue that while knowledge practices derived from any culture are beset with social mystifications, human agents acting within the parameters of their cultural context engage culturally specific processes, in conjunction with others who are similarly located on the hermeneutical horizon, to clarify competing systems of rationality.

A second equally important aim of this preliminary discussion of cultural alterity is to provide a frame of reference for my subsequent critical examination of a body of feminist theories and narrative in this chapter, pertaining to the traditions of feminist *mestizaje/mulatez*. The concepts of disjunctive and multitemporal heterogeneities, as I will show below, help to illuminate the problems that cultural difference poses for subaltern communities. Following this discussion, I draw upon the works of Amalia Mesa-Bains and Ada María Isasi-Díaz to provide a critical review of the history and cultural representations of popular cultural geography within the cultural traditions of *mestizaje/mulatez*. I then analyze how renowned *Chicana* novelist, Ana Castillo, embeds these popular spatial traditions within her narrative, *So Far from God*. I trace the popular spatialized contexts of the female characters within this novel as perspectival interventions, ones that allow for different temporalities to encounter one another. Such interventions serve as sites where the various female characters may become cognizant of different modes of perception and consciousness, and be given the opportunity to ascertain whether those derived from their own culture may prove more useful for their own life options and community survival than those derived from western paradigms.

POSTCOLONIAL AND TRANSNATIONAL FEMINISMS AND THE PROBLEM OF CULTURAL AND MORAL RELATIVISM

Popular cultural expressions that develop out of the syncretic African, indigenous and Anglo cultures of *mestizaje/mulatez* challenge the normative scientific and epistemological frameworks that 'we' in Eurocentric cultures use to develop reasonable and justifiable claims about what constitutes factual, objective knowledge. This is because they make salient the nature and the conditions of knowledge acquisition not as a universal phenomenon, but as context dependent. In other words, knowledge making transpires in relation to specific knowers. Since the significant wane of universalist systems of interpretations used to propose a commonality of thought underlying cultural representations of difference in the last decades due to an increased understanding of cultural difference, theories of relativism, admitting of a wide degree of variation, have taken hold. From fields as various as Anthropology, Ethnology, History, Philosophy, Science, Literary Studies/Cultural studies, scholars have increasingly worked to develop complex theories that explain culturally different conceptualizations of models of thought and morality. Indeed, Lindsay Waters affirms that the problem of cultural incommensurability is arguably "one of the principal ideas for intellectuals and academics in the last thirty-five years" (2001, 135).

The strong relativist position, emblematic of the postmodernists, admits differences in knowledge validation processes and valuation but disallows commonalities. On this view, there is no single history or a single rationality model, but histories and rationalities, whereby all competing claims are approximations that are enabled and constrained by the standards of the culture from which they originate with no one claim being considered truer than the other. Just as knowledge-enhancing descriptions can vary from one social and cultural context to another, so can moral characteristics of actions.

In the West, such a view can result in the adoption of a type of pluralism that has been described as "vulgar relativism" by Bernard Williams and the "incorrigibility thesis" by Charles Taylor (1985, 219; 1985, 123).[3] Such descriptors point to a view of cultural difference that posits either a cross-cultural engagement that ignores the conditions of asymmetries of power between cultures while at the same time demanding exigency to rules based on Western procedural principles, or the impossibility of adjudicating at any level between competing discourses. Cultural differences with regard to knowledge practices and production are simply deemed incommensurable, although each culture is to respect the practices of the other.

On this view of benign toleration, scholars in the West will admit that it is possible to accurately judge the beliefs and values of other cultures based on their own values and perspectives, but still refuse to acknowledge the pertinence of their intellectual modes of inquiry and moral judgments to 'ours.' In effect, we disallow an interference with our own knowledge-making procedures, thereby refusing a relationship across differences based on an accordance of equal status. We are interested in the Other to the extent that we might want to read about, or travel to the culture of the Other, perhaps even occasionally use our scholarship to defend injustices suffered by the Other, but our interests stop at the point in which our everyday practices and worldviews might have to be altered by their perspectives (Schutte 2000, 54–55).

Postcolonial thought in general, including its specific feminist expressions, focuses on the investigation into power relations within various contexts. This body of theory has developed a critique of dominant notions of cultural alterity, providing different visions of and solutions for the relation between the particular and the universal. Postcolonial theories articulate cultural difference in terms of different but interconnecting temporalities. Bhabba speaks of a "multi-accentual temporality" of cultural meaning that "unsettles the liberal ethic of tolerance and the pluralist framework of multiculturalism" (2004, 254). In a 2004 lecture at the Universidad Autónoma Metropolitana (UAM) in Mexico City, liberation philosopher Enrique Dussel offered a positive valorization of difference that he calls the "transmodern."

The concept of the transmodern foregrounds the differentiated, racial, ethnic, gendered cultural Other, both within and across nations. It speaks from a distinct space and time of transformative exteriority, that of the borderlands, and is capable of providing solutions to problems produced by its various cultural dominants. Herein, the Other does not exist in a primitive time, but an 'other' time, spatialized as exterior, that evolves in its inevitable contact with the linear format of European and North American modernity. The transmodern project is liberative, privileging a process that positively valorizes the subalatern collectivity's perspectives and understandings, and uses them to critique dominance within and across temporalities of cultural difference. Postcolonial critic Néstor García Canclini, for his part, coins the term "multitemporal heterogeneity" to indicate the superimposition of temporalities within Latin American societies. The merging of temporalities, he argues, establishes a dynamic link between traditional and modern cultures, while signaling the ongoing relevance of indigenous, colonial, and postcolonial cultural sediments in contemporary society (1995, 46–47).

Dipesh Chakrabarty, is a final and important example. He affirms a coexistence of past time with the present, producing a disjunctive temporality in the present. The only way that another culture from a remote time and space is rendered fully human and intelligible to us is, he posits, if and when we can treat it as if it were our contemporary. The making of history must acknowledge "a plurality of times existing together, a disjuncture of the present with itself" (2000, 109). Chakrabarty uses the metaphor of "time-knots" to provide a visual conceptualization of heterogeneous entangled temporalities that coexist in a shared present. These time-knots are joints of various kinds "from the complex formation of knuckles on our fingers to the joints on a bamboo-stick." Because we are situated within these time-knots, or chronology, Chakrabary goes on to say, "we can can undertake the exercise of straightening out, as it were, some part of the knot"(112). He thus argues that the present is not contemporaneous with itself, but is in some senses "out of joint," with the past, never really remaining purely dead to the present (113).

The *quipu* is a quintessential exemplar of the time-knot, as shown on the front cover of this book. The *quipu*, made out of knotted cord, is an Andean information storage or recording device that dates back to a half millennium before the Inka expansion, the period spanning 1400–1533 (Saloman 2004, 111). Still in use as a communication system during the first period of the *Conquista*, the *quipu* was believed by Spanish chroniclers to deploy standardized patterns of cord designs, which functioned to record important official events much like other recording tools utilized in any imperialist state, including calendars, censuses, inventories, and royal chronicles. Yet, according to *The Cord Keepers,* the pathbreaking work of ethnologist Frank Saloman, such cords were not just chronologies, but also spatialized histories that were to hold together different narrative sites. They were anchored in the particular and the local, that is, they retold narratives that were indexical, indicating how given events were experienced differently in particular places.

While states demanded comparable accounts of different parts comprising the social through standardized practices of their record keepers, the local *quipu* provided for more flexibility, allowing the record keeper the ability to mark the local event as unique. Where the lack of comparability ensued, ambiguity could be resolved or accounted for through face-to-face encounters within the community, since the use of the *quipu* was always within the local context and in this sense served as "chrontopographs" of particular social domains (2002, 16). The different time-knots are not discarded, but rather remain as part of the overarching pattern of the *quipu* record. This Mesoamerican cultural artifact thus points to the human dialectic that holds in a state of tension the particular and the universal, the past and the present.

Postcolonial and transnational feminists have weighed in on and contributed significantly to perspectives on cultural otherness, seeking solutions to the problems that otherness poses for feminist solidarity across differences. With its critical attention to the ways in which women's lives are located within asymmetrical axes of power, this important body of work seeks to illuminate how the project of modernity, with its various conceptualizations of rationality and objectivity, is constitutive of gender and sexual difference. Postcolonial and transnational feminists seek to examine how modernity instantiates itself by creating a necessary contrast between modernity and its 'Other': the feminine and the primitive, racialized Other. They further interrogate how the feminine, situated within different, intersecting, and at times, overlapping temporalities, is itself split and fragmented, a fact that threatens group solidarity based on gender (Felski 2000; Harding 2008). Critical attention is oriented toward unpacking normative academic assumptions such as the concept of neutrality or objectivity of knowledge, which assumes the separation of the subject and object of knowledge, and how such assumptions marginalize and exclude women from the spaces of modernity.

Given the disjunctiveness of different modernities, postcolonialist feminist readings focus on the different effects that such exclusionary practices have on different communities of women. Postcolonial and transnational feminist theorists have sought a range of solutions that cover the full continuum of absolute commensurability to absolute incommensurability. Yet, as Rita Felski notes, there continues to exist "an ongoing tension between the particular and the general, between the 'thick description' of cultural practices that remains faithful to how particular individuals see themselves, and the 'big picture' of transnational structures of inequality that requires a more distanced perspective" (2000, 126–27). Postcolonial and transnational feminists, such as Chandra Talpade Mohanty, (2004) and Gayatri Spivak (1988), privilege localities and micro-narratives as necessary albeit insufficient sites for making difference salient so that differences in power, knowledge, and identity can be better understood cross-culturally. They claim, additionally, that racial, ethnic differences fragment gender as a category of affiliation and politics. Other postcolonial feminists, such as Ien Ang, (1995), eschew feminist theories that seek to assimilate the Other by subsuming it within a transnational feminist community.[4]

With regard to the cultural context of Latinas/os, Latina feminist philosopher Ofelia Schutte analyzes the ethical and pragmatic dilemmas of incommensurability posed by disjunctive temporalities in her analyses of Latina/o migration. Taking one step further García Canclini's notion of multitemporal heterogeneity, she notes that when culturally situated actors become dislocated from their cultures due to processes of colonization or globalization, such as the material displacement and relocation of Latin Americans within U.S. boundaries, this additional mixing of temporalities produces new mergings and discontinuities. The meshing of temporalities in turn engenders innovative systems of relatively mixed cognitions as well as the retention of distinct cognition systems. The result is a shift in disjunctive temporalities, one that changes the relation between the self and the world, "allowing for the recognition of alterity both inside and outside the self" (2000, 51).

A postpositivist realist approach to cultural identity and difference resonates with postcolonial feminist critiques of pluralist conceptions of rationality, questioning the regulative and constraining forces governing the inclusion or exclusion of identities constituted as Other, based on whether or not the perspectives derived from the Other's knowledge cohere with narrative time frames of the West. Postpositivist realism's peculiar points of tension with postcolonialist approaches to identity hinge on the solutions it offers to hybridity. Postpositivist realism is aligned with the forms of postcolonial thought that steer clear from celebrations of hybridity, viewing it neither as a demonstration of achieved transgression of the minoritarian fractured identity, nor as a universal manifestation of the internal fracturing identities in which we all participate within a postmodern world, thereby cancelling out difference.

Postpositivist realism acknowledges social/cultural difference as incommensurable difference yet suggests at the same time that there is a possibility, through de-centered cross-cultural comparative analyses of context-specific social practices, to understand cultural practices that are different, even incompatible with 'ours,' thereby widening the scope of each culture's moral and epistemological vision. On this view, knowledge, while context dependent, is not entirely subjective, nor is it a transparent representation of intrinsic features of our or other's reality.

Since objective knowledge is driven by human agents who construct their understanding, their decision-making procedures, and their actions within the parameters of a social location and cultural context that they inherit, their social practices as well as the beliefs upon which they are legitimized, however unusual they may appear to be relative to 'ours,' have a coherence in terms of the larger system of social practices in which they are produced. As such, they can be analyzed in terms of the adequacy of the justificatory claims of the historical agent, based on the values and beliefs that motivate such processes, including the wellbeing of the agent and her community. I do not want to give to understand here that knowledge is a matter of group consensus. By 'cohere,' rather, I mean that within the context of lived reality, the theories that people construct are rational insofar as they are informed by a whole constellation of epistemic commitments that have been crystallized within temporal spatial relations.

A realist perspective of rational, objective knowledge and human agency does not separate the realm of hard facts from values but rather acknowledges that values are centrally involved in what determines a fact. Values can be reasoned; they contain objective qualities, and are integral to the process of knowing (Harris 2005; Putnam 2002). On this view, social practices and beliefs motivate and accompany the actions of social agents within their own context and location and are therefore open to us for analysis and cross-cultural comparative evaluation, that is, to be judged in terms of the evidence and arguments they provide. Although there is no ideal epistemic agent, given that people's actions fall short of an ideal rationality due to human limitations, that should not be a reason for giving up on the possibility of trying to ascertain knowledge about different cultures within a shared social world. Nor should it be a reason for questioning the cultural assumptions of a given agent, even though, as Satya Mohanty points out, they might not be fully intelligible to us (1997, 136).

This realist view of objective knowledge does not limit its conception of reason and reasonable behavior to a strict correlation with a hyperrationality, based on Enlightenment conceptions, but rather conceptualizes rationality as more broadly inclusive of an array of cultural assumptions and practices as well as values and epistemic commitments that it hopes to clarify and interrogate. For example, as Mohanty points out, in his discussion of Peter Winch's analysis of the Zande practice of magic and ritual, it would be a distortion to simply deem the magical practices of the Zande as an antithesis to the Western category of science. Since we have no category or practice of knowledge practice that resembles Zande magic, it becomes incumbent upon us, if we desire a greater understanding of the Other, to make sense of their practices and beliefs as 'truth-making.' We can do so by examining the resonance of the practice of magic with the broader experiences, discourses, habits, and practices that inform the entire cultural context of the Zande to see how it sheds light on these other elements and how these other elements shed light on the context so as to present a logical consistence. In this manner, we are better able to grasp a different rationality that lies outside our own binary oppositions, for example, between science and non-science (1997, 133–34).

By recognizing that the cultural Other, in this time or in past time, is endowed, as we are, with what Mohanty calls "self-aware historical agency," it becomes possible to see commonalities across our differences, to grant the Other an intelligibility and a reason. This first step is necessary because it then allows for the second and third steps. The second step entails the evaluative judgment of the rationality of the Other, including positing connections, examining the organization of specific actions into the overarching cultural system of which the historical agent forms part as a way of gleaning how decisions and practices are driven by reflection. Clearly such self-reflective processes are not always empirically observable. However, when they are examined against the overall context, such processes can be rendered intelligible.[5]

A third step entails developing cross-cultural hermeneutical specifications of commonalities and differences in order to rupture the parochial underpinnings of our/their distinct rationalities to posit a radical multiculturality in the present. The objective of such a pursuit, as Chakrabarty states, is to release into the space occupied by particular European histories normative and theoretical thought processes enshrined in other existing life practices and their archives. For it is only in this way that we can create plural normative horizons specific to our existence and relevant to the examination of our lives (2000, 20).

With such a process in place, it becomes possible to be more nuanced and less absolutist in cross-cultural comparison for the purpose of achieving cross-cultural interchange and even solidarity. For example, it becomes possible to acknowledge that there are some areas of commensurability across domains of difference, while there are also at the same time, areas of conflict and incompatibility. Herein, the goal would not be to eliminate difference through cultural suppression or enforced assimilation of other schemas of rationality. Nor would it be to embrace cultural pluralism only in those areas of difference that seem to better fit within our overall rationality. Rather, the aim would be to hold different memories and cultural inheritances together, in order to develop a potential for mutual interrogation, or, at the very least, to acknowledge that there might be some points at which contradictory cultural viewpoints could be sustained. The strengths of each perspective could be brought together to form a bridge of understanding, action, and mutual benefit.

This type of work however, also requires that we acknowledge that not all perspectives and beliefs can be as easily mapped as others along a continuum toward commensurability, even when we have effectively undertaken an evaluation that has clarified the rational schemas informing the actions of the cultural Other. Chakrabarty exemplifies the problem of commensurability in his critique of historian Ranajit

Guha's study of the Santals. After examining the differences between Guha's historical depiction of the anti-British uprising of the Santals in 1855 and the Santal's leader's religious explanation, Chakrabarty affirms that there may not be "a third voice that can assimilate the two different voices" (2000, 108).

Given such incommensurability, it becomes necessary to stay with the heterogeneity of the present moment, one that refuses to anthropologize, as Guha the historian does, the Santal people's beliefs in God's instigation of the uprising in order to render their acts and rational justifications intelligible to him.[6] By "staying with the heterogeneity of the present moment," it is possible to look at cultures different from our own as "illuminating possibilities for our own lifeworlds" (112). Keeping this consideration in mind, I now turn to an introduction of Latina popular geography, one that maps out in spatial as well as temporal terms the instantiation of heterogeneous, overlapping non-identical temporalities of *mestizaje/mulatez*, and how they are experienced, represented, and theorized by selected Latina artists, scholars/theologians, and writers.

POPULAR GEOGRAPHY: *DOMESTICANA* AND POPULAR RELIGIOSITY AS SPATIAL PRACTICES

The purpose of the following overview is to bring into purview the submerged and silenced disjunctive temporalities of Latina *mestizaje/mulatez*, represent them as containing a coherent rational view of the world, and retrace the processes that Latina feminists have undertaken to develop and verify their truth claims as they compare their theory-mediated knowledge against other empirical and historical accounts. While Mesa-Bains and Isasi-Díaz provide the frameworks for theorizing popular spatial traditions as a composite set of cultural and rational patterns that inform and give coherence to the lives and values of Latinas, novelist Ana Castillo draws from the repository of these traditions to construct an overarching spatialized context in which she immerses her characters, endowing them with the capacity to use popular traditions, constituted by shared mental constructions, memories, and spaces, as resources of objective knowledge.

Chicana artist and scholar Amalia Mesa-Bains introduced the notion of *domesticana* as a salient cultural expression of feminist *mestizaje*, which she in turn links to Tomás Ybarra-Frausto's conceptualization of *rasquachismo*. A borderlands anti-elitist *chicana/o* aesthetic of irreverence and cultural innovation, *rasquachismo* serves as a resource for cultural affirmation and survival within the context of enforced migration brought about by colonizing, neo-colonizing, and transnational economic processes. *Chicano* cultural workers have developed artistic forms pertaining to a *rasquache* sensibility that are both multicultural and syncretic. They have constructed their works out of the everyday material of life, attempting to make the most out of the least. Herein, these artists exemplify the folk philosophy encapsulated in the expression "*haciendo de tripas corazón*," or 'making slippers out of sow's ears' (Ybarra-Frausto 2003). The materials that are privileged within this artistic sensibility include cast-off remnants and discarded, recycled materials, such as broken mirrors, old tires, and plastic containers. The *rasquache* style is innovative and bold in its staging of the clashing, dissonant encounters between the traditions of a Mexican past from which *Chicanas/os* have been dislocated and cultural elements and objects pertaining to the new spaces and cultures they inhabit.

Domesticana is a *mestiza* feminist aesthetic born out of a *rasquache* sensibility. This feminist aesthetic uses the domestic spaces to which *Chicanas* have been historically relegated to interrogate the tensions such spaces hold as sites of heteropatriarchal violence and domination intrinsic to the community as well as sites of power and contestation against Anglo and *Chicano* heteropatriarchies. *Domesticana* is derived from the *Chicana* lived experience in the so-called private female spaces of home and neighborhood. It grows out of processes of remembering and recording family history and spirituality. The various everyday practices constituting *domesticana* reelaborate domestic rituals, merging glamour, the sacred, and personal style with an ultimate aim to (re)construct histories and identities from a new positionality. It is a set of cultural expressions that function to defiantly assert what is valuable. Using paradox, satire, and humor, *domesticana* ruptures Eurocentric forms of thought that separate the public and private, past and present, and the natural and the supernatural. Within the indigenous and Africanist worldviews comprising *mestizaje/mulatez*, popular traditions carried out in the home, neighborhood, and community merge the world of the mundane with the realm of the supernatural. Within d*omesticana* cultural work as in everyday life, there is no clear demarcation between the world of the living and the dead, the past and the present (Mesa-Bains 2003, 302–08).

Artistic methods of *domesticana* grew organically out of domestic practices of reliquary construction passed on intergenerationally from mother to daughter, including the home altar and yard shrine, practices that are integral to familial spiritual devotion and that serve as a feminine counterpart to masculine rituals identified with official forms of Catholicism (303–04). The home altar, an ongoing storage and recording technology, is composed of decorative elements including devotional icons and memorabilia, as well as formal elements, such as pictures or carvings of saints, family mementos, and various offerings or *ofrendas*. The image of the brown *Virgin of Guadalupe* commonly appears as a central icon in the home altar, indicating women's role as spiritual leader (304). All of these constructions tend to be highly contextualized and temporary or makeshift, indicating the impermanence of the very spaces of identity that *Chicanas* inhabit. In the case of both the altar and the yard shrine, the components constituting these constructions function as a narrative site that tells personal, family, and communal histories from a new location. Mesa-Bains asserts that the assemblage is a *domesticana* methodology that offers a new way of seeing and understanding the self and the community from a different positionality (304).

Other domestic practices of the popular sacred include the enactment of ceremonies within various communal pageants and spectacles, staged within the spaces of neighborhood and community, as well as the cultivation of traditions pertaining to the healing arts. Within official Christianity, as exercised during the Conquest and colonialism, pageantry and spectacle constituted privileged forms of acculturation of indigenous peoples and were used as subjugating tools. In the *domesticana* tradition, there is a parodic, subversive element introduced, one that opens up the possibility for the critique of gender, race, and class subjugation that such official events aimed to reproduce. Ceremonies, such as those celebrated through traditions of the *Día de los muertos*, ('Days of the Dead'), are what Mesa-Bains calls a "spatial memorializing," the practice *Chicanas/os* use to reestablish family histories that have been lost, not only through cultural/spatial dislocation from the spaces where those histories might be remembered, but also through the institutional processes of education and public life in the new, Anglo spaces they inhabit. In the process, they subvert the very institutions that had exploited them. In this way, such processions are transgressive, and have pragmatic ends—to reclaim and reconstitute the spaces they have come to inhabit, marking them as their own (Mesa-Bains 1998).

Domesticana also includes the practice of the homeopathic arts, often combined with popular religious practices (Mesa-Bains 2003, 304). These arts constitute a folk medicinal practice, passed on intergenerationally from older women to younger women through the generations, that views illness and healing not as processes that takes place solely in the body, as do Western medical practices, but as ones that are dependent upon mental and spiritual components of the self as well. The body does not exist separately from the mind and the spirit. The spiritual cleansings or *limpias* conducted by faith healers or *curanderas* is an example of this art, which, while dating back to pre-Hispanic (Aztec and Mayan) cultures, incorporates Catholic religious icons, prayers, and ceremony as well as homeopathic practices.

These traditional forms of the popular sacred combine in *Chicana/o* cultural works, paradoxically, with feminine glamour and hyperfeminization, as well as with other contemporary Anglo cultural elements. Artists cultivating *domesticana* bring together in their work "pop culture discards, remnants of party materials, jewelry, kitchenware, toiletries, saints, holy cards, and *milagros* (toy doll limbs) in combined and recombined arrangements that reflect a shattered glamour" (307). This cultural repository critiques existing histories as well as reflects the reconstitution of erased histories, identities, and modes of inquiry within shifting national and diasporic contexts. It thus facilitates the emergence of new everyday practices, including language, cultural habits, and traditions, as well as new economic projects, that develop as a by-product of these cultural practices.

Popular Religiosity, Latina/o Theology, and Mujerista Theology

Latina/o liberation theologians have also taken as central to their theology the traditions of the popular sacred, noting that such traditions are intrinsic to the everyday lived experiences of Latinas/os. Roberto Goizueta thus affirms that the popular sacred traditions are the constitutive mechanisms by which Latinos shape and reproduce their identity (Goizueta 1995). Feminist scholars working within Latina liberation theological traditions of *mujerista* theology, a liberation praxis that privileges the lived experience of Latinas as a resource for their theology, further develop the notion of contextualized knowledge by bridging it with the concepts of *mestizaje/mulatez* and '*lo cotidiano*" or everyday life.[7] Ada María Isasi-Díaz, a liberation theologian and ethicist of Cuban ancestry, and a political refugee who has been relocated to the United States since 1960, is the progenitor of this branch of Latina theology. *Mujerista* theology centers on embodied *mestizaje/mulatez* as a resource and a practice for gaining knowledge about the context that Latinas share, while acknowledging commonalities and differences among Latina/o communities (Isasi-Díaz 2004a, 44–45). For Isasi-Díaz, the everyday practice of *mestizaje/mulatez* forms the basis of 1) the real lived or enfleshed context of living between at least two cultures and racial economies;

2) a paradigm, that is, a way of representing the lived contexts, and 3) a hermeneutical tool, that is, a way of interpreting lived contexts. In these capacities, *mestizaje/mulatez* functions to inform, motivate, and justify the contextualized practices of '*lo cotidiano*,' or daily life (2004a, 195).[8]

As noted by Isasi-Díaz, popular religious practices informing daily life are palpable not just within Mexican culture, but also within the various ethnicities comprising *latinidad,* and are the most poignant expression of *lo cotidiano.* Popular religiosity is conceived as a syncretic mixing of Eurocentric (Catholic and Protestant) practices with indigenous and African magico-religious ones, and is therefore a paradigmatic expression of *mestizaje/mulatez.* Popular religiosity within a *mujerista* perpspective, with its repository of visual images, ritualized spectacles, and ceremonies, privileges the daily lived experiences of Latina women as a resource for theological reflection as well as epistemological and justification practices. I define *lo cotidiano* within this perspective as a set of reflected-upon, everyday practices undertaken by Latinas for the purpose of challenging the public/private dichotomy that contains the *mestiza/mulata* within Latino and U.S. nations as well as within official Anglo and Latina/o theologies. These popular traditions provide a hermeneutical lens through which grassroots Latinas apprehend reality, enact daily life within the social realm, and make judgments about values and norms imposed upon them by social and religious structures. Their co-participation in these traditions allow Latinas to use the lived, embodied experience of *mestizaje/mulatez* as the context from within which they explain who they are, function within the world, and transform dominant forms of knowledge.

As Isasi-Díaz affirms, *mujerista* theology is a form of critical reflection on and contestation of socio-symbolic institutional systems, beginning with official, hierarchical forms of Catholicism. These symbolic systems impose powerful conceptions of social existence, endowing them with a facticity that was subsequently used to legitimate the *Conquista,* and to acculturate as well as maintain power over the conquered (2004a, 62–65). Nonetheless, as Isasi-Díaz affirms, real enculturation of Hispanic peoples, that is, the process of personalizing the values and beliefs of the conquerors, did not take place. What did develop was a culturization of Christianity. Herein, the symbols and rituals of Christianity took root within the culture of the Americas, where they could now be used along with the repository of traditional practices pertaining to indigenous and African cultures, to construct new meanings (62–64). Within the lived experiences of

Latinas, then, from a *mujerista* theology perspective, there is a juxtaposition or overlapping of socio-symbolic systems and temporalities that gives rise to a "reconceptualization of what is rational," temporalities that go beyond linear logic to include non-Western, pre-Hispanic expressions that form part of the broader rational schemes that frame Latina lives (2004b, 184).

From a *mujerista* theological perspective, the use of such systems by Latinas to achieve more accurate and liberatory knowledge begins with a *praxis*, that is, a critical reflective action that entails examining the historical realities of Latinas. Committed to the liberation of Latinas, a *mujerista* praxis proceeds with 1) an analysis of the impact of structures and ideologies of racism, sexism, and classism on Latinas and the community of which Latinas form part, including the structures and ideologies of the Church; 2) critical self-reflection on the part of each individual comprising the community to understand one's complicity with systems of belief that reproduce structures of oppression; and 3) a process of hermeneutical rediscovery that facilitates social reorganization based on another reality and another rationality to which one must reconnect as part of a historicality of *mestizaje/mulatez*, according to the community's present social and political needs and priorities. The praxiological nature of *mujerista* theology ultimately opens up the possibility for a comparative cross-cultural engagement of a given community of Latinas with other Latina communities that are differentially situated, both nationally and diasporically (2004a, 52–61).

In the next section, I examine how Castillo develops characters that become aware of their immersion in competing and disjunctive rationalities. As they grapple with the particularities of disjunctive cultures, they use everyday popular spatial practices to gain clarity about their own partially conscious feelings and understandings. In doing so, they become better equipped to break out of the public-private dichotomies that contain them, and to construct frameworks that more adequately explain their identities and their social world. I begin with a sketch of the characters and plot summary, and then proceed to my analysis.

Domesticana *and the Popular Religious in* *Ana Castillo's* So Far from God

Castillo's novel represents a hybrid of genres: the *telenovela* or soap opera and a literary realist or historically linear narrative. Set in the early '90s in Tome, a small town in northern New Mexico, a space that embraces the histories of the Spanish, the Mexican, and the

Anglo, the plot centers on the life of Sofi, a *Chicana*, a mother, a farmer, the owner of a local butcher shop, and ultimately, a social activist and mother of saints. As she comes to terms with the deterioration of her marriage, the various calamities faced by her daughters, and ultimately, their deaths, she develops a new capacity or *facultad* to transform herself and her community.

The narrative action begins, however, with Sofi's confusion with regard to her social reality. Her husband's return to the familial home after a long hiatus sparks an identity crisis for Sofi. At the age of fifty-three, Sofi begins to reflect on her family life. Two decades earlier, her gambling husband, Domingo, had hocked her jewelry, sold the ten acres of land her parents had given them as a wedding present, and abandoned her, only to return twenty years later with an unchanged disposition, still calling her "silly Sofi"—even when, as she says, she has "been hanging the rumps of pigs and lambs and getting arthritis from the freezer and praying to God to give [her] the strength to do the best by [her] girls alone..." (1994, 111). Then, there are her four daughters, whose lives, guided by both earthly and supernatural powers, seem to be as misguided and more enigmatic than her own.

Esperanza (Hope), the eldest, majored in *Chicano* Studies in college and subsequently went on to get a Masters in Communication. When she wasn't studying, she participated with her boyfriend Rubén in *chicano* rituals at the Native American church, making love to him, and supporting him economically. She is the *Chicana* with the liberation ethic, who finds that within the *movimimiento* she is anything but liberated. Discovering that for Rubén, she is nothing more than "an unsuspecting symbol, like a staff or a tattle or medicine" (36), a belief that ultimately justifies his sexual and economic exploitation of her, she abandons her family and community. Her alignment with community politics shifts as she assimilates into U.S. culture. Esperanza acts upon what would appear to be a justified belief that she, among her siblings, is the most likely candidate for successful assimilation, given her education. She thus uses her 'hope' in social justice within an assimilated context, and becomes an overseas correspondent for the Gulf War. After months of having the status of "disappeared," and without much apparent action on behalf of the U.S. military or government to locate her, an observation that causes Sofi and Domingo to go to Washington three times to hold the authorities accountable, she is reported dead, even though her body is never recovered.

The second daughter, Caridad (Charity), was a hospital aide. She exercises her 'charity' by giving her body to anyone closely resemblings her husband Memo, who, shortly after their wedding, left her for another woman. The narrator highlights Caridad's sexuality, by stating that while the other female members in her family "all have the flat butt of the Pueblo blood undeniably circulating through their veins, Caridad had a somewhat pronounced ass that men were inclined to show their unappreciated appreciation for everywhere she went" (26) She is attacked one night and left for dead by the *malogra*, a monstrous and otherworldly phantom who strips her of her beauty and sensuality. Following a miraculous healing, Caridad goes to live with an ancient healer or *curandera* to learn of the arts of natural healing and channeling, eventually becoming regarded around the southwest as a legendary figure. During one holy week, she embarks on a pilgrimage inspired by the acts and deeds of the local saints, but never reaches her destination. She reappears, however, one year later, having miraculously survived the harsh wilderness of the region, and is herself hailed as a saint by her people. Soon thereafter, she, along with an ambiguous figure Esmeralda, jumps off the mesa of Sky City, the spiritual center of the Acomo people. The fates of these women bring to life the myth of the sacred sisters who, according to the Acomo Pueblo legends, created the earth in their own feminized image, and then flew off the mesa of Sky City to the earth below.

Fe (Faith), Sofi's third daughter,, has absolute faith in the American dream. She aspires to be perfect both in her bank job and in her construction of the American family, one that means repudiating the tradition of the extended family. Ashamed of her roots and her family relations, with the exception of Esperanza who Fe thinks has really made it as a journalist, Fe believes that if she works hard enough, she can escape second-class citizenship. Through her gaze, the reader sees the community and family as "so self-defeating, so unambitious, and superstitious" (29). She has the lightest skin tone of all of the sisters. She emblematizes the New Mexican practice of claiming pure Spanish ancestry. Her faith 'in the system' leads her to a job in a factory, Acme International, one that fabricated weapons for the Gulf War. Unbeknownst to her, the chemicals in the cleaning products are toxic, leading Fe to experience numerous physical maladies and, finally, and to suffer an untimely and premature death.

Finally, there is La Loca or "*La loca santa*" (the saintly fool). This youngest daughter apparently experiences an epileptic fit at the age of three and dies. Later, however, she awakens in her coffin as the funeral procession enters the local church. She then flies or levitates upward (the narrator is not clear on which), landing on the roof. Henceforth, she refuses to be around people, and stays at home—cultivating local and domestic rituals including playing the fiddle, caring for the horses and peacocks, and helping her mother and sisters through her intuitive knowledge of herbs, curative powers, and culinary talents. She also practices other domestic skills including sewing and caring for the animals. Finally, she performs abortions for her sisters even though she has no training in this or other skills. Though she allows no physical contact through the course of her life, she ultimately succumbs to AIDS.

It is La Loca who informs her mother that Esperanza had died. A lady in white who she saw at the irrigation ditch, and who had come to visit her since she was a child, told her so. Sofi is surprised because she had never told her daughters the story of "*llorona*" or wailing woman, often seen near water, because she never believed in this popular story/myth of *la llorona*, who was destined to suffer throughout eternity as a punishment from God for having drowned her children so that she could run away with her lover (160). In contrast to such negative depictions, Castillo portrays this mythical figure in the narrative as a loving world traveler and companion to the weak, who comes as a kind messenger to alert families of a loss. *La llorona* continues to regularly visit La Loca through her illness and up to her death, along with Esperanza, and they are even joined at times by Caridad, although never by Fe.

It should be clear from this brief summary of the events that transpire in the novel that Castillo introduces a magical-realist mode into her narrative, one that is intrinsically linked to *domesticana* imagery and popular magico-religious traditions. I define magical realism, following Anne Hegerfeldt, as a bi-dimensional mode that evokes and subsequently transgresses narrative conventions aligned with literary realism (2005, 54). It achieves such a transgression through a matter-of-fact narration of what could be deemed by readers as fantastic or bizarre events. The peculiarity of such a mode resides in the fact that the discrepancy between tone and content causes the reader to hesitate—long enough to try to become aware of and analyze reflectively the disparities between different conceptualizations of factuality and belief systems as well as their various justifications (55).

The magical-realist mode in Castillo's narrative draws upon *domesticana* representational vocabularies for its expression, creating for the reader a hermeneutical encounter with a complex of competing rationalities. Such an encounter enjoins the reader to examine the boundaries of what is considered rational and irrational across cultural contexts that coexist within the same place. This in turn causes both characters and readers to confront disjunctive mental constructions, and to interrogate what counts as knowledge inside and outside of 1) rational-scientific discourse, based on observational evidence that derives from a secular view of human existence and its positive relationship with a Western conception of modernity; 2) historiography, which conforms to scientific criteria by requiring these very same mechanisms of external legitimation equated with positivist science; and 3) literary realism, a narrative mode that instantiates its worldview by yoking itself to discourses of truth derived from History and Geography, in order to meet the reader's expectations that the fictional world is a copy of our own (Hegerfeldt 2005, 72–76).

The reader's encounter with the magical-realist mode in Castillo's narrative provides an opportunity to consciously examine what interests and purposes lie beneath a powerful desire to reconcile apparently incompatible beliefs and understandings derived from different worldviews and rationalities, even when nothing in the text would warrant us doing so, by seeking to extend the logical schemas that Western historical, scientific, and religious discourses provide—a desire that is purposefully thwarted by Castillo. The characters undergo an analogous process. Herein, Castillo draws upon the magical-realist mode in order to introduce a series of interactions and events to which characters react using differing rational schemas, some pertaining to Western traditions and others pertaining to Mesoamerican traditions. The decisions they make as well as the justificatory practices that guide the outcomes of the various life events they must confront oblige them to assess the varying degrees of reasoned judgment that each culture offers, in terms of enhancing their own welfare and that of their community. In the process, they discover rational schemas that are incompatible and others that are complementary to one another. In both cases, such discoveries enjoin the characters and readers to ponder the possibilities of the translatability of rational schemas.

In what follows, I exemplify the cross-cultural assessments that the characters and readers become obliged to undertake through my analysis of three major constellations of events: a) the birth, illness, and death of La Loca, events that are framed within a popular religious temporal cycle and space; b) Sofi's candidacy as the mayor of Tome; and c) two popular religious events: the *Via Crucis* procession that La Loca leads during holy week, and a pageant celebrated in the closing pages of the novel that inaugurates the Conference of the Mothers of Daughters of Martyrs and Saints (M.O.M.A.S.).

The Life and Death of La Loca. The thematization of cultural alterity is triggered with the first death and resurrection of La Loca that begins the narration as well as the second death of La Loca that brings the novel to completion. These episodes illuminate the ways in which the characters find themselves caught throughout the narrative between the views and belief systems of official Christology, defended by the institution of the Catholic Church, and popular, syncretic religious traditions; and between scientific-empirical traditions of Western medicine and magico-religious *domesticana* conceptions of the body and bodily health. In the first pages of Castillo's narrative, the local priest, Father Jerome, adhering to official Catholic sacramental procedures of the funeral ceremony, admonishes Sofi on her grief, stating that it reflects a lack of faith in God's will. When the lid of the coffin pushes open just seconds later, the priest attempts to approach La Loca, but the baby girl rejects his intent to gain access to her as she levitates up to the church roof. The priest and the mother of the girl diverge on their interpretations of these events while a doctor who is subsequently called in offers his own explanation and other villagers offer theirs. Father Jerome draws upon his interpretive authority as priest to limit the potential power such acts evoke. He suggests that La Loca's return to life and her levitation might be due to an act of Satan and not of God, and that he alone is invested in the power to make such a call, as well as to act as her intermediary by praying for her.

Sofi, however, rejects his interpretive authority, as her daughter had done, but in a more earthbound manner: She swears at the priest, charging at and beating him at the same time. She screams that this miracle is the work of God. Her behavior, the others present observe, could surely cause her excommunication. Shortly thereafter, the official word of the doctors is that her child is an epileptic, an assessment that explained the resurrection but not the levitation. When mother and daughter arrive home, everyone in the community regards her as a saint, naming her "*la loca santa*" (the saintly fool), both because of her miraculous resurrection and levitation, as well as for her subsequent otherworldly behavior.

While the author immerses us in these first pages into a world that might appear to us to be totally bizarre due to the staging of these apparently fantastic events, such hermeneutical contentions, the indicators of different rational schemas as well as of different interests and priorities, have historical precedence. There have been numerous accounts of levitation recorded in Christianity as well as in Islam since the first century, and levitation continues to be practiced today in shamanism, as documented by noted anthropologist Mircea Eliade (1989). Most notably within the Hispanic tradition, Saint Teresa of

Ávila was reported to have levitated a foot and a half above the ground for up to a half hour. Her powers were also subject to the evaluative assessments of the ecclesiastical authority of the Church. Ultimately, she was not found guilty of heresy but rather her levitating acts occurred during her raptures, when her soul achieved that perfect union with God. Forty years following her death, she was canonized in 1622 (Bilinkoff 2008, xxv). Not only have such levitating acts been subject to verification through papal authority, but the possibility of levitation has been examined by physicists in the Western world. In recent decades, for example, scientists have found a way to levitate objects, using the forces of quantum mechanics.

Of course my point here is not to resubmit La Loca's levitating act to the current evaluative practices of the scientific community nor to the rigor of past evaluative assessments of papal authority with regard to mystical thought. Instead, I merely wish to indicate that events, actions, or practices that do not pertain to the lived experiences of a given culture may appear bizarre initially. Yet when upon further examination, we can determine that they fit within the parameters of the broader social and cultural practices in which the given event unfolds, they become intelligible to us. Such practices, when taken up by people in different manners and contexts, become translatable, offering possibilities for *their* practices to become part of *our* lived experience. I also seek to indicate that people's understandings and beliefs, derived from their lived experiences, whether within Western or non-Western contexts, justify their practices, including acts and decisions, insofar as such practices produce real effects on their lives.

As Isasi-Díaz notes with respect to Latinas, religiosity, defined as the everyday practice of Latinas, is integral to Latinas' struggle for survival. Their critical reflection on matters of ultimate concern, as historical and moral agents, is informed by the hermeneutical constructs available within that cultural context. As outlined by Clifford Geertz, such a context can be characterized as "a system of symbols which acts to establish powerful, pervasive, and long-lasting moods and motivations...by formulating conceptions of a general order of existence and clothing these conceptions with such an aura of factuality that the moods and motivations seem uniquely realistic" (1973, 90). Once identified, these contexts become open to us for cross-cultural hermeneutical comparison with our own truth-making procedures and justificatory practices.

Within La Loca's community, her levitating act is interpretable as a precocious act of rationality, insofar as it points to a willful separatist praxis, derived from the infant's radical suspicion of modern society for its insidious effects on her community. As a bi-dimensional character, La Loca's actions must be understood as existing with a literary realist frame, that is, within a historical or chronological dimension. Also, however, she takes on a magical dimension, as do other characters in the narrative, through a magical-realist technique that Hegerfeldt calls "literalization" (Hegerfeldt 2005, 54–57). This technique transforms abstract ideas as well as mental constructions pertaining to members of a community, linked to memories of past or current communal traditions and experiences, into concrete phenomena, often through personification. Perspectives from a concrete 'somewhere' become embodied. As Hegerfeldt affirms, through literalization, "emotions can be touched and smelled, memories are looked for in literal corners or become cooking ingredients" (57).

La Loca literally cloisters herself within the domestic sphere. Even as she lies dying of AIDS, a disease, ironically, contracted through human contact, she refuses to be seen by Anglo doctors, just as she had refused to be touched by Father Jerome. She had witnessed the cannibalization of Fe's body due to toxic poisoning, which caused extreme fatigue, headaches, a nose ring, hair and nail loss, bad breath, miscarriages, infertility, and, finally, cancer. She also witnessed Fe's medical mistreatment, which included a surgical scraping of her entire body in order to remove cancerous moles, and an ensuing infection that was caused when a catheter guideline remained lodged in her head. This, the narrator tells us, "was enough to keep her far away from anyone wearing anything that even looked like a smock as long as she lived" (230). La Loca did, however, allow Dona Felicia, the *curandera*, to provide her with *limpias* and a vast array of remedies that she had gathered from all of the faith healers in the region. She also allowed Dr. Tolentino the Filipino Psychic Surgeon, to provide a "psychic surgery" on her, one that began with prayers and ended with the 'surgeon' plunging his full fist into an opening he had made in la Loca's stomach, an act that Sofi thought must be an hallucination. Nonetheless, the psychic surgeon, upon seeing Sofi's disbelieving look, warned her: "Don't forget your faith, señora…" (229).

Much like the levitation, the psychic surgery is an act that does not fall into the Western everyday experience and would therefore be considered a sort of hocus-pocus. Castillo embeds these events into the linear narrative in a matter-of-fact manner, as is typical of the magical-realist mode. She uses this bi-dimensional mode to critique the so-called rationality of Western institutions of health and work, foregrounding and exposing thus the endemic deleterious effects of modernity: medical torture and labor exploitation. By extending the description of La Loca's demise, and characterizing it as one in which La Loca is surrounded not only by family but by healers that cause her to feel "alleviated" from her suffering (230), the reader is obliged to consider the nature of such communal care practices in light of the West's contemporary medical practices.

Psychic surgery, often referred to as a "laying on of hands," is a form of spiritual healing practiced primarily in the Philippines that dates back to the sixteenth century, although it has been practiced around the world since biblical times. Viewed more recently as fraudulent among Western medical practitioners, the Filipino practice has come under investigation by Western legal and medical organizations since the 1970s. Throughout the '80s, many of its practitioners have been prosecuted. The polemic investigations around psychic surgery, otherwise called fourth-dimension surgeries, hinge on the question of whether or not the surgeries are sleight-of-hand or in fact real surgical interventions and extractions of toxic or infected matter. The conclusions of studies addressing this critical question are diverse. Obviously, a review of them falls outside of the scope of this study. What is of import here, however, is that statistically, patients with diverse illnesses, both in kind and in gravity, have been healed by such surgeries.

Moreover, during the same period that psychic surgeries were falling under heavy scrutiny and persecution by the medical community, reports were being published about medical experiments conducted by American doctors for the purpose of investigating the placebo effect. In these experiments, some patients suffering from *angina pectoris* were treated through real surgical intervention while others with the same disease underwent, unbeknownst to them, placebo surgeries. These latter patients were put to sleep with anesthesia and then given a surface incision, which was subsequently sutured. It was found that a significant number of these patients were healed (Martin 1999).

We could add to these new medical practices other emerging trends in Western medical practices. Throughout the '70s, Dr. Dolores Krieger, a Ph.D. in nursing and a professor of education at New York University, introduced to her graduate students a 'laying on of hands' technique, or what she called a "therapeutic touch," a technique that was later taught in nursing schools around the country. She claimed and demonstrated in her workshops that a transfer of energy that was curative took place between nurse and patient. In a recent newspaper article published by the Associated Press, medical writer Maurianne Gordon notes that at a major trauma hospital in Baltimore, nurses are deploying a hands-on medical therapy called Reiki therapy that heals or alleviates suffering through invisibile energy fields. She notes that this form of therapy has had positive healing effects on patients by creating biochemical changes (Gordon 2008). Due to increased demand for alternative forms of medical therapy, patients at hospitals around the nation are offered "complementary and alternative medicine" (CAM). Clearly, the psychic surgeries, which are often viewed as relegated to primitive societies, when viewed in the light of placebo surgeries and other current medical trends, seem to have the capacity to illuminate possibilities for our own medical practices, where patients often suffer extreme physical and psychic pain as a result of normative medical treatment.

Sofi as Mayor of Tome. A second constellation of apparently fantastic events revolves around Sofi's conversion from housewife and mother to mayor of the village of Tome, an event that amazes her neighbor/ *comadre* and her husband, Domingo, both of whom believe that her imagination and fantasizing have caused her to go mad. Up to the moment at which her neighbor tells her that her husband is going to take her to the dance in Belén, shortly after Domingo arrives back home, Sofi seems to have as her only moral and hermeneutical compass the various cultural representational systems that were available in her hybridized *mestiza* space: the *telenovela* and classic drama of Hollywood film and music. Her neighbor's reference to the local Saturday night dance obliges Sofi to hearken back to her meeting with her husband at the same dance, thirty-eight years earlier, when she saw Domingo, alternately, as Franky, Omar Sharif, Rudy Valentino, and Brett Butler.

She remembers her *quinceañera* or coming of age ball, when not even her father's stern admonitions could prevent her from seeing her 'Franky.' Although her family and her friends wanted her to have nothing to do with him, for her, he was all sweetness or "*miel* in the flesh" (104). She is both seen by him as and herself as hyperfeminized. She remembers that on that long-awaited day, she embodied the ideal representation of glamour. Her clothes, jewels, flower decorations, and cake—were all fit for a bride (107) Yet at the same time that Domingo pedestalized her, she recalls, he also infantilized her, calling her, even in the courtship days, "silly Sofi." Sofi realizes, additionally, that she had been an active co-participant in recreating herself and her relationship to fit the local, popular portrayals of gender roles encountered in the Mexican *telenovela*.

Her romantic relationship and those of her daughters in Tome are superimposed on the *telenovela*'s central themes of seduction, betrayal, jealousy, and corruption, as well as its various central motifs, often pertaining to the feminine sphere, including miracles, myths, gossip, recipes, and local color. Her love for Domingo was like that experienced by Cleófilas, protagonist of "Women Hollering Creek,"a love that "Cleófilas has been waiting for, has been whispering and giggling for...passion in its purest crystalline essence. The kind the books and songs and *telenovelas* describe when one finds, finally, the great love of one's life, and does whatever one can, must do, at whatever the cost" (Cisneros 1991, 44).

According to its critics, the *telenovela* represents an image of an ideal, imagined Mexican nation and has an impulse toward closure. As bad people are punished, and good people are rewarded, the moral values and idealized worldview of the nation are reinstantiated. The *telenovela*, affirms Francisco Javier Torres Aguilera, can be understood as a privileged vehicle for the reproduction of the more problematic beliefs around the Mexican nation, including racial, sexual, and class hierarchies (1994, 13). In her work *Plotting Women: Gender and Representation in Mexico*, Jean Franco notes that within the Mexican *telenovela*, women are often cast stereotypically as infantilized, or, alternately as one or the other part of the binary *Malinche/Guadalupe*. As the *Malinche*, she is a glamorous, seductive figure, competing for a man's attention. Her acts represent the morally fallen nation. Alternately, in her role as the self-abnegating, long suffering and de-sexed Virgin *Guadalupe*, she represents the focus on family, community, and a new nation, founded on a mixed racial heritage (1989, xviii). In this regard, the *telenovela* should be viewed as the ideological mechanism for reproducing existing Mexican hegemonic structures in new, culturally pluralistic spaces.[9]

In Castillo's novel, the melodramatic plot is instantiated only to be disrupted, and, along with it, the race, class, gendered hierarchies it reproduces. Sofi is the liminal, borderlands agent of *domesticana,* a *Guadalupe* figure—the ideal mother whose apparent central mission is to embody idealized love and fulfill familial duties, which in her case, and with much irony on the part of the author, requires that she work not only at home but, due to the fact that she was abandoned by a gambling husband, also in her parent's butcher shop. She can thus maintain her family economically. In her embodiment of *domesticana*, Sofi, as the image of hyperfeminized glamour, lies shattered. She is a parody of glamourized *mestiza* femininity. Decades following her *quinceañera*, she stands in front of her husband, her hands bloodied from her work at the butcher shop, still reflecting on her 'last dance.' When he asks her "What are you thinking about silly Sofi" she reminds herself and him that no one in her family liked him ever, and adds: "And don't call me 'silly Sofi' no more neither" (109).

Ultimately, as the *domesticana*/magical-realist narrative imposes itself, supplanting the linear one, however, Sofi comes to embody a living family altar, producing saintly daughters who make tangible the values, beliefs, and practices of her community, and who serve, along with her, as recorders of erased memories that will now be made available as resources of forgotten knowledge by the community. Sofi, the iconic *Guadalupe* figure, begins to assume a spiritual leadership, but in a way that breaks open the stereotypical role of the domesticated woman. She is analogous to another male figure in the narrative, Francisco, the *santero*, who is endowed with the special ability to carve wooden saints in perfect replication of the saint's appearance. His artistic creations do not derive from individual talent, nor does he accrue individual social capital from his work because, as the narrator tells us, "[h]is expert hand was not guided by the aesthetic objectives of artists, but by the saint himself in heaven, as permitted by God, because that wood-turned-*bulto* would become the saint's own representation on earth to aid those who were devoted to him" (96).

Unlike Francisco, however, Sofi does not painstakingly carve the *bultos* or figures of saints from wood. Instead, as mother, she reproduces saintly daughters out of her own body, a space that, as Marita Sturken notes, is "the most intimate and domestic" (1997, 229). These saints, who personify, externalize, concretize, or make literal the various abstract qualities or values that justify particular cultural behaviors, dispositions, and practices, facilitate her discovery or recovery of wisdom. With her recovered knowledge, Sofi becomes equipped to construct a new narrative of her identity as well as to recontextualize the dilemmas of her ancestors' dislocation caused by enforced migration. In her reconstructions, informed by her interpretation of her daughters' lives, she is able to test out her understandings of her gendered, classed, and raced identity, derived from stereotypical representations of the *telenovela,* the Mexican part of herself, or of Hollywood film, the Anglo part of herself, and, ultimately, is able to incorporate her indigenous identity, erased by both Anglo and Mexican norms. After having discarded the pedestalized glamorous figure of the feminine, reproduced in the *telenovela,* as well as the perpetually infantilized representation, she begins to recognize the spuriousness of the de-sexed *Guadalupe* identity, constructed within patriarchal Christianity as a maternal figure deprived of a sexual identity. She recognizes with rage the futility of twenty years of celibacy, and the tragic intergenerational effects of the *Malinche/Guadalupe* dichotomy on the self and the nation (112).

She first realizes that she has been an active co-participant in reproducing the stereotypical feminine images of the *telenovela* by raising daughters who, like her, are seduced and abandoned by husbands or lovers, becoming sell outs to their family and community. Like their mother, Fe and Caridad have forgotten their indigenous roots, believing, as their grandmother had insisted, that "they were Spanish, descendants of pure Spanish blood" (26). She is able to see how all of her daughters, except La Loca, who remained confined in the familial home, sacrificed their lives to their male partners, to be adored, and then abandoned. All of them have interpreted their experiences as *telenovela* stories and Hollywood plots that replaced their own memories. She comes to realize that Domingo's internalization of systems of racialized oppression have caused him to have a lack of faith with respect to his own capacities, and to believe that the world is governed by the mystery of luck rather than self-worth, which causes him to become a passionate gambler. She comes to discover that, like her, he saw himself as a figure in one of the *telenovelas* that he spends all day watching from his Lazy Boy, that is, when he was not gambling.

While she witnesses the disintegration of her daughters' lives, that of her own, and her community, she begins to envision a potential restitution of the *Malinche* or de-sexed *Guadalupe* figure she and her daughters have been condemned to represent. This vision is sparked by one among a long unending set of domestic dysfunctions, an event that becomes the proverbial last straw in terms of Sofi's subjugation to her domestic role: the wringer breaks. Having invited her neighbor/*comadre* to come over, she sits her down in her kitchen, and, over coffee, tells her that she has decided to become the mayor of Tome, even though there had never been one before.

Sofi is not acting out some fantasy as her *comadre* believes, but simply demonstrating that the confinement of the practice of Christian feminine virtues to the domestic sphere, identified with her daughters, is neither effective in providing positive identity formation for women, nor in serving the needs and priorities of the community, a community that is mired by hopelessness and apathy caused by economic disenfranchisement and its exacerbated racial-ethnic minority status. For the last half century, the community members have not been able to live off the land, the *comadre* muses while she listens to Sofi's plans, because the 'outsiders' had come in and overused it, so that it was no longer good for grazing livestock or farming (139). Unable to find their livelihood there, the young people had no choice but to leave for Albuquerque or the Army. Those who did remain were the ones who had fallen prey to drug use, as drugs had been introduced to them in their schooldays (148).

Sofi implements a *domesticana* vision as she takes the practices of such virtues out of the home, and into the public square. As a magical-realist figure, she makes tangible her daughter's virtues with an aim to transform herself and her community. In responding to her and her daughters' lives, Sofi pushes beyond her identity crisis. Sofi learns from Esperanza not only an ultimate refusal to be exploited by the males of her own culture, a changed attitude not lost on her husband, but also on how to implement *Chicana* insurgency and a 'hope' for social justice in order to bring about what Esperanza calls "community improvement" (138). But Sofi also realizes that she must seek hope in a manner that actually uplifts all those who pertain to her own community, particularly women, and that she must make use of her own community, rather than the U.S. government, to create economic opportunity.

From Caridad, Sofi learns how to be a redemptive cultural nationalist and *creatrix*, resuscitating the collectivist indigenous beliefs of her people; the beliefs that had been cut off by the Conquest and colonization. But she does so in a manner that produces tangible outcomes for her people. From Fe, she learns that it is counterproductive to one's survival to invest one's absolute faith in the hegemonic rationality of Western modernity, one whose institutions extend the false hope of the American Dream. Though Fe's job at Acme International holds the promise of such an achievement, Fe does not survive long enough to enjoy a second wedding anniversary nor her newly acquired automatic dishwasher, microwave, Cuisinart, and VCR (171). From La Loca, the separatist and Christ-like figure, Sofi learns to define herself not as the mere keeper of an altar and religious/cultural history that imprisons and demonizes women, but by her salvific, transformative function. But she enacts this function, unlike La Loca, in the public, institutional sphere of the community. She also learns from La Loca, untutored in and untouched by the ways of the world, that sometimes one is better able to penetrate profounder social truths when one is not encumbered with worldly learning and conventions.

The saints that are the major figures in Sofi's living altar, spatialized as the constitutive outside of the nation and confined within the domestic, now take center stage. As the concretization of mental constructions that constitute another rationality, these saintly figures hold together the past with the present and death with life by transmitting memories to the imagination of those that survive them, memories that inform their values, and motivate them to action. Such is the power of the altar and the alter keeper, who is to maintain the altar and exhibit it for the sake of community survival.

From a postpositivist realist perspective, Sofi has come to understand that goods and resources are disbursed (or not) according to identity categories, reproduced and legitimized within various cultural representations. Drawing upon the epistemic value of identity, Sofi discovers that the raced, classed, and gendered identities that had been variously imposed upon her—the exceptional Spaniard, the *mestiza-india*, the pedestalized *Guadalupe*, her evil counterpart *la llorona* (the wailing woman), who comes out at night to kill children, and the infantilized "silly Sofi"—fail to adequately refer to the social location to which her identity is indexed.

Sofi thus experiences dissonance with the gendered identity articulated by the Catholic Church, used as a socializing mechanism within the family—a dissonance that La Loca had noted from the time she was three. She remembers the fear of excommunication that her mother used to control her behavior, and that kept her clinging to a marriage that was annihilating her. With her mother now long deceased, she ultimately decides to serve her husband divorce papers. Sofi also ponders her long-held understandings of her raced and classed identities. She had always considered herself to be among one of the first pure Spanish descendants in the region, and as such, of landed aristocracy. She finally understands that she is just a *Chicana-india* woman. She finds evidence of this status not only in the flat Indian butts of three of her daughters, but also in the fact that when her husband gambled away her property and she went to the judge who had won it to get it back, she could not claim that it pertained to her family. The original deeds had either not been honored when New Mexico had become annexed to the United States through the Treaty of *Guadalupe* or, in her case, she simply could not produce the deed even though her family had lived on that land through the generations.

Sofi further came to understand the broader effects of racial oppression that came with the Annexation, namely, the change in her and her community's identity to a minority racial status, one that, as noted by Vigil and Henley, "had severe implications on *chicano* social, economic, and political life, as well as the nature of their macrostructural identity" (2002, 411). She experiences this as the victim of horizontal violence when, upon going to Judge Julano to claim her entitlement to the land, he simply stated, using a legalist tone, that "he won the property fair and square" in the cockfight, even when, as Sofi points out, cockfights are in fact illegal (216).

Drawing upon collectivist forms of thinking intrinsic to pre-Hispanic indigenous cultures that have been suppressed by the dominant individualist forms of economic survival promoted by U.S. capitalism, Sofi begins a grassroots project of reclaiming and marking the spaces that had been taken. In doing so, she facilitates a transformation of her people. To insure her nation's survival, something that she cannot expect the Church or the state to do, she re-introjects and implements the epistemological insights of her daughters in order to transcend their lives. She is the incarnation of wisdom as her name represents, carrying within the saintly qualities she engendered— hope, charity, faith, and the wise folly that results as a consequence of exercising these virtues in a tainted world.

Having clarified the erroneous nature of her assumptions about *Chicana* womanhood, Sofi is thus equipped to lead a struggle for economic self-sufficiency for the inhabitants of Tome. With her neighbors she undertakes the ambitious project of starting a sheep-grazing wool-weaving enterprise, one that not only involves effort and time, but also ends up "changing their whole way of thinking so that they could do it" (146). Neighbors who inherited land from homesteading ancestors but were no longer using it sold or bartered it off for services in shares to skilled neighbors who had no land. In bartering, people were able to purchase equipment. They began to work for the cooperative by learning some aspect of the business: wool scouring, weaving, and the selling of wool products. In the second year, a group of women began a wool-weaving cooperative. Due to the wide range of skills learned, they were able to acquire college credit from the local junior college and even earn an associate's degree in business.

What seems like an utterly improbable utopian economic restructuring plan undertaken by Sofi and the women of Tome is in fact patterned after and based on the real-life story of a cooperative that was developed by a group of women in al village in Northern New Mexico.[10] The undertaking of such an unlikely project in this diasporic location of New Mexico illuminates the coexistence and simultaneity of disjunctive time frames or time-knots that coexist in the present and that open up on to each other. Sofi's project is a merger of collectivist, anticapitalist practices, motivated by pre-Hispanic belief systems that cannot be subsumed by historical discourse as simply a past reality, with structures pertaining to Eurocentric modernity. The structures of higher education provide a systematically coordinated educational formation. For those within Sofi's community who so desire it, they can become credentialed, making possible their integration as citizens into the social fabric of U.S. society where they can choose to either reproduce official organizational structures, or use their own multitemporal experience to fuel changes within U.S. institutions in a manner that would be transformative for Latina/o communities more broadly.

Elaborating a vision for the future, Sofi implements what Isasi Díaz calls a *mujerista* praxis of justice. This praxis starts with an interrogation of the impact of structures and ideologies of racism, sexism, and classism on Latinas and the community of which Latinas form part, beginning with the colonial and imperialist projects of the Church and state, and extending their transformative practices to include a critique of other modern institutions, including the U.S. military, health, work, and the economy. Sofi's activism then proceeds as she draws in other community members so that they too can reflect on their different positionalities within such systems and their varying degrees and kinds of internalization that has in turn led to their acquiescence to their minority status within them. The praxis culminates, finally, in a process of hermeneutical rediscovery that facilitates a social reorganization.

Within this newly organized oppositional body politic, everyone is recognized as having strengths and assets that they may pool together to form structures that are to some extent but not completely compatible with those of the cultural dominant. Such a praxis is justified and achieved by means of a changed faith, a belief in another way of thinking, that is, another rationality to which the community has reconnected in order to meet the community's present social and political needs. The grassroots community, or what Isasi-Díaz calls "*comunidades de fe*," is based on a common good. In such a community, everyone must participate in the production of goods that will sustain life in the community. And this "'common good' is to be judged by the rights and participation of the poorest in society" (2004a, 58).

Pageantry and Spectacle: The Various Endings of the Novel. Sofi's economic self-sufficiency project inspires La Loca to take on her own community project. In the advanced stages of her illness, La Loca leads the *Via Crucis*, or Way of the Cross Procession, one that marks the death and resurrection of Jesus. This is the only occasion on which La Loca ever leaves the house "except at the age of three when she was taken to a hospital in Albuquerque and her death diagnosis was reevaluated as epilepsy" (238). She now moves out of the private, domestic sphere of home where she has hidden away from people, and makes her "debut," understanding that the evil of race, class, and gender oppression affecting her and her community—that she has smelled and steered clear from since she was born—is not something that she can simply hold at bay for herself and her family. Rather, she now sees herself as part of a community and inexorably affected by it. The illness with which she is stricken is symbolic of her participation in her community's afflictions. She now uses her analysis of social and historical structures to move others to consciousness. She foregrounds the implications of structural inequality on their lives. She encourages them, as Isasi-Díaz recommends, to "actualize [their] sense of *comunidades de fe* by setting up communities which are praxis-oriented, which bring together personal support and community action" (2004, 57).

The procession that La Loca leads, as a Jesus figure, the first fool for God, is like no other, the narrator tells us, bringing into the popular religious frame of reference the concerns not just of Hispanic families, but also of the Native families that lived in the region. She thereby moves those that form part of the procession to be a part of the economic and social processes of communal recovery. She enjoins them to reclaim the lands that not only had been taken from them, but that had also been spoiled with toxic waste dumps from the factories they had constructed there, which were killing their people. The participants use the procession to mark a space as a private but also a public geography in a manner that brings into purview a "relationship to a shared community with others who hold some of the same values about family and history" (Mesa-Bains 1998, 4). The narrator begins a description of the *mestiza* ceremony as follows:

> When Jesus was condemned to death, the spokesperson for the committee working to protest dumping radioactive waste in the sewers addressed the crowd.
> Jesus bore His cross and a man declared that most of the Native and *hispano* families throughout the land were living below poverty level, one out of six families collected food stamps. Worst of all, there was an ever-growing number of *familias* who couldn't even get no food stamps 'cause they had no address and were barely staying alive with their children on the streets.
> Jesus fell,
> and people all over the land were dying from toxic exposure in factories.
> Jesus met his mother, and three Navajo women talked about uranium contamination on the reservation...and the babies they gave birth to that were born with brain damage and cancer.... (243)

As the narrative unravels, a final pageant is staged, the conference of the world-famous organization of Mothers of Martyrs and Saints

(M.O.M.A.S.), of which Sofi is founder and *presidenta* (247). The celebration is held biannually, coinciding with a national and a global event, the World Series and the Olympics. On these occasions, the mothers of saints meet to discuss important matters relevant to their communities and to enjoy reunions with their daughters, who come back from the dead "to converse with their moms" and bring "all kinds of news and advice" (251). Thus, in closed attendance with other mothers of saints and martyrs who participate in the conference, Sofi gains the opportunity to see all of her daughters, except for Fe, who has so thoroughly given up her culture in order to assimilate into American society that there is nothing left of her to come back.

Although not overtly referenced in the narrative, the M.O.M.A.S. conference pertains to the Day of the Dead or *el día de los muertos,* and the Assumption that marks the resurrection of Mary, the first mother of a martyr—feast days that coincide respectively with the World Series and the Olympics. They are what Schutte refers to as the "unsaid" in the encounter of incommensurable cultures. In such encounters, Schutte notes, it becomes incumbent upon the person who wants to understand what *is* being said or performed as linked and fitting into a larger system of cultural signifiers to which it is attached and to which it refers, "denoting or somehow pointing to what remains unsaid" (2000, 55–56). In the case of Castillo's narrative, this would entail the reader or observer of the celebrations fitting what is observed—the M.O.M.A.S. conference—into what is not viewed (the background assumptions), but still provides coherence to the performance. What is not viewed includes not only the wider cyclical and transformative context of *el día de los muertos* traditions, but also the overarching rationality that proceeds from a different temporality that is cotemporaneous with the secular linearity of events that history embraces as its only subject.

It becomes incumbent, moreover, upon the person who is a member of the cultural dominant who wants to understand the culture of the Other to be willing to undertake this process of contextualizing an event, as well as translating it, in order to really figure out what is being said and how what is said can take on meaning and value within the dominant culture. In this manner, the member of the culturally dominant group subverts the power she has to turn away from the subject without full understanding, making the Other appear as incompetent or nonsensical (Schutte 2000, 57). Castillo seems to revel in this final trickster play with her readers, challenging them to take a leap in consciousness, as her counterpart, Francisco does, when he chases Esmeralda and Caridad off the cliff at the Acomo village, prompting them to leap in fulfillment of their mission for their people.

Within the narrative itself, the outsiders or tourists choose to dismiss the M.O.M.A.S. conference as a serious manifestation of *chicana* culture. Although the onlookers are prohibited from entering the site of the conference, from their position on the outside they draw upon the so-called rational schemas pertaining to Western modernity, in particular, from a mimetic model of commoditization and reproduction, that has what Michael Taussig calls "the capacity to Other" (1993, 19). This is evidenced in an ever-increasing presence of vendors around the conference, who sell trinkets to eager onlookers—"useless products and souvenirs," the narrator tells us, such as "your T-shirts with such predictable stenciled phrases as 'The Twenty-third Annual Convention of M.O.M.A.S., Flushing, NY,' or 'Perros Bravos, Nuevo León,' or 'Las Islas Canarias'" (249–50). Such acts of commoditization by members of the culturally dominant group serve the purpose of bringing the Other into their own sphere (assimilation) by erasing the difference that they cannot hold within themselves, in effect, turning the event into a World Series. They stand in stark contrast to and in conflict with the acts and rituals of the Day of the Dead traditions as they are depicted in the cultural work and texts of *Chicanas*, wherein the female icons representing both life and death serve as a point of reflection on the crushing dominance of patriarchy and Eurocentrism.

CONCLUSION

The erasure that results from such appropriating tactics is not complete, however. Castillo has explained so thoroughly the rational schemas of her characters and made available, for those who care to listen, their justificatory processes, that the throwing away of identities simply because they become subject to the appropriation strategies of the cultural dominant would, as I hope to have shown, be viewed as completely unwarranted. The everyday practices of *domesticana* make possible new modes of liberating consciousness and praxis. However mystifying they may appear to Western eyes, the decisions and actions of Sofi and her community have a coherence, that is, they fit within the rational schemas of the larger system of social practices in which they are produced.

I end this study with Castillo's narrative because it powerfully illuminates the role that identities play in providing epistemological resources that minoritian communities, feminists, and scholars of social inequality can use more broadly to achieve objective knowledge across cultural and social differences, and to cultivate processes for shared understanding across different cultural contexts. An analysis of the popular practices implemented by the protagonist in Castillo's narrative reveals that Sofi uses the cultural mechanisms and lived experiences that she has at her disposal from within her location to negotiate an identity more in accord with who she thinks she is. Through the deployment of *domesticana,* a set of everyday embodied practices that form part of a *mestiza* cultural representational system, she gains access to the epistemological possibilities of lived experience in order to overcome distorted understandings of her self. She also reestablishes the historical relationship that binds her to her community, and defends the interests of that community. Castillo implements Isasi-Díaz's notion of the identity narrative as one that, "puts sinews and flesh on the dry bones of reason and creed" (2004, 48).

Castillo's narrative also illuminates the possibilities and the difficulties of cross-cultural understanding in the context of incommensurable difference. Incommensurability develops as an intrinsic process for *mestizas.* Insofar as they have non-identical identities— Spanish, Mexican, and indigenous, commensurability is a process that *mestiza* feminists must undertake for the purpose of restitution and recovery. But cross-cultural understanding also develops across the divide of Anglo and *mestiza* cultures when the female characters in Castillo's narrative demand to have their incommensurable difference acknowledged in their encounters with U.S. structures and institutions. They thus challenge those of us who pertain to the culturally dominant to apprehend them from that positionality of difference, as well as acknowledge their refusal of the assimilative, subsuming gesture. Moreover, rather than indicating that we are all the same in our fractured identities, the narrative shows that the subaltern's efforts to move their own social and cultural practices into ever-widening publics increase the possibility of making such practices available to dominant institutions, which in turn offer the opportunity for institutional change.

In the encounter with the cultural Other, however, as Castillo's characters remind us, there is also an increased possibility that the Other's practices will be appropriated, radically decontextualized, and commoditized. In this regard, the deployment of multicultural practices by the cultural dominant is never the same as their deployment by the subaltern. In the case of the former, the deployment of cultural forms and practices pertaining to other cultures does not represent a threat to the cultural dominant's rational schemas. As a case in point, the anesthesia chief of the University of Maryland Medical Center can say he is a fan of Reiki therapy due to its positive effects on the patients and in the same breath call it "mystical mumbo jumbo" (Marchione 2009). For the subaltern, on the contrary, the accelerated deployment of one's own traditions and practices is essential to the process of cultural cross-fertilization, as García Canclini, states, given the contradictory hegemony of Western societies and the ongoing relegation of the culture of the Other to a subordinate status, based on race, class, and gender differences. Indeed, the insistence on the part of subaltern communities to maintain non-assimilative dispositions along with the cultivation of cultural cross-fertilization, as exemplified in Sofi's leadership, makes possible the cultural Other's material and cultural survival.

The non-assimilating stance that Castillo espouses in this narrative, one that characterizes the texts and cultural work of other *mestiza* feminists and womanists, should not be viewed as a factor that places constraints on the achievement of the feminist goal of solidarity. For if as a member of the white wing of feminist movement I can acknowledge the stakes of incommensurable difference, I can then work to identify areas of shared understanding of the culturally differentiated Other as well as undertake a project of hermeneutic self-recognition in the discourses of the Other. African American philosopher George Yancy illustrates the importance of such a project with a personal anecdote in which he describes sitting in a graduate class in African American literature. He focuses on the anger he felt when he noticed that during a class discussion that centered on Frederick Douglass's *Narrative of the Life of Frederick Douglass, An American Slave, Written by Himself* and Harriet Jacob's *Incidents in the Life of a Slave Girl*, the white students in the class did not interpolate themselves in the text. They thereby avoided the hermeneutical task of interpreting their own whiteness as implicated in a historical trajectory of structural white power of which they were the beneficiaries. They simply had not thought about it in that way, viewing themselves instead as 'good whites,' thereby unable "to locate their own center of power" (2004, 4).

Hermeneutical self-recognition is available to 'us' in the excellent condition in which Flannery O'Connor's house remains to this day, as noted in Walker's essay on this author and in the literary canon to which she was exposed as student, that correlated to her own hermeneutical traditions. It is available in the description of Sofia's wild look, when Celie asks her to be obedient in her subjugation; and in Miz Millie's containment of Sofia and Eleanor Jane's unquestioning acceptance of the presence of Sofia in her household. It is available in Fe's bright and shiny new appliances that she never gets a chance to enjoy; in her unquestioning faith in "the system"; and in the catheter guideline lodged in her head. It is also present in the ideology of *blanqueamiento* that causes Miriam Jiménez Román and Sandra María Estéves to struggle to understand and make present to themselves their Africanness. It is present, as final examples, in Anzaldúa's self-loathing and in the imagined mythical national unity that the *mestiza/mulata* is to symbolize in the project of nation building. Such processes of hermeneutical self-recognition make whiteness visible as an identity that is socially constructed, but that is also real. Whiteness refers outward, to social categories in the world. Yancy explains the objective status of racial identity as follows: "Whiteness's *reality* gets concretized through complex systems of advantage that have accrued over time, systems of differential power (whites benefiting more than nonwhites) created and maintained by whites who see it as their natural (God-given) right to be at the apex of natural and historical evolution" (2004, 15).

Besides seeing myself as implicated in the discourses of the cultural/racial Other, and therefore integral to it, I must also further acknowledge the incommensurability of discourses and identities, and, therefore, my inability to translate every propositional statement of the Other. This inability does not represent an obstacle to my understanding of the Other, however, for that would oblige me to read my expectations into everything, thereby maintaining myself enclosed in my own hermetic circle of subjective understanding, my own center of power. To say that it is now impossible for me to understand someone differently located because there are some things I do not understand would free me from the social and ethical responsibility of having to work to understand the Other in order to evaluate my own truth claims. Recognizing simultaneously the translatability of meaning as well as incommensurable difference—the unfamiliar and the unassimilable—is what allows feminist cross-cultural engagement to remain an open-ended activity so that mutual interrogation can take place, in the name of gaining a more objective knowledge of diverse women's lives.

NOTES

1 INTRODUCTION: RECONCEPTUALIZING IDENTITY POLITICS IN A POST IDENTITY POLITICS AGE

1. For a cogent depiction of these issues, see Felski (2000, 196–98).
2. This plea to get beyond identity politics is framed in a variety of ways, some more sympathetic than others, but all equally adamant. See, for example, Benhabib (1995), Felski (1989), and Halberg (1989).
3. For further background information on pragmatism and its relation to realism and naturalism, see Shook (2003).
4. The work of second-generation womanist scholars has pivoted on the notion of universality. See, for example, Floyd-Thomas (2006b).
5. My department, at the time I wrote this chapter, was not called "Ethnic Studies" but it did house programs that focused on social inequality, such as Women's Studies, Africana Studies, Native-American Studies, and Appalachian Studies, among others.

2 REIMAGINING IDENTITY POLITICS IN THE NEW MILLENNIUM: A POSTPOSITIVIST REALIST APPROACH

1. I also use continental philosophical theories, namely, phenomenology, in chapter 5. However, I show how this approach resonates with post-positivist realism.
2. My reading of Wiegman and Friedman might be interpreted as an attempt to engage in a personal polemics or what Wiegman refers to as "academic methodologies of intellectual murder," (234, note 16). In fact, my goal is to pursue an investigation of the broader implications of recent theoretical turns in academic feminism that have had a widespread impact on these fields, and that have led the scholars espousing them to achieve critical renown. Wiegman, for example, was the Margaret Taylor Smith Director of Women's Studies at Duke from 2001–07 and co-director of the Dartmouth Summer Institute on American Studies from 1998–2004; Susan Stanford Friedman is the Virginia Woolf Professor of English and Women's Studies.
3. For an overview of the complex relationships between feminism and postmodernism, see Linda J. Nicholson's edited collection, *Feminism/Postmodernism*, 1990.

4. In Chapter 6 of *Fighting Words*, 1998, Collins incorporated intersectionality as a complement to standpoint theory, allowing for greater complexity in conceptualizing identity and social power.
5. See Felski, 1989, for a similar conceptualization of counterpublics.
6. The use of the 'Fro' as a representational strategy, while not widely disseminated, does provide us with an instance, nonetheless, of the ways in which subaltern groups negotiate social capital within cultural representation.
7. Both of these scholars also note the ways in which a politics of respectability was a double-edged sword: Black club and church women used respectability as a discourse of resistance but by buying into negative stereotypes about Black women and using them to regulate Black female behavior, they reproduce the white hegemonic gaze. See Higginbotham (1993, 196); and White (2001, 36–37).
8. In her 1997 essay, "To Catch a Vision," Barkley Brown examines the over-emphasis on the liberal notion of individual liberty as a basic tenet for measuring emancipation, one that obscures the value of collective responsibility within the African American community as the privileged means of strategizing freedom.
9. Inclusion and unity are central tenets in feminist thought and praxis. The National Women's Studies Association, for instance, reflects the notion of unity and inclusivity as noted in its online organizational documents (www.nwsa.org). The concept of difference is referenced as if it were already assumed and understood—as if now inclusivity and difference are natural partners. And the "women" in Women's Studies in general continues to stand in for *all* women, without the naming being problematized, other than, as Wiegman suggests, to eliminate 'women' altogether.

3 WOMANISMS AT THE INTERSTICES OF DISCIPLINES, MOVEMENTS, PERIODIZATIONS, AND NATIONS

1. In her discussion of hook's notion of "postmodern blackness," Kimberly Chabot Davis argues for a modification of postmodern theories that would permit such theories to accommodate cultural modes of expression with an "overt political agenda of social protest" (1998).
2. In her study of modernism and postmodernism as these aesthetic movements apply to the work of African American artists, Ann Gibson argues that postmodern African American artists produce art that rejects Eurocentric culture in favor of adhering to a core African culture. But in doing so, they historicize African cultural values in order to make relations of power salient as well as highlight the diversity of expressions within U.S. Black cultural production (1995, 84–90).
3. The view of American cultural production as postmodern indicates a need to redefine these periodizing concepts. For an extensive review

of the complexities of creating periodizations, see Dubey (2003, 17–40).

4. Several critics have pointed to the calcification of the racial politics of modernism as represented in the Black cultural nationalism of the '60s as the cause of the rise of postmodernist cultural expressions. See Hogue (1996, 6); Lubiano (1991, 66); and Soja and Hooper (1993, 187–88).

5. Layli Phillips' edited anthology, *The Womanist Reader* (2006), provides multiple definitions of womanism and also includes samples of various types of womanist scholarship within and across disciplines.

6. Collins carves out the exact meaning of oppositionality as it relates to Black feminist thought: "remaining oppositional involves challenging the constructs, paradigms, and epistemologies of bodies of knowledge that have more power, authority, and/or legitimacy than Black feminist thought" (1998, 88).

7. For a review of some of the salient criticisms aimed at Afrocentrism by Black feminists, see Collins (1990, 155–83). For a review of some of the criticism lodged against Afrocentrism by womanists, see Sanders (1995).

8. James' continuum does not, however, help to differentiate womanism and Black feminism. This is because she sees both of these movements positioned somewhere in the middle of this continuum, with Black women working in conventional feminist parameters and radical, and more progressive Black women working at the end of the spectrum.

9. Although Asante clearly rejects Christianity as a religious option for Afrocentric people, he does cite, as Cheryl Sanders points out, the Black church traditions to illustrate Afrocentric values, spirituality, and culture (1995, 159–60). A prime example of this is the witness of the spirit or the collective amen as the assertion of 'truth' of the Black church community. These expressive modalities are analogous to and interconnected with the witness of history—the collective stories, traditions, and rituals of African Americans that come to constitute a spiritual communication, mediated by the collectivity, and as a criterion for validation of new knowledge (Sanders 159–61).

10. As womanist theologian Linda Thomas affirms, (1988/89), an overwhelming majority of womanist scholars of religion rely on written texts for their reconstruction of Black women's knowledge, primarily fiction, biography, and autobiography.

11. Layli Phillips points out that actually the first time that Walker coins the term "womanism" is in 1979, in her short story "Coming Apart," published in Laura Lederer's anthology *Take Back the Night* (2006, xix).

12. These terms refer to inherited and internalized white supremacist frameworks that use skin color or physical characteristics as a means for ascribing virtue or human worth in ways that are segregating,

hierarchalizing, and dehumanizing. For a review of these phenomena as they affect Black women, see Arthur P. Davis (1962).

13. For some of the problems that arise when using a womanist perspective in theology and ethics, see Sanders et. al (1989).

14. I discuss Gadamer's hermeneutics again in chapter 5, as an analytical approach that can be used in conjunction with phenomenology.

15. William Wilkerson affirms that it is possible to determine accuracy of an interpretation when we see that an interpretation can stand the test of time, that is, when the interpretation can be subject to continued verification (2000, 265).

16. Ann duCille refers to these appropriating processes as the *"Driving Miss Daisy* syndrome,"* (1996, 109). She defines this as "an intellectual sleight-of-hand that transforms power and race relations to make best friends out of driver and driven, master and slave, boss and servant, white boy and Black men" (109–10).

17. My struggle to reinterpret difference as both historically grounded and at the same time decentered and destabilized is captured in a more recent terminology, that of "transdifference"—a term that, as Breinig and Lösch affirm, "does not do away with the originary binary inscription of difference, but rather causes it to oscillate. Thus, the concept of transdifference interrogates the validity of binary constructions of difference without completely deconstructing them. This means that difference is simultaneously bracketed and yet retained as a point of reference" (2002, 23).

18. For more on the ethnocentric gaze of this film, see Grewal and Kaplan (2006, 379–401).

4   STORYTELLING AS EMBODIED KNOWLEDGE: WOMANIST PRAXIS IN ALICE WALKER'S *THE COLOR PURPLE*

1. Much of the scholarship applying a womanist lens to Black women's writings have emphasized the compensatory efforts on the part of Black women writers, that is, their concentrated efforts to correct denigrating stereotypes by replacing them with positive renderings and celebratory affirmations of Black women's lives, values, and perspectives. This line of scholarship tends to emphasize unproblematically the truthful reinterpretations supplied by Black women writers. Katie Cannon, for example, asserts: "The work of Black women writers can be trusted as seriously mirroring Black reality" (1988, 90). Angelene Jamison-Hall's emphasis on the womanish attitude in her 1993 essay "She's Just Too Womanish for Them: Alice Walker and *The Color Purple*," is another example of this type of celebratory orientation.

2. There is a history of womanist scholarship that places Walker as well as her more immediate model, Zora Neale Hurston, within

a cosmological tradition of mediumship or "conjuring." Within this context, the author, as well as her female characters, are or become endowed with magical properties originating in an African cosmological system. This sociosymbolic space allows the writer to encapsulate the wisdom, power, and authority of the oral folk tradition within the text. Through storytelling, the author, as well as her female protagonists, pass down the ancient power through the generations, allowing Black women to transform their lives. See, for example, Pryse and Spillers (1985, 10–15). Gay Wilentz, (1992), also identifies storytelling with Afrocentric systems disrupted by slavery, but reinstated in Black women's writings within the lives of the female protagonists.

3. Such an approach, involving the shifting and interrogating of perspectives, is intrinsic to a womanist analysis of texts. In her edited anthology, for example, Layli Phillips duly notes that a major focus of womanism is the shaping and reshaping of thought processes and relationships, (2006, xxx). However, the celebratory tendency within womanist analyses of Black women's writings tends to obscure the epistemic processes of interpretation, processes that involve error as much as accuracy, and the ensuing continuity of oppression and horizontal violence. Historians of Black historiography writing in the '90s have similarly noted the exaggerated emphasis on slave resistance in the works of historians of the '80s, works that failed to take seriously the absolute repressiveness of plantation life. Baptist and Camp focus instead on the paradoxes of a simultaneous accommodation to and resistance against enslavement in bondspeoples' lives (2006, 2–3). Finally, this very effort to emphasize the celebration of Black women's realities, values, and experiences is what Mae Henderon critiques. She cogently argues that a focus on "felicitious-images" causes Black critics to "risk reducing the complexity and misconstructing (or misconstruing) the totality of our experiences" (1989, 162).

4. There is a growing body of scholarship on the neo-slave narrative as a discourse emerging from the Black Power movement. For a thoroughgoing overview of this scholarship, see Ashraf H. A. Rushdy's work, *Neo-slave Narratives: Studies in the Logic of a Literary Form*, (1999).

5. For a review of this controversy, see Shapiro (1975).

6. For a review of this historiography, see Beaulieu (1999), Baptist and Camp (2006), Carby (1987) and Fabre and O'Meally (1994).

7. Gabrielsen Scholl classifies the novel as a Christian parable (1991); Hite as a variant of the Shakespearean romance (1990); hooks as a fictive autobiography and parody of the slave narrative (1990b); and Katz as an epistolary fiction and *Buldungsroman* (2000). In her collection of prose, *In Search of our Mothers' Gardens*, however, Walker locates the novel within a historical narrative tradition and also within a tradition linked to the slave narrative tradition (1983, 5 and 355).

8. Angela Davis points out that the white slave master reduced the sexual act to an animal-like act for the symbolic purpose of conquering

the potential resistance or insurgency of the Black female slave. In Walker's text, we see the internalization of these strategies in Pa and Mr.___'s performance of male supremacy of southern culture, at the expense of Black women (1971).

9. For a review of these motifs, see Olney (1985, 152–53). As these relate to women-authored slave narratives, see Davis (1971); and Carby (1987, 50–55).

10. W.E.B. Du Bois's *Black Reconstruction in America* (1935) spawned a major historiographic turn in the study of Reconstruction and race among American historians. In this work, Du Bois attempted no less than to dislodge and reinterpret the hegemonic historical image of the plight of Black people in America, in effect, by creating counter-memories of the self and of community in order to rescue Black history in America from structural amnesia. For a thorough discussion of the import of this work in its connection to the tensions between history and memory, see David W. Blight's essay "W.E.B. Du Bois and the Struggle for American Historical Memory" (1994).

11. Wendy Wall asserts that the letters are in fact the surrogate body for Celie, that both allow her to deflect and express suppressed emotions. For Mr.___, stealing the letters (the female body) is a form of circumscribing or constricting the body, denying phallic desire—an act that Wall likens to the African practice of clitoridectomy (1988, 87).

5   Latina/o *Mestizaje/Mulatez:* Vexed Histories, Ambivalent Symbolisms, and Radical Revisions

1. All translations in this chapter are mine.
2. Cited by Cazeaux (2007, 70).
3. For an in-depth review of these features, see Nicol (2008).
4. The bibliography on this writer is voluminous. A review of even the most important critical works falls outside of the scope of this study. For some recent scholarship on the notions of space and place in Anzaldúa's works, see Oliver-Rotger (2003) and Sadowski-Smith (2008).
5. For more on the notion of *susto* as a folk *chicano* concept, see Castro (2001, 216).
6. These writers did not appear out of a vacuum, but were, rather, influenced by *Nuyorican* writers of the civil rights era, who cultivated a cultural nationalist perspective, such as Piri Thomas and Nicholasa Mohr. For more on this trajectory, see Lisa Sánchez González (2001). For an overview of the different deployment of these metaphors within Puerto Rican women's writings, see Domínguez Miguela (2001).
7. For more on mixed-race formations of Puerto Ricans, see Negrón-Mutaner and Grosfoguel (1997), and Wade (1997).

6 CONSTRUCTING IDENTITY(IES) THROUGH *LO COTIDIANO*
('EVERYDAY PRACTICE'): A POSTPOSITIVIST REALIST APPROACH
TO POPULAR SPATIAL TRADITIONS IN AMALIA MESA-BAINS'
DOMESTICANA AESTHETIC, ADA MARÍA ISASI-DÍAZ'S *MUJERISTA*
THEOLOGY, AND ANA CASTILLO'S *SO FAR FROM GOD*

1. All translations in this chapter are mine.
2. An earlier version of this chapter, entitled "Revisiting Identity Politics in Contemporary *Mestiza* Thought: The Case of *Domesticana*," appears in the volume *Identity, Migration and Women's Bodies as Sites of Knowledge and Transgression* (Borrego and Romero Ruiz 2009).
3. For a more in-depth review of these concepts, see Shrage (1994, 22–30).
4. For a more extended review of these arguments, see Felski (2000, 124–30).
5. Mohanty calls the subjection of rational schemas to context a "context-sensitive" reason (1997, 142).
6. By "anthropologize," Chakrabarty simply means to provide some equivalent human-centered rather than God-centered explanation to the motivation for the Santal people's entrance into battle so that the historian can incorporate it into his or her discourse.
7. *'mujer'* signifies 'woman' in Spanish.
8. For a review of the range of thought on Latina/o popular religiosity, see Gonzales (2002).
9. For a more extensive elaboration on and analysis of the gender, sexual, and family ideologies inherent in melodrama, and the myriad ways in which such ideologies drive popular culture as well as contemporary U.S. political discourse, see Alexander-Floyd (2009).
10. For more on the development of this community project, see Ochoa (1995).

WORKS CITED

Ahmad, Aijaz. 1995. The politics of literary postcoloniality. In *Race and Class* 36 (3): 1–20.

Alarcón, Norma. 1997. The theoretical subject(s) of *this bridge called my back* and Anglo-American feminism. In *The Second Wave: A Reader in Feminist Theory*. Ed. Linda J. Nicholson. 288–99. New York: Routledge.

Alcoff, Linda Martin. 1996. *Real Knowing: New Versions of the Coherence Theory*. Ithaca, New York: Cornell University Press.

———. 1997. Cultural feminism versus post-structuralism: The identity crisis in feminist theory. In *The Second Wave: A Reader in Feminist Theory*. Ed. Linda J. Nicholson. 330–55. New York: Routledge.

———. 2000. Who's afraid of identity politics? In *Reclaiming Identity: Realist Theory and the Predicament of Postmodernism*. Ed. Paula M. L. Moya, and Michael R. Hames-García. 312–41. Berkeley: University of California Press.

———. et al. eds. 2006. *Identity Politics Reconsidered*. New York: Palgrave Macmillan.

———. 2006. *Visible Identities: Race, Gender, and the Self*. New York: Oxford University Press.

Aldama, Frederick Luis. 2003. *Postethnic Narrative: Magicorealism in Oscar "Zeta" Acosta, Ana Castillo, Julie Dash, Hanif Kureishi, and Salman Rushdie*. Austin, TX: University of Texas Press.

Alexander-Floyd, Nikol G. 2007. *Gender, Race, and Nationalism in Contemporary Black Politics*. New York: Palgrave MacMillan.

———. Alexander-Floyd, Nikol G., and Evelyn M. Simien. 2006. "What's in a name?" reconsidered: Exploring the contours of Africana womanist thought. *Frontiers: A Journal of Women's Studies* 27(1): 67–89.

———. "But I voted for Obama": Post-civil rights, postfeminist ideology in *Grey's anatomy*, *Crash* and Barack Obama's 2008 presidential campaign. Presented at the Annual Meeting of the National Conference of Black Political Scientists. March 13–21.

Alexander, M. Jacqui, and Chandra Talpade Mohanty. 1997. Genealogies, legacies, movements. In *Feminist Genealogies, Colonial Legacies, Democratic Futures*. Ed. Jacqui Alexander and Chandra Talpade Mohanty. xiii–xlii. New York: Routledge.

Allan, Tuzyline Jita. 2000. *The color purple*: A study of Walker's womanist gospel. In *Alice Walker's* The Color Purple: *Modern Critical Interpretations*. Ed. Harold Bloom. 119–38. Philadelphia: Chelsea House Publishers.

Allen, Robert, and Antoinette LaFarge. 2006. A meditation on virtual kines-thesia. *Extensions: Online Journal of Embodiment and Technology* (3). Available at http://www.performancestudies.ucla.edu/extensionsjournal/allenlafarge.htm.

Ang, Ien. 1995. I'm a feminist but...: "Other" women and postnational feminism. In *Transitions: New Australian Feminisms*. Ed. Barbara Caine and Rosemary Pringle. 57–73. New York: St. Martin's Press.

Appadurai, Arjun. 1988. Putting hierarchy in its place. *Cultural Anthropology* 3(1): 36–49.

Antonio, Robert J. and Douglas Kellner. 1994. The future of social theory and the limits of postmodern critique. In *Postmodernism and Social Inquiry*. Ed. David R. Dickens and Andrea Fontana. 127–52. New York: The Guilford Press.

Anzaldúa, Gloria, 1987. *Borderlands/La Frontera: The New Mestiza*. San Francisco: Aunt Lute Books.

———. ed. 1999. *Making Face/Making Soul Haciendo Caras: Creative and Critical Perspectives by Women of Color*. San Francisco: Aunt Lute Books.

Baker, Houston, Jr. 1995. Critical memory and the Black public sphere. In *The Black Public Sphere: A Public Culture Book*. Ed. The Black Public Sphere Collective. 4–38. Chicago: The University of Chicago Press.

Baptist, Edward E., and Stephanie M. H. Camp, ed. 2006. *New Studies in the History of American Slavery*. Athens, Ga: The University of Georgia Press.

Baudrillard, Jean. 1983. *In the Shadow of the Silent Majorities...or the End of the Social*. Trans. Paul Foss, Paul Patton, and John Johnston. New York: Semiotext.

Beaulieu, Elizabeth Ann. 1999. *Black Women Writers and the American Neo-Slave Narrative: Femininity Unfettered*. Westport, CO: Greenwood Press.

Bell, Bernard W., Trudier Harris, William J. Harris, R. Baxter Miller, Sandra A. O'Neale, and Horace Porter, ed. 1998. *Call and Response: The Riverside Anthology of the African American Literary Tradition*. Boston: Houghton Mifflin Company.

Bell, Bernard W. 1987. *The Afro-American Novel and Its Tradition*. Amherst: The University of Massachusetts Press.

———. 2004. *The Contemporary African American Novel: Its Folk Roots and Modern Literary Branches*. Boston: The University of Massachusetts Press.

Bell, Erica Townsend. 2007. *Identities Matter: Identity Politics, Coalition Possibilities and Feminist Organizing*. Ph.D diss., Department of Political Science, Washington University. St. Louis, Missouri.

Benhabib, Seyla. 1992. *Situating the Self: Gender, Community and Postmodernism in Contemporary Ethics*. New York: Routledge.

———. 1995. From identity politics to social feminism: A plea for the nineties. *Philosophy of Education* 1(2): 14.

Berlant, Lauren. 2000. Race, gender, and nation in *The Color Purple*. In *Alice Walker's* The Color Purple: *Modern Critical Interpretations*. 3-28. Philadelphia: Chelsea House Publishers.

Bhabba, Homi. [1994] 2004. *The Location of Culture*. Oxford and New York: Routledge.

Bilinkoff, Jodi. 2008. Introduction. In *The Book of Her Life by Teresa of Ávila*. Trans. Kieran Kavanaugh, and Otilio Rodríguez. Indianapolis, IN: Hackett Publishing.

Blassingame, John W. 1979. *The Slave Community: Plantation Life in the Antebellum South*. Oxford: Oxford University Press.

Blight, David W. 1994. W. E. B. Du Bois and the struggle for American historical memory. In *History and Memory in African-American Culture*. Ed. Genevieve Fabre, and Robert O'Meally. 45-71. Oxford: Oxford University Press.

Bloom, Harold, ed. 2000. *Alice Walker's* The Color Purple: *Modern Critical Interpretations*. Philadelphia: Chelsea House Publishers.

Bobo, Jacqueline, ed. 2001. *Black Feminist Cultural Criticism*. Malden, MA: Blackwell.

Brah, Avtar. 1996. *Cartographies of Diaspora: Contesting Identities*. London: Routledge.

Brake, Michael. 1985. *Comparative Youth Culture: The Sociology of Youth Cultures and Youth Subcultures in America, Britain, and Canada*. London: Routledge.

Breinig, Helmbrecht, and Klaus Lösch. 2002. Introduction: Difference and transdifference. In *Multiculturalism in Contemporary Societies: Perspectives on Difference and Transdifference*. 11-36. Erlangen: Univ. Bibliothek.

Brodkin, Karen. 1998. *How Jews Became White Folks and What That Says about Race in America*. New Brunswick, New Jersey: Rutgers University Press.

Browdy de Hernandez, Jennifer. 1998. Mothering the self: Writing through the lesbian sublime in Audre Lorde's *Zami* and Gloria Anzaldúa's *Borderlands/la frontera*. In *Other Sisterhoods: Literary Theory and U.S. Women of Color*. Ed. Sandra Kumamoto Stanley. 244-63. Champaign, Illinois: University of Illinois Press.

Brown, Elsa Barkley. 1995. Negotiating and transforming the public sphere: African-American political life in the transition from slavery to freedom. In *The Black Public Sphere: A Public Culture Book*. Ed. The Black Public Sphere Collective. 111-50. Chicago: The University of Chicago Press.

———. 1997. To catch the vision of freedom: Reconstructing southern Black women's political history, 1865-1880. In *African-American Women and the Vote 1837-1965*. Ed. A. Avakian et al. 66-99. Amherst: University of Massachusetts Press.

Brown, Monica. 1998. Neither here nor there: Nuyorican literature, home, and the "American" national symbolic. *JSRI Research and Publications Working Paper Series*. 42 (February).

Browne, Joy Elizabeth. 1995. Theology and literary criticism in the womanist mode. *Journal of the Interdenominational Theological Center* (*JITC*)
22(2): 115–28.

Butler, Johnnella E. 2006. African American literature and realist theory:
Seeking the "true-true." 171–92. In *Identity Politics Reconsidered*. Ed.
Linda Martin Alcoff, Michael Hames-García, Satya P. Mohanty, and
Paula M. L. Moya. New York: Palgrave Macmillan.

Butler, Judith. 1990. *Gender Trouble: Feminism and the Subversion of Identity*.
New York: Routledge.

Cabral of Guinea Bissau, Amilcar. 1973. *A Return to the Source*. New York:
Monthly Review Press.

Cannon Katie G. 1988. *Black Womanist Ethics*. Atlanta, Georgia: Scholars
Press.

———. 1996. *Katie's Canon: Womanism and the Soul of the Black Community*.
New York: Continuum.

———. 1998. Remembering what we never knew. *Journal of Women and
Religion* 16: 167–77.

———. 2006. Structured academic amnesia: As if this true womanist story never
happened. In *Deeper Shades of Purple: Womanism in Religion and Society*. Ed.
Stacey M. Floyd-Thomas. 9–23. New York: New York University Press.

Cano Alcalá, Rita. 2003. A *Chicana* hagiography for the twenty-first cen-
tury: Ana Castillo's *locas santas*. In *Velvet Barrios: Popular Culture and
Chicana/o Sexualities*. Ed. Alicia Gaspar de Alba. 3–15. New York:
Palgrave Macmillan.

Carby. Hazel V. 1985. "On the threshold of woman's era": Lynching, empire,
and sexuality in Black feminist theory. *Critical Inquiry* 12: 262–77.

———. 1987. *Reconstructing Womanhood: The Emergence of the Afro-
American Woman Novelist*. Oxford: Oxford University Press.

Castillo, Ana. 1994. *So Far from God*. New York: Plume Press.

———. 1995. *Massacre of the Dreamers: Essays on Xicanisma*. New York:
Plume Press.

Castro, Rafaela G. 2001. *Chicano Folklore: A Guide to the Folktales, Traditions,
Rituals and Religious Practices of Mexican Americans*. Oxford: Oxford
University Press.

Cazeaux, Clive. 2007. *Metaphor and Continental Philosophy: From Kant to
Derrida*. New York: Routledge.

Chakrabarty, Dipesh. 2000. *Provincializing Europe: Postcolonial Thought
and Historical Difference*. Princeton, New Jersey: Princeton University
Press

Chandler, James, Davidson, Arnold I., and Harootunian, Harold D. ed.
1994. *Questions of Evidence: Proof, Practice and Persuasion across the
Disciplines*. Chicago: University of Chicago Press.

Christian, Barbara. 1985. Trajectories of self-definition: Placing contemporary Afro-American women's fiction. In *Conjuring: Black Women, Fiction,
and Literary Tradition*. Ed. Pryse, Marjorie, and Hortense J. Spillers.
233–48. Bloomington: Indiana University Press.

———. 1987. The race for theory. *Cultural Critique* 6: 51–63.

Cisneros, Sandra. 1991. Women hollering creek. In *Women Hollering Creek and Other Stories*. New York: Random House.

Clinton, Catherine. 1994. With a whip in his hand: Rape, memory, and African-American women. In *History and Memory in African-American Culture*. Ed. Genevieve, Fabre and Robert O'Meally. 205–18. Oxford: Oxford University Press.

Cohen, Jean. 1996. Mobilization, politics, and civil society: Alain Touraine and social movements. In *Alain Touraine*. Ed. John Clark, and Marco Diani. 173–204. London: Falmer Press.

Colebrook, Claire. 2002. *Gilles Deleuze*. New York: Routledge.

Collins, Patricia Hill.1986. Learning from the outsider within: The sociological significance of black feminist thought. *Social Problems* 33 (6): 14–32.

———. 1990. *Black Feminist Thought: Knowledge, Consciousness, and the Politics of Empowerment*. New York: Routledge.

———. 1998. *Fighting Words: Black Women and the Search for Social Justice*. Minneapolis, MN: University of Minnesota Press

———. 2004. Comment: Where's the power? In *Feminist Standpoint Theory Reader: Intellectual and Political Controversies*. Ed. Sandra Harding. 247–54. New York: Routledge.

The Combahee River Collective, A Black feminist statement. [1977] 1982. *But Some of Us Are Brave: All the Women Are White, All the Blacks Are Men: Black Women's Studies*. Ed. Gloria T. Hull, Patricia Bell Scott, and Barbara Smith. Westbury, 13–22. New York: The Feminist Press.

Connerton, Paul. 1990. *How Societies Remember*. Cambridge: Cambridge University Press.

Copeland, M. Shawn. 2006. A thinking margin: The womanist movement as critical cognitive praxis. In *Deeper Shades of Purple: Womanism in Religion and Society*. Ed. Stacey M. Floyd-Thomas. 226–35. New York: New York University Press.

Cornell, Drucilla. 1993. *Transformations: Recollective Imagination and Sexual Difference*. New York: Routledge.

Crenshaw, Kimberle W. 1991. Mapping the margins: Intersectionality, identity politics, and violence against women of color. *Stanford Law Review* 43 (6): 1241–99.

Dávila, Arlene. 2004. *Barrio Dreams: Puerto Ricans, Latinos, and the Neoliberal City*. Berkeley: University of California Press.

Davies, Carole Boyce. 1994. *Black Women, Writing and Identity: Migrations of the Subject*. London: Routledge.

Davis, Amanda J. 2005. To build a nation: Black women writers, Black nationalism, and the violent reduction of wholeness. *Frontiers: A Journal of Women's Studies* 26 (3): 24–53.

Davis, Angela. 1971. Reflections on the Black woman's role in the community of Slaves. *The Black Scholar* 3(4): 2–15.

Davis, Arthur P. 1962. The black-and-tan motif in the poetry of Gwendolyn Brooks. *CLA* 6: 90–97.

Davis, Charles T., and Henry Louis Gates, Jr., ed. 1985. *The Slave's Narrative*. Oxford: Oxford University Press.

Davis, Kimberly Chabot. 1998. "Postmodern blackness": Toni Morrison's *Beloved* and the end of history-novel by Black female author. *Twentieth Century Literature*, 44: 242–60.

Dickens, David R. and Andrea Fontana, ed. 1994. *Postmodernism and Social Inquiry*. New York and London: The Guilford Press.

Douglas, Kelly Brown, and Cheryl J. Sanders. 1995. Introduction. *Living the Intersection: Womanism and Afrocentrism in Theology*. Ed. Cheryl J. Sanders. 9–17. Minneapolis, MN: Augsburg Fortress Press.

Duany, Jorge. 2007. Nation and migration: Rethinking Puerto Rican identity in a transnational context. In *None of the above: Puerto Ricans in the Global Era*. Ed. Frances Negrón-Muntaner. 51–63. New York: Palgrave MacMillan.

Dubey, Madhu. 2002. Contemporary African American fiction and the politics of postmodernism. *Novel: A Forum on Fiction* 35 (2–3): 151–168.

———. 2003. *Signs and Cities: Black Literary Postmodernism*. Chicago: Chicago University Press.

Du Bois, W.E.B. 1935. *Black Reconstruction in America: an Essay toward a History of the Part Which Black Folk Played in the Attempt to Reconstruct Democracy in America, 1860–1880*. New York: The Free Press, Simon & Schuster.

duCille, Ann. 1994. The occult of true Black womanhood: Critical demeanor and Black feminist studies. *Signs* 19 (3): 591–629.

———. 1996. Postcolonialism and Afrocentricity: Discourse and dat course. In *Skin Trade*. 120–35. Cambridge, MA: Harvard University Press.

Duggan, Lisa. 2003. *The Twilight of Equality? Neoliberalism, Cultural Politics, and the Attack on Democracy*. Boston: The Beacon Press.

Dussel, Enrique. 2004. Transmodernity and interculturality: An interpretation from the philosophy of liberation. Lecture, UAM (Universidad Autonoma Metropolitana) Iztapalapa , Mexico City. Available at http://www.enriquedussel.org/txt/Transmodernity%20and%20Interculturality.pdf

Dyck, Elizabeth, and Pamela Moss. 2002. *Women, Body, Illness: Space and Identity in the Everyday Lives of Women with Chronic Illness*. Lanham, MD: Rowman and Littlefield.

Ebert, Teresa L. 1996. *Ludic Feminism and after: Postmodernism, Desire, and Labor in Late Capitalism*. Ann Arbor: The University of Michigan Press.

Echols, Alice.1989. *Daring to Be Bad: Radical Feminism in America, 1967–1975*. Minneapolis, MN: University of Minnesota Press.

Eliade, Mircea. [1951] 1989. *Shamanism: Archaic Techniques of Ecstasy*. London: Penguin Arkana.

Elkins, Stanley M. 1968. *Slavery: A Problem in American Institutional and Intellectual Life*. Second Edn. Chicago: The University of Chicago Press.

Estéves, Sandra María. 1994. Not neither. *Stone on Stone/Piedra a Piedra*. Ed. Zoe Anglesey. Seattle, WA: Open Hand Publishing Company.

Fabre, Genevieve, and Robert O'Meally, ed. 1994. *History and Memory in African-American Culture*. Oxford: Oxford University Press.

Felski, Rita. 1989. *Beyond Feminist Aesthetics: Feminist Literature and Social Change*. Cambridge: Harvard University Press.

———. 2000. *Doing Time: Feminist Theory and Postmodern Culture*. New York: New York University Press.

Fields, Barbara Jeanne. 1982. Ideology and race in American history. In *Region, Race, and Reconstruction: Essays in Honor of C. Vann Woodward*. Ed. J. Morgan Kousser, and James M. McPherson. 143–77. Oxford: Oxford University Press.

Flores, Juan. 1993. *Divided Borders: Essays on Puerto Rican Identity*. Houston, TX: Arte Público Press.

Floyd-Thomas, Stacey M. 2006a. *Mining the Motherlode: Methods in Womanist Ethics*. Cleveland, OH: Pilgrim Press.

———. ed. 2006b. *Deeper Shades of Purple: Womanism in Religion and Society*. New York: New York University Press.

Fogel, Robert William, and Engelman, Stanley L. [1974] 1995. *Time on the Cross: the Economics of American Negro Slavery*. New York: W. W. Norton & Company.

Foucault, Michel. 1977. *Language, Counter-Memory, Practice*. Trans. Donald F. Bouchard, and Sherry Simon. Ithaca, NY: Cornell University Press.

Foster, Frances Smith. 1993. *Written by Herself: Literary Production by African-American Women, 1746–1892*. Indianapolis: Indiana University Press.

Franco, Jean. 1989. *Plotting Women: Gender and Representation in Mexico*. New York: Columbia University Press.

Fraser, Nancy. 1995. Politics, culture, and the public sphere: Toward a postmodern conception. In *Social Postmodernism: Beyond Identity Politics*. Ed. Linda J. Nicholson, and Steven Seidman. 287–312. Cambridge: Cambridge University Press.

Friedman, Susan Stanford. 1998. *Mappings: Feminism and the Cultural Geographies of Encounter*. Princeton, New Jersey: Princeton University Press.

Fuss, Diana. 1989. *Essentially Speaking: Feminism, Nature, and Difference*. New York: Routledge.

Gadamer, Hans Georg. 1993. *Truth and Method*. Second Edn. Trans. Joel Weinsheimer, and Donald G. Marshall. New York: Crossroad Press.

Gagnon, Monika Kin. 2000. *Other Conundrums: Race, Culture, and Canadian Art*. Vancouver: Arsenal Pulp Press/Artspeak/KAG.

García Canclini, Néstor. 1995. *Hybrid Cultures: Strategies for Entering and Leaving Modernity*. Minneapolis, MN : University of Minnesota Press.

Gates, Jr. Henry Louis. 1984. The blackness of blackness: A critique of the sign and the signifying monkey. In *Black Literature and Literary Theory*. Ed. Henry Louis Gates, Jr. 285–321. New York: Methuen Press.

————. 1988. *The Signifying Monkey: A Theory of Afro-American Literary Criticism.* New York: Oxford University Press.

————. 1991. Critical Fanonism. *Critical Inquiry* 17 (3) (Spring): 457–70.

Geertz, Clifford. 1972. *The Interpretation of Culture.* New York: Basic Books.

Genovese, Eugene D. 1974. *Roll, Jordan Roll: The World the Slaves Made.* New York: Random House.

Gibson, Ann. 1995. The African-American aesthetic and postmodernism. In *African American Visual Aesthetics: A Postmodernist View.* Ed. David C. Driskell. 81–100. Washington: Smithsonian Institution Press.

Gibson, James J. 1975. Note on proprioception in relation to somaesthesis, self-awareness, and introspection. Available at http://huwi.org/gibson/proprioception.htm.

Giddings, Paula. 1984. *When and Where I Enter: The Impact of Black Women on Race and Sex in America.* New York: William and Morrow Company.

Giles, Freda Scott. 1995. Methexis vs. mimesis: Poetics of feminist and womanist drama. In *Race/Sex: Their Sameness, Difference, and Interplay.* Ed. Naomi Zack. 175–82. New York: Routledge.

Gillman, Laura, and Stacey M. Floyd-Thomas. 2001. Bounded cultures. Presented at the National Women's Studies Association, June 13–17.

————. 2002. Subverting forced identities, violent acts, and the narrativity of race: A diasporic analysis of Black women's radical subjectivity in three novels acts. *Journal of Black Studies* 32 (5): 528–56.

————. 2005. "The whole story is what I'm after": Womanist revolutions and liberation feminist revelations through biomythography and emancipatory historiography. *Journal of Black Theology* 3 (2): 176–99.

Gillman, Laura. 2007. Beyond the shadow: Re-scripting race in women's studies. *Meridians* 7 (2): 117–41.

Goizueta, Roberto S. 1995. *Caminemos Con Jesús: A Hispanic/Latino Theology of Accompaniment.* New York: Orbis.

Gonzales, Michelle. 2002. Latino/a theology: Doing theology latinamente. In *Dialog: A Journal of Theology* 41(1): 63–72.

Gordon, Lewis R. 2002. Sociality and community in black: A phenomenological essay. In *The Quest for Community and Identity: Critical Essays in Africana Social Philosophy.* 105–23. Ed. Robert E. Birt. Lanham: Rowman and Littlefield.

————. 2008. *An Introduction to Africana Philosophy.* Cambridge: Cambridge University Press.

Grosfoguel, Ramón. 2003. *Colonial Subjects: Puerto Ricans in a Global Perspective.* Berkeley: University of California Press.

Grosz, Elizabeth. 1994. *Volatile Bodies: Toward a Corporeal Feminism.* Bloomington: Indiana University Press.

Gunning, Isabelle R. 1998. Cutting through the obfuscation: Female genital surgeries in neo-imperial culture. In *Talking Visions: Multicultural Feminism in a Transnational Age.* 203–24. New York: The M.I.T. Press.

Gutman, Herbert. 1977. *The Black Family in Slavery and Freedom, 1750–1925.* New York: Vintage Books.

Gwaltney, John Langston. 1980. *Drylongso: A Self Portrait of Black America.* Rpt. New York: Random House.

Halberg, Margareta. 1989. Feminist epistemology: An impossible project? *Radical Philosophy* 53: 3–7.

Hall, Stuart. 1988. New Ethnicities. *ICA Document* 7. 27–31. London: ICA.

———. 1993. What is this "black" in black popular culture? In *Black Popular Culture: A Project by Michele Wallace.* Ed. Gina Dent. 21–53. Seattle: Seattle Bay Press

———. ed. 2003. *Representation: Cultural Representations and Signifying Practices.* London: Sage Publications.

Haraway, Donna. 1990. A manifesto for cyborgs: Science, technology, and socialist feminism in the 1980s. In *Feminism/Postmodernism.* Ed. Linda J. Nicholson. 190–233. New York: Routledge.

Harding, Sandra. 1986. *The Science Question in Feminism.* Ithaca: Cornell University Press.

———. 1993. Rethinking standpoint epistemology: "What is strong objectivity?" In *Feminist Epistemologies.* Ed. Linda Alcoff and Elizabeth Porter. 48–92. New York: Routledge.

———. 2004. Introduction: Standpoint theory as a site of political, philosophic, and scientific debate. In *The Feminist Standpoint Theory Reader: Intellectual and Political Controversies.* Ed. Sandra Harding. 1–16. New York: Routledge.

———. 2008. *Sciences from below: Feminisms, Postcolonialities, and Modernities.* Durham: Duke University Press.

Harper, Phillip Brian. 1994. *Framing the Margins: The Social Logic of Postmodern Culture.* New York: Oxford University Press.

Harris, Robert A. 2005. A summary of the fact/value dichotomy. *VirtualSalt.* Web.

Harris, Rose M. 1999. Signifying race and gender: Discursive strategies in feminist theory and politics, Ph.D diss., Department of Political Science, Rutgers University, New Brunswick, New Jersey.

Harvey, David. 1989. *The Condition of Postmodernity.* Baltimore: The Johns Hopkins University Press.

Hegerfeldt, Anne C. 2005. *Lies That Tell the Truth: Magic Realism Seen through Contemporary Fiction from Britain.* Amsterdam: Rodopi.

Henderson, Mae. 1989. Response to Houston A. Baker, Jr.'s "There is no more beautiful way: Theory and the poetics of Afro-American women's writing." In *Afro-American Literary Study in the 1990s.* Ed. Baker, Jr. Houston A. and Patricia Redmond. 155–63. Chicago: The University of Chicago Press.

———. 1991. Speaking in tongues: Dialogics, dialectics, and the Black woman writer's literary tradition. In *Changing Our Own Words: Essays on Criticism, Theory, and Writing by Black Women.* Ed. Cheryl A. Wall. 16–37. New Brunswick, NJ: Rutgers University Press.

Hesse, Barnor. 1993. Black to front and black again: Racialization through contested times and spaces. In *Place and the Politics of Identity*: Ed. Michael Keith, and Steve Pile. 162–181. London: Routledge.

Higginbotham, Evelyn. 1993. *Righteous Discontent: The Women's Movement in the Black Baptist Church, 1880–1920*. Cambridge, MA: Harvard University Press.

Hill, Peter C., and Hood, Ralph W. Jr., 1999. *Measures of Religiosity*. Birmingham, Alabama: Religious Education Press.

Hine, Darlene Clark. 1979. Female slave resistance: The economics of sex. *Western Journal of Black Studies* 3(2): 123–27.

Hite, Molly. 1990. Romance, marginality, and matrilineage: *The color purple* and *Their eyes were watching God* . In *Reading Black, Reading Feminist*. Ed. Henry Louis Gates, Jr. 431–453. New York: Penguin Books.

hooks, bell. 2000. *Feminist Theory: From Margin to Center*. Cambridge, MA: South End Press.

———. 1990a. Postmodern blackness. In *Yearnings*. 23–31. Boston: South End Press.

———. 1990b. Writing the subject: Reading *The color purple*. In *Reading Black, Reading Feminist*. Ed. Henry Louis Gates, Jr. 454–70. New York: Penguin Books.

Hogue, W. Lawrence. 1996. *Race, Modernity, Postmodernity: a Look at the Histories and Literatures of People of Color since the 1960s*. New York: Suny Press.

Hudson-Weems, Clenora. [1993] 2006. Africana womanism. In *The Womanist Reader*. Ed. Layli Phillips. 44–56. New York: Routledge.

Hutnyk, John. 1997. Adorno at womad: South Asian crossovers and the limits of hybridity-talk. In *Debating Cultural Hybridity: Multi-Cultural Identities and the Politics of Anti-Racism*. Ed. Pnina Werbner and Tariq Modood. 106–36. London: Zed Books.

Hutton, Patrick. 2000. Recent scholarship on memory and history. *The History Teacher* 33 (4): 533–48.

Isasi-Díaz, Ada-María. 2004a. *En La Lucha/in the Struggle: Elaborating a Mujerista Theology*. Minneapolis, MN: Fortress Press.

———. 2004b. *La Lucha Continues: Mujerista Theology*. Maryknoll, NY: Orbis Books.

Jacobs, Harriet. [1861] 2004. *Incidents in the Life of a Slave Girl, Written by Herself*. New York: Basic Civitas.

Jacques, Michele. 1995. Testimony as embodiment: Telling the truth and shaming the devil. *The Journal of the Interdenominational Theological Center* (JITC) 22(2): 129–45.

James, Joy. 1999. *Shadowboxing*. New York: St. Martin's Press.

Jameson, Frederic. 1984. Postmodernism; or, the cultural logic of late capitalism. *New Left Review* 146: 53–92.

Jamison-Hall, Angelene. 1993. She's just too womanish for them: Alice Walker and *The Color Purple*. In *Censored Books: Critical Viewpoints*. Ed. Nicholas J. Karolides, et al. 191–200. Metuchen, New Jersey: The Scarecrow Press.

Jenson, Jane. 1985. Struggling with identity: The women's movement and the state in Western Europe. In *Women and Politics in Western Europe*. Ed. Sylvia B. Bashevin. 5–18. London: Frank Cass and Company Ltd.

Jiménez Román, Miriam. [1998] 2001. Allá y acá: Locating Puerto Ricans in the diaspora(s). *Diálogo* (5). Center for Latino Research, Chicago, IL: De Paul University.

Jones, Jacqueline. 1985. *Labor of Love, Labor of Sorrow: Black Women, Work, and the Family, from Slavery to the Present*. New York: Random House.

Katz, Tamar. 2000. Show me how to do like you: Didacticism and the epistolary form in *The color purple*. In *Alice Walker's* The Color Purple: *Modern Critical Interpretations*. Ed. Harold Bloom. 67–76. Philadelphia, MA: Chelsea House Publishers.

Keating, AnaLouise. 2006. From borderlands and new *mestizas* to *nepantlas* and *nepantleras*: Anzaldúan theories for social change. *Human Architecture: Journal of the Sociology of Self-Knowledge* 4 (Summer): 5–16.

King, Lovalerie. 2004. African-American womanism: From Zora Neale Hurston to Alice Walker. In *The Cambridge Companion to the African American Novel*. Ed. Maryemma Graham. 233–52. Cambridge, UK: Cambridge University Press.

Kolawole, Mary E. Modupe. 1997. *Womanism and African Consciousness*. Trenton, new Jersey: Africa World Press.

Levin, Amy K. 2003. *Africanism and Authenticity in African-American Women's Novels*. Gainesville, FL: University Press of Florida.

Lloréns, Hilda. 2006. Dislocated geographies: A story of border crossings. *Small Axe* 19 (10) 1: 74–93.

Low, Setha M., and Denise Lawrence-Zuñiga. 2003. *The Anthropology of Space and Place: Locating Culture*. Malden, MA: Blackwell Publishers.

Lubiano, Wahneema. 1991. Shuckin' off the African-American native other: What's "po mo" got to do with it? *Cultural Critique* 18: 149–186.

———. 1995. The postmodernist rag: Political identity and the vernacular in *Song of Solomon*. In *New Essays on* Song of Solomon. ed. Valerie Smith. 93–116. Cambridge: Cambridge University Press.

Marchione, Marilynn. 2009. Alternative medicine goes mainstream. *Associated Press* (June 9).

Martin III, Harvey J. 1999. Unraveling the enigma of psychic surgery. *Journal of Religion and Psychical Research* 22 (3): 168–74.

Martínez, Jacqueline M. 2000. *Phenomenology of Chicana Experience and Identity: Communication and Transformation in Praxis*. Lanham, MD: Rowman and Littlefield.

Massey, Doreen. 1993. Politics and space/time. In *Place and the Politics of Identity*. Ed. Michael Keith, and Steve Pile. 141–61. London: Routledge.

McKay, Nellie. 1990. Crayon enlargements of life: Zora Neale Hurston's *Their eyes were watching God* as Autobiography. In *New Essays on* Their Eyes Were Watching God. Ed. Michael Awkward. 51–70. Cambridge, UK: Cambridge University Press.

McLaren, Peter. 1994. Multiculturalism and the post-modern critique: Toward a pedagogy of resistance and transformation. In *Between Borders: Pedagogy and the Politics of Cultural Studies*. Ed. Henry A. Giroux, and Peter McLaren. 192–222. New York: Routledge.

Merleau-Ponty, Maurice. 1962. *Phenomenology of Perception*. New York: Routledge and Kegan Paul Press.

Meese, Elizabeth. 1986. *Crossing the Double-Cross: The Practice of Feminist Criticism*. Chapel Hill: University of North Carolina Press.

Mesa-Bains, Amalia. 1998. Artists working in social space: A theoretical approach. Presentation for the National Graduate Seminar of The Photography Institute of Columbia. Published in the *TPI* Journal *TPI-NGS*.

———. 2003. *Domesticana*: The sensibility of *Chicana rasquachismo*. In *Chicana Feminisms: A Critical Reader*. Ed. Gabriela F. Arredondo, et al. 298–315. Durham: Duke University Press, 2003.

Mignolo, Walter D. 2000. *Local Histories/Global Designs: Coloniality, Subaltern Knowledges, and Border Thinking*. Princeton, New Jersey: Princeton University Press.

Miguela, Antonia Domínguez. 1994. Postmodernism in the social sciences. In *Postmodernism and Social Inquiry*. 1–24. New York: The Guilford Press.

———. 2001. Bridges in the air: Literary tropes for border identity in U.S. Puerto Rican literature. *The Atlantic Literary Review*. 2(4): 60–71.

Mitchell, Angelyn. 2002. The freedom to remember: Narrative, slavery, and gender. In *Contemporary Black Women's Fiction*. New Brunswick, New Jersey: Rutgers University Press.

Mitchem, Stephanie Y. 2002. *Introducing Womanist Theology*. Maryknoll, NY: Orbis Books.

Mohanty, Chandra Talpade. 2004. *Feminism without Borders*. Durham, North Carolina: Duke University Press.

Mohanty, Satya P. 1997. *Literary Theory and the Claims of History: Postmodernism, Objectivity, Multicultural Politics*. Ithaca: Cornell University Press.

———. 2000. The epistemic status of cultural identity: On *Beloved* and the postcolonial condition. In *Reclaiming Identity: Realist Theory and the Predicament of Postmodernism*. Ed. Paula M. L. Moya, and Michael R. Hames-García. 29–66. Berkeley: University of California Press.

Morrison, Toni. 1987. The site of memory. In *Inventing the Truth: The Art and Craft of Memoir*. Ed. and Intro. William Zinsser. 103–24. Boston: Houghton.

Mouffe, Chantal. 1995. Feminism, citizenship, and radical democratic politics. In *Social Postmodernism: Beyond Identity Politics*. Ed. Linda J. Nicholson, and Steven Seidman. 315–31. Cambridge, UK: Cambridge University Press.

Moya, Paula M.L., and Michael R. Hames-García, ed. 2000a. *Reclaiming Identity: Realist Theory and the Predicament of Postmodernism*. Berkeley: The University of California Press.

———. 2000b. Introduction: Reclaiming identity. In *Reclaiming Identity: Realist Theory and the Predicament of Postmodernism*. Ed. Paula M. L. Moya, and Michael R. Hames-García. 1–28. Berkeley: The University of California Press.

———. 2002. *Learning from Experience: Minority Identities, Multicultural Struggles*. Berkeley: University of California Press.

Moynihan, Daniel Patrick. 1965. The Negro family: The Case for National Action. Washington, D.C.: Office of Policy Planning and Research. United States Department of Labor.

Munn, Nancy D. 2003. Excluded spaces: The figure in the Australian aboriginal landscape. In *The Anthropology of Space and Place: Locating Culture*. Ed. Setha M. Low, and Denise Lawrence-Zuñiga. 92–109. Malden, MA: Blackwell.

Munt, Sally R. Framing intelligibility, identity, and selfhood: A reconsideration of spatio-temporal models. Available at http://www.reconstruction. ws/023/munt.htm

National Women's Studies Organization. 2007. *Mapping Women's and Gender Studies Data Collection*. Available at www.nwsa.org/research/ programadmin/database/index.php.

Negrón-Mutaner, Frances, and Ramón Grosfoguel, ed. 1997. Introduction. In *Puerto Rican Jam: Essays on Culture and Politics*. 1–36. Minneapolis: University of Minnesota Press.

Nicholson, Linda J., and Nancy Fraser. 1990. Social criticism without philosophy. In *Feminism and Postmodernism*. 19–38. Ed. Linda J. Nicholson. New York: Routledge.

Nicholson, Linda J., and Steven Seidman, ed. 1995. *Social Postmodernism*. Cambridge, UK: Cambridge University Press.

Nicol, Jennifer J. 2008. Creating vocative texts. *The Qualitative Report* 13(3): 316–33.

Nora, Pierre. 1989. Between memory and history: *Les lieux de memoire*. *Representations* 26. Special Issue: *Memory and Counter-Memory* (Spring): 7–24.

Ochoa, María. 1995. Cooperative re/weavings: Artistic expression and economic development in a Northern New Mexican village. *Perspectives in Mexican American Studie*s 5: 121–50.

Oliver-Rotger, María Antonia. 2003. *Battlegrounds and Crossroads: Social and Imaginary Space in Writings by Chicanas*. New York: Rodopi.

Olkowski, Dorothea. 1999. *Gilles Deleuze and the Ruin of Representation*. Berkeley: University of California Press.

Olney, James. 1985. "I was born": Slave narratives, their status as autobiography and as literature. In *The Slave's Narrative*. Ed. Charles T. Davis, and Henry Louis Gates, Jr. 148–75. Oxford: Oxford University Press.

Omi, Michael, and Howard Winant. [1986]1994. *Racial Formations in the United States: From the 1960s to the 1980s*. New York: Routledge.

Pandya. Vishvajit. 1990. Movement and space: Andamanese cartography. *American Ethnologist* 17(4): 775–97.

Parry, Benita. 1987. Problems in current theories of colonial discourse. *Oxford Literary Review* 9: 27–58.

Peet, Richard. 1998. *Modern Geographical Thought*. Oxford, UK: Blackwell Publishers.

Phillips, Layli, ed. 2006. *The Womanist Reader*. London: Routledge.

Pryse, Marjorie. 1985. Introduction: Zora Neale Hurston, Alice Walker, and the "ancient power" of Black women. In *Conjuring: Black Women, Fiction, and Literary Tradition*. Ed. Pryse Marjorie, and Hortense J. Spillers. 1–24. Bloomington: Indiana University Press.

Putnam, Hilary. 2002. *The Collapse of the Fact/Value Dichotomy and Other Essays*. Cambridge, MA: Harvard University Press.

Quiñones Rivera, Maritza. 2006. From Trigueñita to Afro-Puerto Rican: Intersections of the racialized, gender, and sexualized body in Puerto Rico and the U.S. mainland. *Meridians* 7(1): 162–82.

Ransby, Barbara. 2000. Afrocentrism, cultural nationalism, and the problem with essentialist definitions of race, gender, and sexuality. In *Dispatches from the Ebony Tower: Intellectuals Confront the African American Experience*. Ed. Manning Marable. 216–23. New York: Columbia University Press.

Rawick, George. 1972–79. *The American Slave: A Composite Autobiography*. Westport, Conn.: Greenwood Press.

———. 1973. *From Sundown to Sunup and the Dialectic of Marxian Slave Studies*. Westport, Conn.: Greenwood Press.

Riggs, Marcia Y. 1994. *Awake, Arise, and Act: A Womanist Call for Black Liberation*. Cleveland OH: Pilgrim Press.

Rodríguez, Clara E. 1994. Challenging racial hegemony: Puerto Ricans in the United States. In *Race*. Ed. Steven Gregory, and Roger Sanjek. 131–45. New Brunswick, New Jersey: Rutgers University Press.

———. ed. 1997. *Latin Looks: Images of Latinas and Latinos in the U.S. Media*. Boulder, Co: Westview Press.

Romani, Celina. 1992. Neither here nor there yet. *Callaloo* 15(4): 1034.

Rorty, Richard. 1979. *Philosophy and the Mirror of Nature*. Princeton, New Jersey: Princeton University Press.

Rosenthal, Sandra B. 2003. The pragmatic reconstruction of realism: A pathway for the future. In *Pragmatic Naturalism and Realism*. Ed. John R. Shook. 43–54. Amherst, New York: Prometheus Books.

Roth, Benita. 2004. *Separate Roads to Feminism: Black, Chicana, and White Feminist Movements in America's Second Wave*. Cambridge, UK: Cambridge University Press.

Rovira, Carlos. 2005. *El grito de lares*: The birth of Puerto Rico's fight for independence socialism and liberation magazine (September): Online edition: http://socialismandliberation.org/mag/index.php?aid=459.

Rushdy, Ashraf H. A. 1999. *Neo-Slave Narratives: Studies in the Social Logic of a Literary Form*. New York and Oxford: Oxford University Press.

———. 2000. Relate sexual to historical: Race, resistance, and desire in Gayl Jones's *Corregidora*. *African-American Review* 34(2) (Summer): 273–97.

Sadowski-Smith, Claudia. 2008. *Border Fictions: Globalization, Empire, and Writing at the Boundaries of the United States*. Charlottesville: University of Virginia Press.

Sálazar, Claudia. 1991. A third world woman's text: Between the politics of criticism and cultural politics. In *Women's Words: The Feminist Practice of Oral History*. Ed. Shema Berger and Daphne Patai. 93–105. New York: Routledge.

Sale, Maggie. 1992. Call and response as critical method: African-American oral traditions and *Beloved*. *African American Review* 26.1 (Spring): 41–50.

Saloman, Frank. 2004. *The Cord Keepers: Khipus and Cultural Life in a Peruvian Village*. Durham, North Carolina: Duke University Press.

San Juan, E. Jr. 2002. *Racism and Cultural Studies: Critiques of Multiculturalist Ideology and the Politics of Difference*. Durham, North Carolina: Duke University Press.

Sánchez González, Lisa. 2001. *Boricua Literature: A Literary History of the Puerto Rican Diaspora*. New York: New York University Press.

Sanders, Cheryl J., Katie G. Cannon, Emile M. Townes, M. Shawn Copeland, bell hooks, and Cheryl Townsend-Gilkes. 1989. Roundtable discussion: Christian ethics and theology in womanist perspective. *Journal of Feminist Studies in Religion* 5: 83–112.

Sandoval, Chela. 1991. U.S. third world feminism: The theory and method of oppositional consciousness in the postmodern world. *Genders* 10 (Spring):1–24.

Scholl, Diane Gabrielsen. 1991. With ears to hear and eyes to see: Alice Walker's parable *The color purple*. *Christianity and Literature* 40(3): 255–66.

Schrage, Laurie. 1994. *Moral Dilemmas of Feminism: Prostitution, Adultery, and Abortion*. New York: Routledge.

Schutte, Ofelia. 2000. Cultural alterity: Cross-cultural communication and feminist theory in north-south contexts. In *Decentering the Center: Philosophy for a Multicultural, Postcolonial, and Feminist World*. Ed. Uma Narayan, and Sandra Harding. 47–66. Bloomington, IN: Indiana University Press.

Scott, Joan. 1991. The evidence of experience. *Critical Inquiry* 17 (Summer): 773–97.

Seremetakis, Nadia. 1994. Gender studies or women's studies: Theoretical and pedagogical issues, research agendas and directions. *Australian Feminist Studies*. (Summer): 107–118.

Shapiro, Herbert. 1975. The confessions of Nat Turner: William Styron and his critics. *Negro American Literature Forum* 9 (4) (Winter): 99–104.

Shohat, Ella. 1998. Introduction. In *Talking Visions: Multicultural Feminism in a Transnational Age*. Ed. Ella Shohat. 1–63. Cambridge, MA: MIT Press.

Shook, John R., ed. 2003. *Pragmatic Naturalism and Realism*. Amherst, New York: Prometheus Books.

Smith, Dorothy E. [1972] 2004. Women's perspective as a radical critique of sociology. In *The Feminist Standpoint Theory Reader: Intellectual and Political Controversies*. Ed. Sandra Harding. 21–53. New York: Routledge.

Smitherman, Geneva. 1977. *Talkin' and Testifyin': The Language of Black America*. New York: Houghton-Mifflin

Soja, Edward, and Barbara Hooper. 1993. The spaces that difference makes: Some notes on the geographical margins of the new cultural politics. In *Place and the Politics of Identity*. Ed. Michael Keith, and Steve Pile. 183–205. London: Routledge.

Spivak, Gaytri Chakravorty, 1988. Can the subaltern speak? In *Marxism and the Interpretation of Culture*. Ed. Cary Nelson, and Lawrence Grossberg. 271–313. Urbana/Chicacago: University of Illinois Press.

Stewart, Dianne M. 2006. Dancing limbo: Black passages through the boundaries of place, race, class, and religion. In *Deeper Shades of Purple: Womanism in Religion and Society*. Ed. Stacey Floyd-Thomas. 82–97. New York: New York University Press.

Stone, Alison. 2004. Essentialism and anti-essentialism in feminist philosophy. *Journal of Moral Philosophy* 1(2):135–53.

Sturken, Marita. 1997. *Tangled memories: The Vietnam War, the Aids Epidemic and the Politics of Remembering*. Berkeley: University of California Press.

Styron, William. 1967. *Confessions of Nat Turner*. New York: Random House.

Sudbury, Julia. 1998. *Other Kinds of Dreams: Black Women's Organizations and the Politics of Transformation*. London: Routledge.

Taussig, Michael. 1993. *Mimesis and Alterity: A Particular History of the Senses*. New York: Routledge.

Taylor, Charles. 1985. Philosophy and the human sciences. *Philosophical Papers*, 2. Cambridge: Cambridge University Press.

Taylor, Diana. 2003. *The Archive and the Repertoire: Performing Cultural Memory in the Americas*. Durham: Duke University Press.

Thernstrom, Abigail, 2009. Commentary: Identity politics in the age of Obama. Available at http://www.cnn.com/2009/POLITICS/06/04/thernstrom.identity.politics/

Thomas, Linda. E. 1988/89. Womanist theology, epistemology, and a new anthropological paradigm. *Crosscurrents* 48(4) (Winter): 488–99.

Thornton, R. 1988. Culture. In *South African Keywords*. Ed. E. Boonzaier, and E. Sharp. 17–27. Cape Town: David Philip.

Torres Aguilera, Francisco Javier. 1994. *Telenovelas, televisión y comunicación*. Ed. Coyoacán. Mexico: D.F. : Ed. Coyoacán

Torres, Arlene, and Norman E. Whitten. 1998. *Blackness in Latin America and the Caribbean*. Vol 1. Bloomington, IN: Indiana University Press.

Townes, Emilie. 1995. *In a Blaze of Glory: Womanist Spirituality as Social Witness*. Nashville, TN: Abingdon Press.

Townsend-Gilkes, Cheryl. 1995. We have a beautiful mother: Womanist musings on the Afrocentric idea. In *Living the Intersection: Womanism and Afrocentrism in Theology.* Ed. Cheryl J. Sanders. 21–42. Minneapolis, MN: Augsburg Fortress Press.

Van Manen, Max. 1997. From meaning to method. *Qualitative Health Research* 7(3): 345–69.

Vigil, James Diego, and Hanley, Gisella. 2002. *Chicano* macrostructural identities and macrohistorical cultural forces. *Journal of Historical Sociology* 15(3): (September) 395–426.

Wade, Peter. 1997. *Race and Ethnicity in Latin America.* London: Pluto Press.

Walker, Alice. 1982. *The Color Purple.* New York: Pocket Books.

———. 1983. *In Search of Our Mothers' Gardens: Womanist Prose.* San Diego: Harcourt Brace and Company.

———. 1985. Interview. In *Black Women Writers at Work.* Ed. Claudia Tate. 175–87. New York: Continuum.

Wall, Wendy. 1988. Lettered bodies and corporeal texts in *The color purple. Studies in American Fiction* 16(1): (Spring) 83–97.

Waters, Lindsay. 2001. The age of incommensurability. *Boundary* 2 28(2): 133–72.

West, Cornel. 1992. The new cultural politics of difference. In *Out There: Marginalization and Contemporary Cultures.* Ed. Ferguson, Russell, Martha Gever, Trinh T. Minh-ha, and Cornell West. 19–36. Cambridge, MA: The M.I.T Press. New York: The New Museum of Contemporary Art.

Whalen, Carmen Teresa. 2005. Colonialism, citizenship, and the making of the Puerto Rican diaspora: An Introduction. In *The Puerto Rican Diaspora: Historical Perspectives.* Ed. Carmen Teresa Whalen and Victor Vázquez Fernandez. 1–42. Philadelphia, PA: Temple University Press.

White, Deborah Gray. 1985. *Ar'n't I a Woman? Female Slaves in the Plantation South.* New York: W. W. Norton & Company.

White, E. Frances. 2001. *Dark Continent of Our Bodies: Black Feminism and the Politics of Respectability.* Philadelphia: Temple University Press.

Wilkerson, William S. 2000. Is there something you need to tell me? Coming out and the ambiguity of experience. In *Reclaiming Identity: Realist Theory and the Predicament of Postmodernism.* Ed. Paul M. L. Moya, and Michael R. Hames-García. 251–78. Berkeley: University of California Press.

Wiegman, Robyn. 1995. *American Anatomies: Theorizing Race and Gender.* Durham: Duke University Press.

Wilentz, Gay. 1992. *Binding Cultures: Black Women Writers in Africa and the Diaspora.* Indianapolis: Indiana University Press.

Williams, Bernard. 1985. *Ethics and the Limits of Philosophy.* Cambridge, MA: Harvard University Press.

Williams, Delores S. 1987. Womanist theology: Black women's voices. *Christianity and Crisis* 47 (March 2): 66–70.

———. 1995. Afrocentrism and male-female relations in church and society. In *Living the Intersection: Womanism and Afrocentrism in Theology.* Ed. Cheryl J. Sanders. 43–56. Minneapolis, MN: Augsburg Fortress Press.

Willis, Susan. 1991. I shop therefore I am: Is there a place for Afro-American culture in commodity culture? In *Changing Our Own Words: Essays on Criticism, Theory, and Writing by Black Women.* Ed. Cheryl A. Wall. 173–95. New Brunswick: Rutgers University Press.

Winant, Howard. 2004. *The New Politics of Race: Globalism, Difference, Justice.* Minneapolis: University of Minneapolis Press.

Yancy, George. 2004. Fragments of a social ontology of whiteness. In *What White Looks Like: African-American Philosophers on the Whiteness Question.* Ed. George Yancy. 1–23. New York: Routledge.

Ybarra Frausto, Tomás. 2003. Notes from Losaida: A Foreword. In *Velvet Barrios: Popular Culture and Chicana/o Sexualities.* Ed. Alicia Gaspar de Alba. v–viii. New York: Palgrave Macmillan.

Young, Iris Marion. 1995. Gender as seriality: Thinking about women as a social collective. In *Social Postmodernism.* Ed. Linda J. Nicholson, and Steven Seidman. 187–215. Cambridge, UK: Cambridge University Press.

INDEX